ETIENNE DELESSERT

Birds of Prey

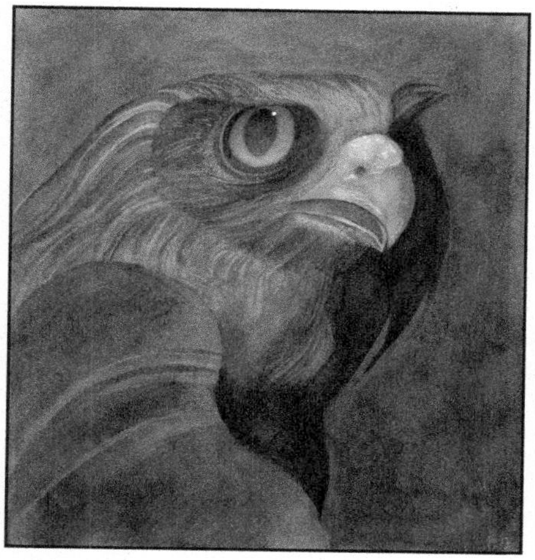

Trump

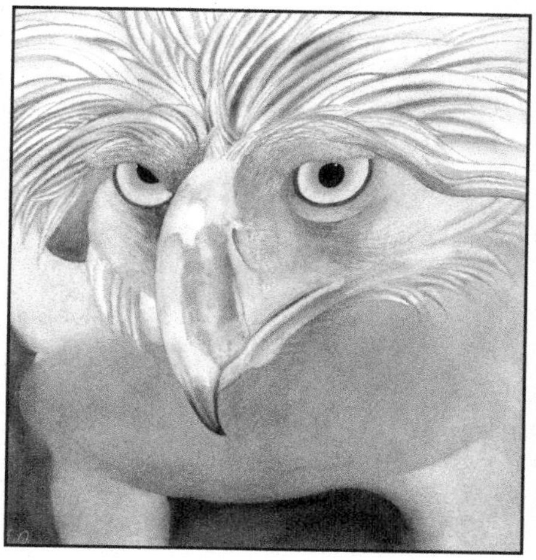

Conway

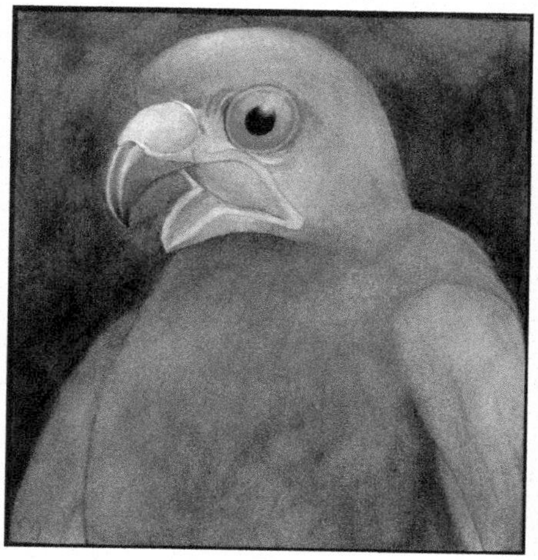

Pence

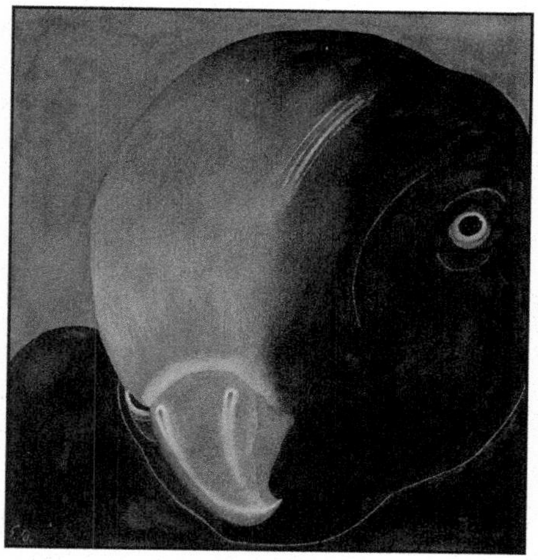

Mnuchin

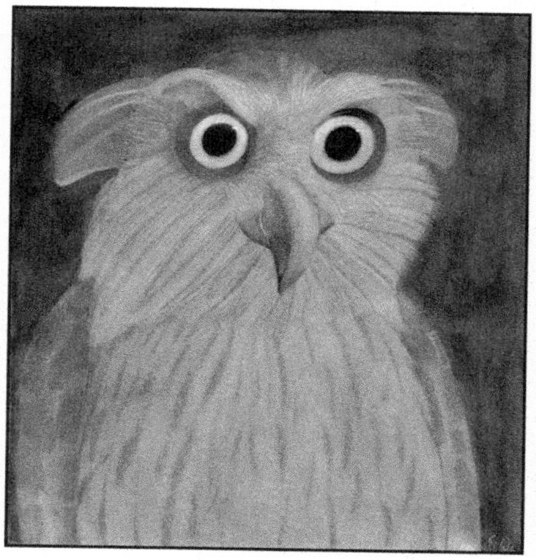

Bannon (resigned)

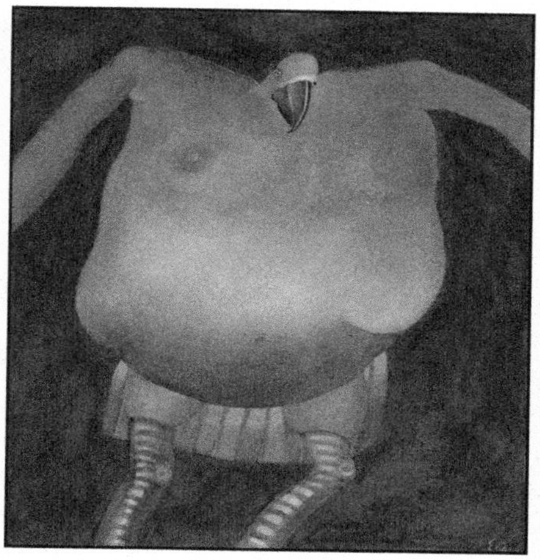

Bannon (drunk)

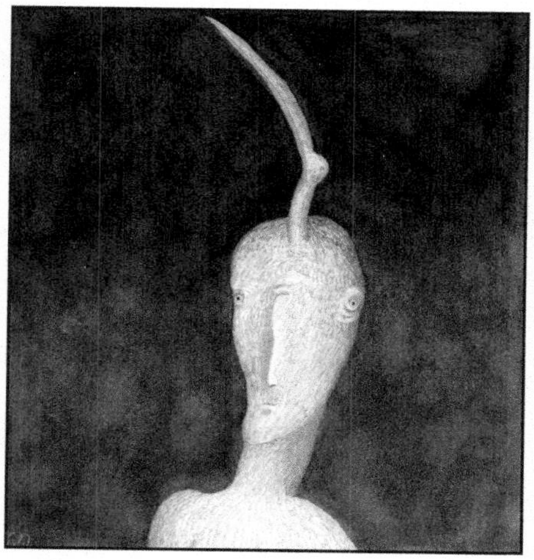

Miller

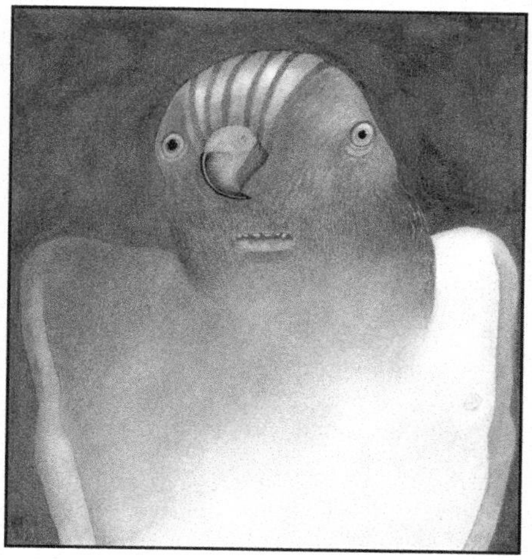

Flynn (fired)

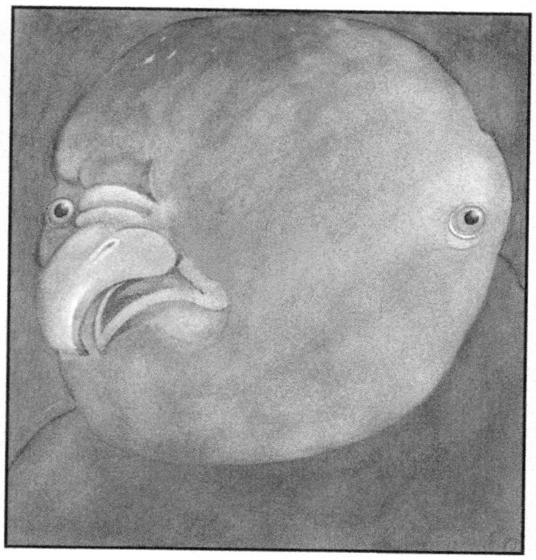

Spicer (resigned)

BY MICHAEL GERBER

DING DONG

A (very classy) fable for our times

Once upon a time there was a great and powerful kingdom. Though not totally peaceful, it was more peaceful than most; its Emperors tried hard to do the right thing, usually, and sometimes even succeeded. It was a lucky land.

One spring, however, its fortunes turned. A ship bearing cargo from the East contained a pestilence, which spread far and wide. The sitting Emperor, who had been a reasonably good Emperor, died; as did the person expected to succeed him — and so forth and so on, until the throne ended up in the hands of a distant relation, a vain and dim-witted merchant widely considered to be a mountebank.

This poor reputation made the new Emperor even more determined to show his enemies — which he defined as "everyone" — how wonderful and special he was. He decided to throw the most lavish coronation the Empire had ever seen; putting the affairs of state on hold, the Emperor oversaw every detail personally. Finally, he was down to the last item: his outfit.

Merchants from all around the Empire came to offer up their goods. They knew that the Emperor's taste was rather garish, so each of them tried to outdo the other until the Emperor was practically drowning in bolts of silk, luxurious pelts and fabrics that sparkled like the night sky. Finally one outfit seemed to stand out above all the others, a velvet and ermine number so encrusted with gems you could barely lift it.

MICHAEL GERBER

(@mgerber937) is Editor & Publisher of *The American Bystander*.

"I'll take it," the Emperor snarled, for he snarled at everyone. "For free. You'll be paid in exposure."

To his credit, the clothier did not lose his temper; he was much too sly for that. Paid in exposure, eh? A plan formed.

"My dear Emperor," the man purred, "this was a test. These raiments, though fine, are not the finest in the land — but by picking them you show yourself to be a man of unparalleled taste and refinement. There is an ensemble, one I've been working on for years, that is classier by far. So classy, in fact, that only the classiest people can even see it."

The Emperor stopped frowning. "Did you bring it?" he asked.

The next morning, the Emperor and the clothier boarded his splendid gilded carriage. During the short ride to the Grand Cathedral, the clothier helped the Emperor out of his old outfit, and into his new, much classier one. Just as they pulled up to the Grand Cathedral, the clothier leaned over. "Sire, let me adjust your hat."

"Thanks," the Emperor growled, for he growled at everyone. "How do I look?"

"Unforgettable," the clothier said.

When the Emperor emerged from his carriage, there were gasps. For a moment, the Emperor was unsure; the clothier leaned out of the window. "They are gasping in wonder, your Highness."

"Obviously," the Emperor snapped, and strode confidently down the red carpet toward the church. The throngs packed in behind grim-faced soldiers were silent; not a flag waved, not a word was spoken.

At the church door, a child of one of the imperial chambermaids broke the silence. "Look, Mom!" she cried. "He's naked! *The Emperor is naked!*"

The little girl wormed her way between the soldiers. Giggling, she ran up to the Emperor, and grabbed his scrawny member. "Mom, look!" She pulled it like the bell in the Empress's bedroom. "Ding-DONG. Get it? Ding-dong!" Then the girl collapsed on the ground laughing because this was the funniest thing ever.

Perhaps it was the titters in the crowd, or perhaps the Emperor had a thing about females, but his face turned a very unattractive shade of puce. "*Pikemen!*" he roared. "Capture her! Be rough!"

The nearest pair of pikemen moved rather slowly — roughing up little girls was not why they'd gone to the Piking Academy — but they shoveled her up, gently, using the flat blade of their pikes like a spatula. The little girl was escorted, still giggling, to the Tower.

The next day, everyone tried to figure out what had happened. Some said he was a new Emperor, and didn't understand the nuances of the job. He's got his own style, others said, remember that Emperor who didn't like to wear a hat?

Seven percent of the Emperor's subjects dismissed it as "an honest mistake."

Another 9 percent, secret nudists, said, "That's exactly why I like him!"

But the leading theory, held by fully 12 percent of the Emperor's subjects, was this: they didn't believe he'd been naked at all. They dismissed the whole thing as a plot to make him look foolish. And no amount of evidence could convince them, including time-lapse photos of the Emperor's genitals getting sunburned. "Obvious fakes," they said.

Though the remaining 72 percent of the country thought the Emperor a fool, some kindhearted folks tried to meet him halfway. In a spirit of amity and patriotism, they began going bottomless, which made both sides hate them and led to many painful splinters.

The Castle went on the offensive. "So-called elites need to wake up to the fact that their fashion-backward 'values' don't play to the average citizen," said the Emperor's chamberlain. Overnight, the imperial court all adopted the new dress code. This was stomach-turning, except in the case of the Empress, whose approval rating skyrocketed.

Encouraged by the Emperor, whole districts suddenly became hotbeds of pugnacious nudity. Some became worried by this, and humbly petitioned the Emperor. "In summer, O.K. — but what happens in fall?" they wrote. "Or, God forbid, winter?" The Emperor wouldn't even receive their petition; he knew what side they were on, and privately began discussing ways to throw everyone wearing pants into prison.

Fall came, and some citizens did die, mostly babies and old people, but this changed fewer minds than you'd think. Camping became less popular, as did dining alfresco. Then winter came, and people died in droves. Eventually, the Emperor's support began to wane. And when a wicked flu came through the kingdom, even the Emperor himself got it.

"I just can't seem to get warm," the Emperor said, lying naked on his bare mattress (the clothier had made him a *really classy* sheet and duvet combo which, to its credit, had been delightfully cool in summer. Now, however, the Emperor felt every draft. "This place is a dump," the Emperor griped weakly. "I should knock it down and rebuild it...out of gold or something."

"Your Highness," the Lord Chamberlain said, "why not go back to your old pajamas, old bedclothes — just until you get better. No one need know."

Normally this would've loosed a torrent of abuse, but the Emperor was too weak. "Not...classy...enough," he whispered.

"At least let me move you close to the fire," the chamberlain said. Now whether this was an honest mistake, or payback for some private humiliation, we will never know. But it seems that, sometime in the night, a stray spark spat out of the fire and ignited the Emperor's bed. Others whisper that the kindling was the Emperor's pubes, dried by exposure to the sun — but this was never proved. What is sure is that he was found the next morning, burned to a crisp.

The Emperor rested in state, in the Rotunda of the Grand Cathedral, dressed in the outfit that had sealed his fate. Naked supporters filed by, those that had survived; in their eyes, the Emperor was a martyr. They vowed, in his memory, to go naked for the rest of their lives. Which, it being December, were not long.

And what happened to the little girl? She and her family tried to live quietly for a while. But people egged their house and fed their cows grass that made the milk stinky, and generally made life intolerable. So they moved to a kingdom to the north, or maybe it was the south, and got along quite well. The little girl grew up to run a very classy humor magazine called — you guessed it — *Ding Dong*. Her scathing-yet-hilarious front-of-book essays solved every conceivable political problem, and everyone everywhere lived happily after ever. ▇

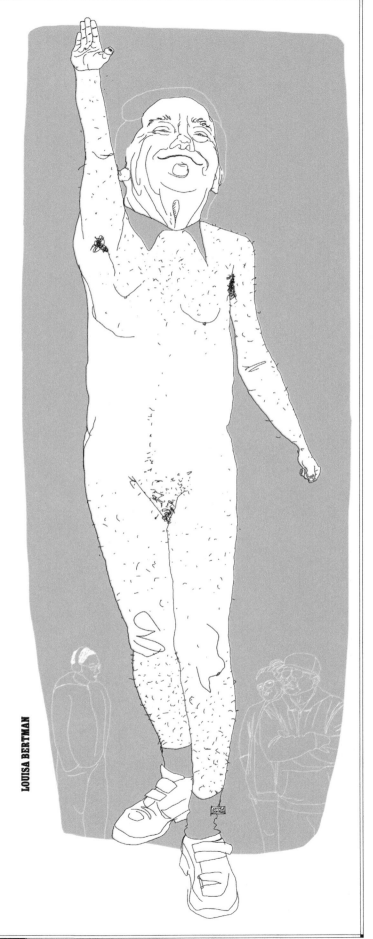

LOUISA BERTMAN

3

TABLE OF CONTENTS

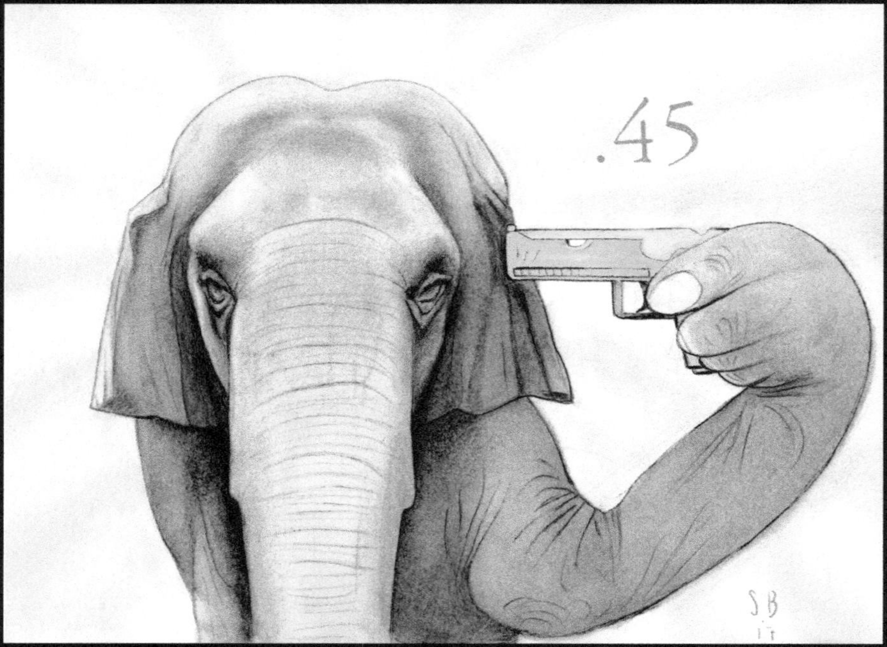

.45

STEVE BRODNER

DEPARTMENTS

GALLIMAUFRY

SHORT STUFF

FEATURES

The AMERICAN
BYSTANDER

#5 • Vol. 2, No. 1 • Summer 2017

EDITOR & PUBLISHER
Michael Gerber
HEAD WRITER Brian McConnachie
SENIOR EDITOR Alan Goldberg
DEPUTY EDITORS
Michael Thornton, Ben Orlin
CONTACTEE Scott Marshall
ORACLE Steve Young
STAFF LIAR P.S. Mueller
LIASONS James Folta (*New York*)

CONTRIBUTORS
Jeremy Banks, Andrew Barlow, Ron Barrett, Charles Barsotti, Louisa Bertman, Chris Bonno, George Booth, Andy Breckman, Steve Brodner, Dylan Brody, M.K. Brown, David Chelsea, Seymour Chwast, River Clegg, Howard Cruse, John Cuneo, Etienne Delessert, Nate Dern, Scott Dikkers, Chris Dingman, Randall Enos, Liana Finck, Drew Friedman, Tom Gammill, James Finn Gardner, Rick Geary, Alan Goldberg, Sam Gross, Tom Hachtman, Jack Handey, Todd Hanson, Tim Harrod, Ron Hauge, Sam Henderson, Scott Jacobson, J. Jonik, Ted Jouflas, Farley Katz, Joe Keohane, Adam Koford, Ken Krimstein, Stephen Kroninger, Peter Kuper, Todd Levin, Merrill Markoe, Matt Matera, Amanda Meadows, Hana Michels, Joe Oesterle, Josh Perilo, Dennis Perrin, Ethan Persoff, Andy Prieboy, Mike Sacks, Jacob Sager Weinstein, Katie Schwartz, Cris Shapan, Mike Shiell, Michael Sloan, J.D. Smith, Rich Sparks, Nick Spooner, Ed Subitzky, Steve Torelli, Tom Toro, Ted Travelstead, Evan Waite, D. Watson, J.A. Weinstein and Jack Ziegler.

COPYEDITING
Cheryl Levenbrown, God bless 'er

THANKS TO
Kate Powers, Jessica Ziegler, Rae Barsotti, Lanky Bareikis, Jon Schwarz, Alleen Schultz, Molly Bernstein, Joe Lopez, Eliot Ivanhoe, Neil Gumenick, Thomas Simon, Greg and Patricia Gerber and many, many others.

NAMEPLATES BY
Mark Simonson

ISSUE CREATED BY
Michael Gerber

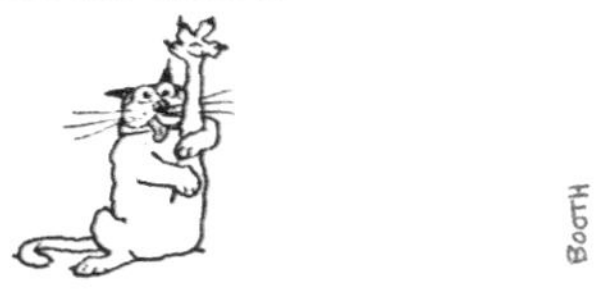

BOOTH

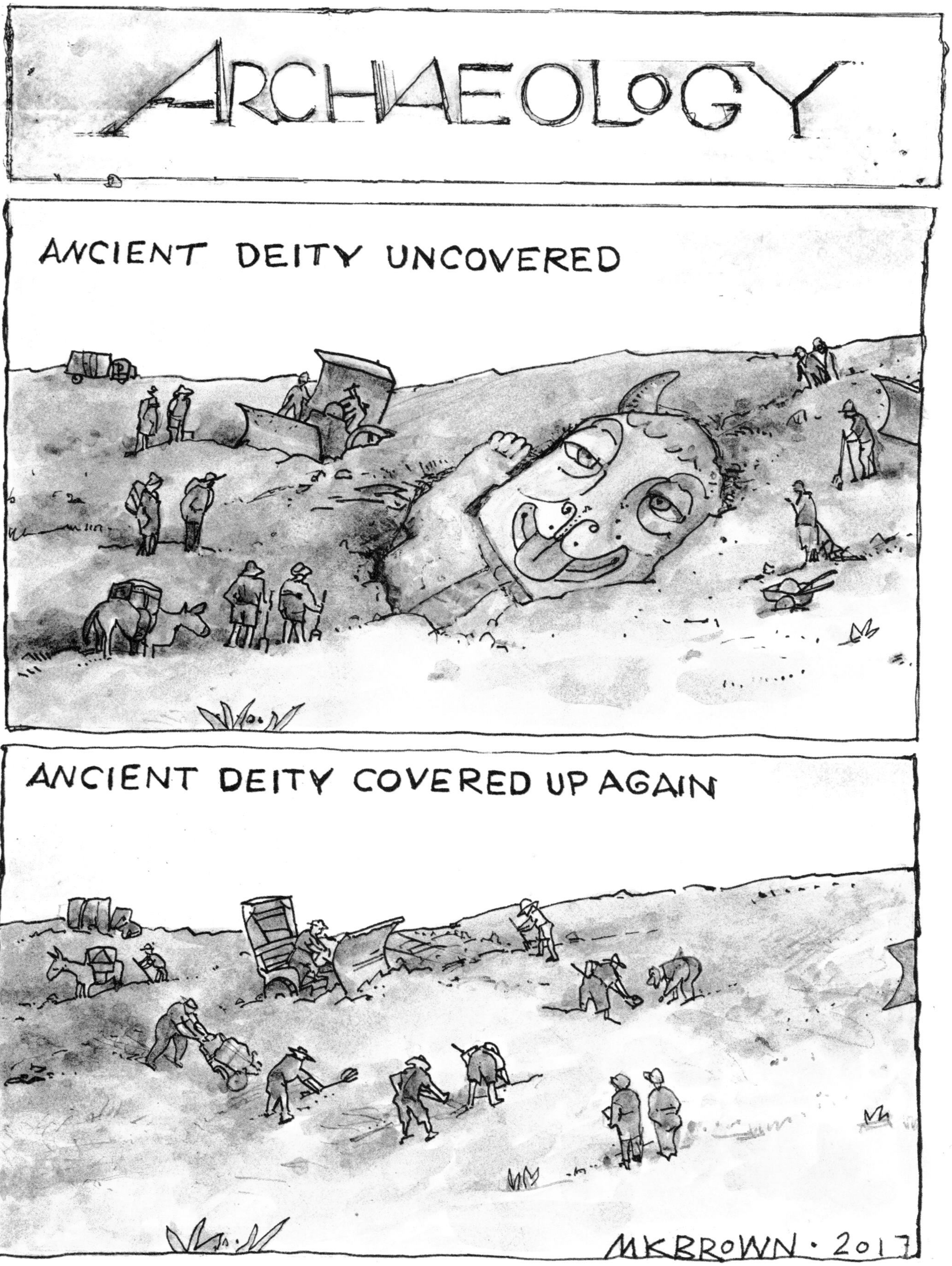
ARCHAEOLOGY
ANCIENT DEITY UNCOVERED
ANCIENT DEITY COVERED UP AGAIN
MKBROWN · 2017

CARTOONS & ILLUSTRATIONS BY
L. Atkinson, C. Barsotti, J. Banx, L. Bertman, C. Bonno, G. Booth, A. Breckman, S. Brodner, M.K. Brown, D. Chelsea, S. Chwast, J. Cuneo, E. Delessert, L. Donnelly, B. Eckstein, R. Enos, L. Finck, D. Friedman, M. Gerberg, S. Gross, L. Guyer, R. Hauge, J. Jonik, T. Jouflas, F. Katz, K. Krimstein, S. Kroninger, P. Kuper, S. Lautman, S. Mack, P.S. Mueller, J. Oesterle, A. Prieboy, C. Shapan, M. Shiell, M. Simonson, R. Sparks, N. Spooner, S. Torelli, T. Toro, D. Watson, and J. Ziegler.

"The other one's on the ground in Afghanistan."

COVER

We first saw this cover in the delightful booklet that Jack Ziegler's daughter Jessica prepared for his memorial service, held at New York's Society of Illustrators on June 17, 2017. We immediately began a campaign of highly targeted whining, and Jessica rightly identified us as an organization whose good taste in cartoonists is excelled only by its ability to be annoying. So she agreed; then Scott Marshall did his usual magic. She and the rest of the Ziegler family have our deep thanks. Once a Bystander, always a Bystander, Jack.

ACKNO WLEDG MENTS

All material is ©2017 its creators, all rights reserved; please do not reproduce or distribute it without written consent of the creators and *The American Bystander*. The following material has previously appeared, and is reprinted here with permission of the author(s): Stan Mack's "Compulsion" first appeared in *The Village Voice*. "Wedding Info: V. Important! <3" is from the book *The Best American Emails*. "Woody Allen and Dr. Moreno's Theater of the Psychodrama" appeared in the book *John Wilcock: The New York Years*.

———◆———

THE AMERICAN BYSTANDER, Vol. 2, No. 1, (978-0-692-94389-2). Publishes ~4x/year. ©2017 by Good Cheer LLC. No part of this book can be reproduced, in whole or in part, by any means, without the written permission of the Publisher. For this and other queries, email *Publisher@ americanbystander.org*, or write: Michael Gerber, Publisher, *The American Bystander*, 1122 Sixth St., #403, Santa Monica, CA 90403. Subscribe at www.patreon.com/bystander. Other info can be found at www.americanbystander.org.

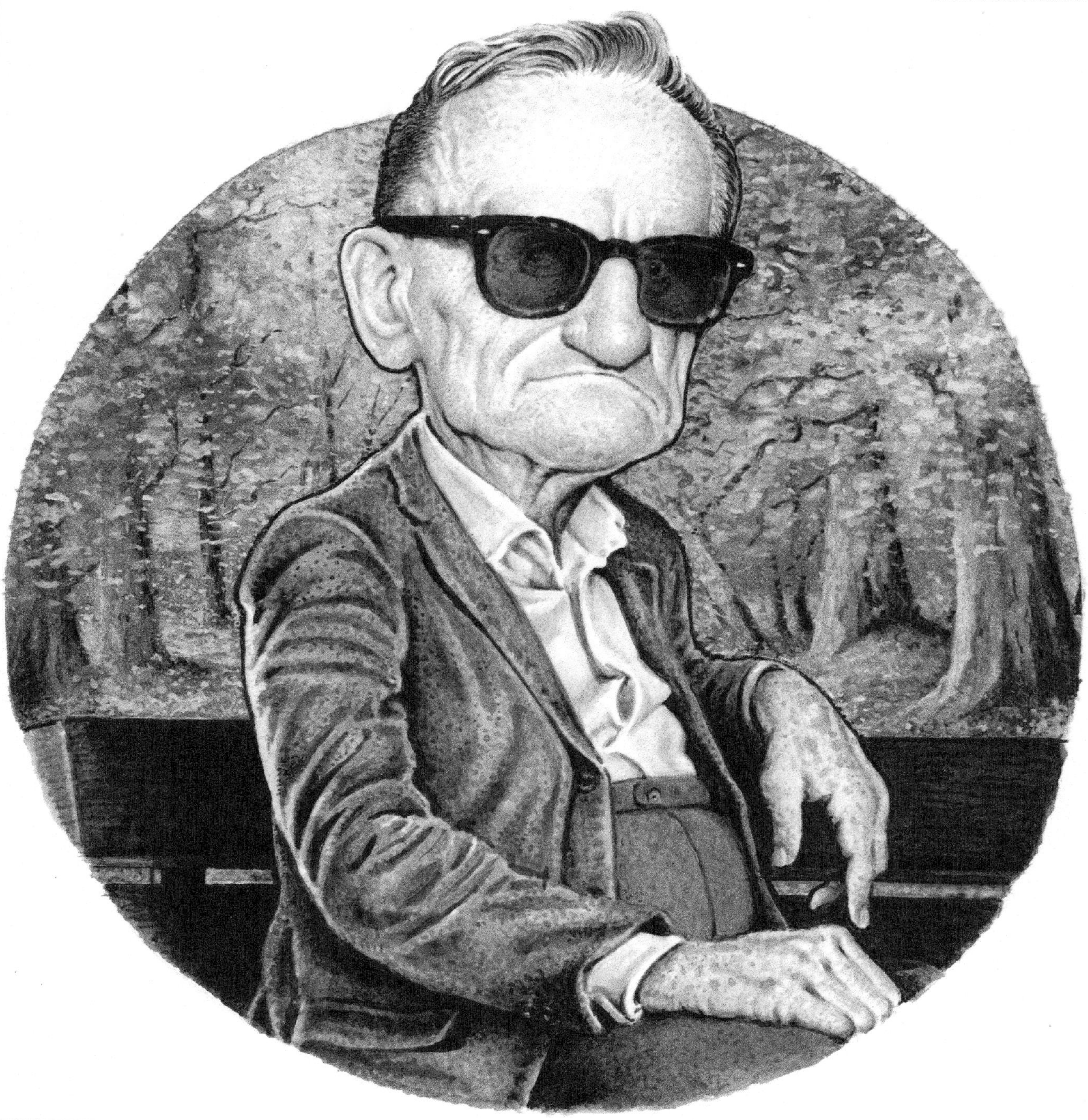

American Bystanders #2

Longfellow "Sparky" Yutzman

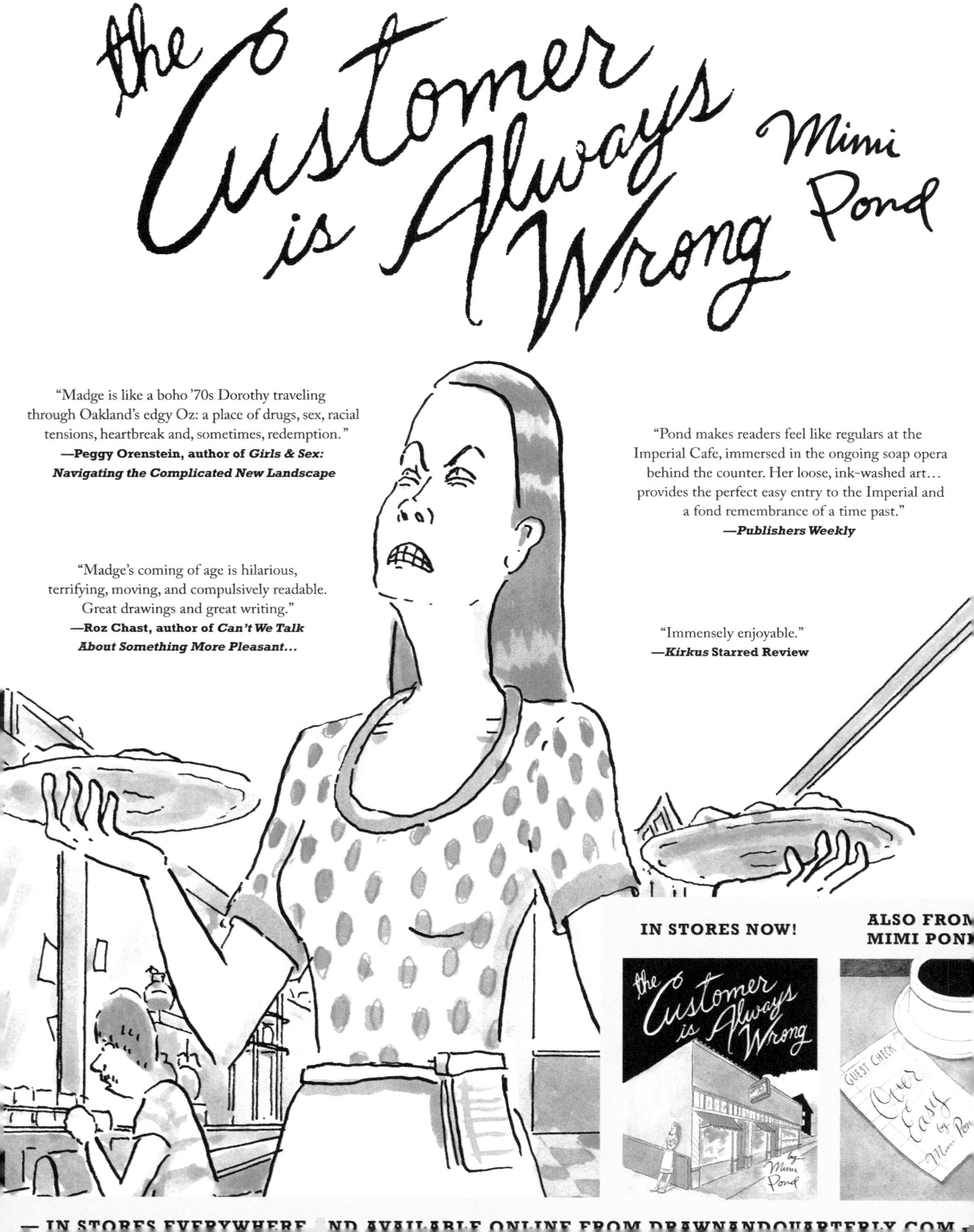
the Customer is Always Wrong
Mimi Pond
"Madge is like a boho '70s Dorothy traveling through Oakland's edgy Oz: a place of drugs, sex, racial tensions, heartbreak and, sometimes, redemption."
—Peggy Orenstein, author of *Girls & Sex: Navigating the Complicated New Landscape*
"Pond makes readers feel like regulars at the Imperial Cafe, immersed in the ongoing soap opera behind the counter. Her loose, ink-washed art… provides the perfect easy entry to the Imperial and a fond remembrance of a time past."
—*Publishers Weekly*
"Madge's coming of age is hilarious, terrifying, moving, and compulsively readable. Great drawings and great writing."
—Roz Chast, author of *Can't We Talk About Something More Pleasant...*
"Immensely enjoyable."
—*Kirkus* Starred Review
IN STORES NOW!
the Customer is Always Wrong
by Mimi Pond
ALSO FROM
MIMI PON
GUEST CHECK
Over Easy
— IN STORES EVERYWHERE ND AVAILABLE ONLINE FROM DRAWNANDQUARTERLY.COM

NEWS & NOTES

Gerber-2 asks, "Were you at our first-ever live reading? Did you see that couple in the corner?"

The Bystander boys, after a boisterous (but not too boozy) staff lunch, 4/25/17. From left: Gerber-2, McConnachie, Goldberg.

It has come to our attention that a rumor has taken hold in certain quandrants of our readership: that *Bystander*'s Editor & Publisher, **MICHAEL GERBER**, is in fact an ongoing experiment undertaken by a group of computer scientists at the University of Illinois. According to Alex Jones, "This so-called 'Michael Gerber' doesn't exist. He's a computer program, a rudimentary form of A.I., artificial intelligence, designed to make humanity obsolete."

The scientists, the story goes, were so incensed by the election of Donald Trump, they dusted off a bunch of Nixon-era cybercivics software designed to create "virtual citizens." In this way, democracy can be controlled without the obvious tell of stripping anyone of the right to vote.

"Whenever a candidate is running that the eggheads don't like," Jones says, "they release a swarm of these 'bots,' who all vote 'intelligently'... The humor magazine thing, that's just a stalking horse, a dry run for 2020. And you better believe the program's totally off-the-books. The scientists are settling a bet. 'I bet you can't do it.' 'I bet I can.' That's how nerds fight."

Like all truly great conspiracy theories, its surface logic is appealing and almost impossible to refute. After all, what person would be so misguided as to run a print humor magazine these days? If you had the smarts to do it, you'd also know it was impossible. Flesh-and-blood people need to eat, pay bills; *ergo*, it has to be some sort of replicant.

Frustrated and out of ideas, the shadowy *Bystander* High Command sent Mr. Gerber to New York in April, May and June, in hopes that a critical mass of contributors and subscribers would meet him, be convinced, and this rumor would be put to rest. It didn't work. "He's obviously an actor." "I saw that guy spinning a sign outside Verizon two weeks ago." "Boy, his mask is really glued on *tight*."

Bulgarian fake news sites and the world's biggest bot-net are now spewing a variation on the theory: A humorist named Michael Gerber did exist, but was killed in a car crash shortly after publication of the first *Barry Trotter* book. ("That's why the last two sucked.") The theory asserts that agents of MI-5 acted on secret orders from the British royal family, which was concerned Gerber-1 would lampoon more

and more books until Britain's cultural patrimony would be in ruins. The man running *Bystander* is "Gerber-2," the winner of a 2003 lookalike contest announced by Orion Books, but then supposedly canceled for "lack of interest."

Before we get to Gerber-2's account of our first-ever live event, we'd like to extend a special *Bystander* welcome* to a few of the contributors making their debuts in this issue. Readers of the now online-only *Village Voice* will remember cartoonist **STAN MACK** (Page 24). We are delighted to have Stan aboard, and are more determined than ever to thrive in this era of dwindling outlets for high-quality work.

Another downtown paper, *The Soho Weekly News*, was the original home for **TOM HACHTMAN**'s lovely "Gertrude's Follies" (Page 69). Tom is teaming up with beloved *Bystander* **SAM GROSS**, and it's a winning combination.

Finally, readers of *The National Lampoon* will certainly remember **ED SUBITZKY**, who was all over that august publication (and its audio offshoot, the *Radio Hour*). We've been politely pursuing Ed since before Issue #1, and we're delighted that he's joined the fold. Welcome, fellas — and to all you other newbies as well. Now, Gerber-2, the floor is yours.

Thanks, disembodied institutional voice. Humor magazines are — no blame, no shame — an introverted pleasure. So I wasn't being entirely Eeyorish convincing myself that nobody would show for *Bystander*'s first-ever reading, held in the East Village this past June 15th. I walked into the HiFi bar full of Kaufmanesque contingency plans: Maybe we'd end up playing charades, or I'd take the audience to Katz's. ("I'll have one egg cream, and 27 straws.")

Turns out the straws weren't necessary. The modest back room of the bar — about the size of a squash court, with a tiny stage at one end — was packed as full as the overnight train to Mumbai. I practically had to shout credentials just to make it through the crowd. **JAMES FOLTA** said, "I've spent a lot of time at HiFi,

EVAN WAITE

* We're not going to get into what precisely a "Bystander welcome" entails, but it for sure involves asking you for $20 via Kickstarter.

and I have to say beyond any doubt the *Bystander* show was the sweatiest I've ever been in that place."

Luckily, the mood was friendly — *very* friendly. "Sitting on laps was in full effect," **M. SWEENEY LAWLESS** said. I don't know if any babies were conceived, it was hard to see from the stage. Mike the bartender was doing his best to make conditions favorable.

After my rather shambling introduction — saved when the crowd broke into a rousing rendition of "Happy Birthday" (as I revealed in Issue #4, Donald Trump and I share June 14) — the cartoonist **PETER KUPER** started us off right. "I had spent months preparing a PowerPoint show on the history of aquatic insects (it runs 2.5 hours) but when the computer failed to work, I was forced to tell a short comedie tale of a flight I took to Istanbul. It was clear the audience was deeply disappointed; I look forward to a future event where my complete historic analysis of the *Corixidae* (among many other fascinating creatures) can be presented in full."

The first half continued brilliantly, with **TIM HARROD** delivering a rendition of his Paul Bunyan piece from *Bystander* #4 that made me wish he'd do a children's album. **LEE SACHS** followed up admirably; this being downtown, where pretentious restaurants sprout like mushrooms, "Monk Chin" wrung many laughs of recognition from the throng. Then **EVAN WAITE** read something I liked so much I bought it on the spot (you can read it on Page 20). After Ms. Lawless detonated the absurd and, frankly, irresponsible Goldilocks mythos with gum-chewing swagger, the crowd was spent from laughter (and God knows what else). So we gave them 10 minutes to refill their drinks and think about what they'd done.

My wife, Kate, got me a glass of water, and as I looked out upon the churning wall of subscribers, my mischievous brain squirted out a thought: *What if I need to pee?* Would the staff form a *cordon sanitare* between myself and the audience as I relieved myself in a cup? For what we pay?

Then it was onto Round 2. First, I asked some friends in the audience to coax co-founder **ALAN GOLDBERG** to the stage. Alan was the man who brought **BRIAN**

M^cCONNACHIE and I together, then kept the *Bystander* project on track when I was recovering from an illness. He does a million things to keep *Bystander* going, including co-writing our crossword, but he'd be the last one to tell anybody. So I had to. "Alan's too shy to say this," I said, "but without him, this magazine wouldn't exist." The crowd showered him with applause, enough, I hope, for Alan to forgive me (at least a little bit).

I read a few "regrets" sent in by staffers (reproduced on Page 77), and then stepped aside for the real talent. James Folta read the comments he received on a recent piece; and then **DENNIS PERRIN** read an excerpt of his memoir, *JanitorGod*. Dennis's book has a wonderful effect on audiences. It makes them so happy and grateful their lives don't suck.

Those of us wanting to sell goods and services to **RIVER CLEGG** were treated to a hilarious (and very useful) essay on how to do just that. Then came **J.A. WEINSTEIN**, who had this to say: "I killed; veritably challenged those who followed me to kill on the level that I killed or hail a hansom cab and go home. **STEVE YOUNG** and **TODD HANSON** promptly killed: killing on a level of killing greater than even my killing."

Yes, Steve Young — one of my ringers. Back in 2014, I'd seen him emcee a show at Cinefamily here in Los Angeles, where he told jokes, did patter, played guitar and sang. On this evening, he read the piece on Page 30, to much, much applause.

By now it was 9:30, and time to wind things up. Faces were flushed from laughter and heat, and there was at least one couple who looked definitely ready to commit a health code violation. When I first considered doing a reading, I asked a few staffers for suggestions. "Get Todd Hanson," **P.S. MUELLER** said to me, "and make him your closer." I did, and he was. I didn't think Todd's article "Sic Semper Papyrus" from Issue #2 could be any funnier, but turns out it's even better when Todd reads it aloud.

And with that, I banged the gavel, and everyone dispersed. I think Kate shot most of the night on her phone; if there's interest, maybe we'll put it up. Looking back, I'm truly grateful for two things in particular. First, that the whole evening was suffused with the *Bystander* spirit: a mellow, unhurried geniality and wit, blossoming unexpectedly in a small corner of the world. And second, that I didn't have to pee.

We'll do more readings, for sure in New York and L.A., where so many of you are — and if those of you in other locales are interested, drop me a line at publisher@americanbystander.org. **B**

After **STEVE BRODNER**'s *wonderful cover for Issue #4, we had to ask, "What's your secret?" This was his reply. Turns out, behind every great artist is...a dog.*

BY TODD HANSON

THE CRUELEST MONTH

Burning and burning in the shimmering haze / The falcon lies deep-fried before the falconer

#1: LAMENT

My God hath curs'd me with this hellish heat
And air so still and lusterless it seems
To lack even the oxygen enough
To fire the neurons of the brain's gray mass

And sustain life.
Oh woe! Humidity
Descends upon my slack and morbid form
And causes sick'ning rivulets to drain
From me as I lay sprawl'd on this sofa, doomed.

Noon's furious meridian is cross'd.
The flaming chariot of Helios,
Ablaze in sky o'erhead, a hammer-blow
Upon the blasted anvil of this world.

And yet, the sunbeam's rays seem fallen not
From Heav'n above, but risen up from Hell,
A vast and stinking continent of filth,
Fierce fire, and foul contagion's evil fume.

So thus this oven of a chamber seems
Waged war upon by Heav'n and Hell alike.
Here in these tortur'd rooms like glowing coals
What respite is there ever to be found?

Why, ask I, hath this planet meted out
A punishment so dire and cruel as this?
How can it be this Earth, which we were born
Into without our knowledge or consent

Should persecute us with such merciless
And unrelentingly sadistic aim?
Alas! Alack! My soul-spent sorrows grow.
I hate the New York City summer so!

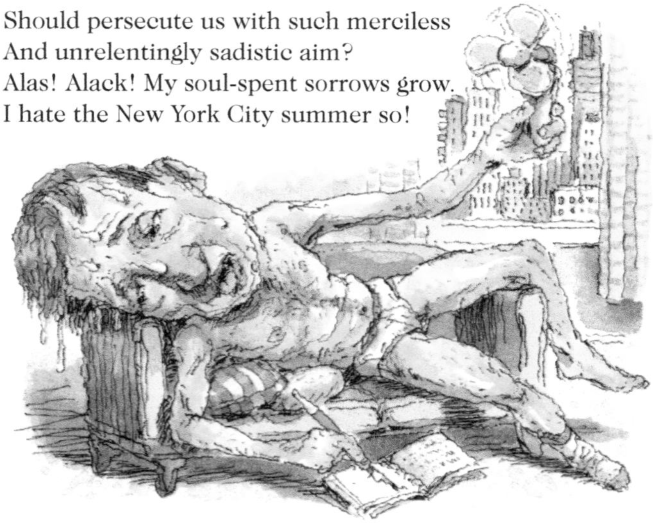

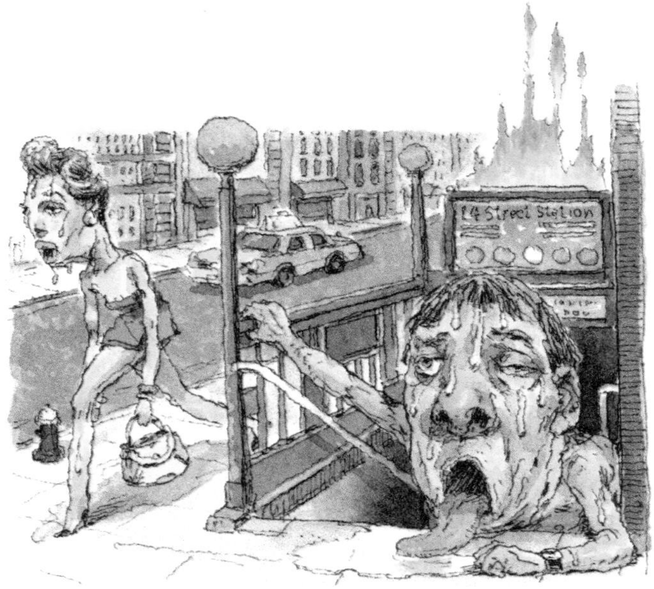
14 Street Station

JOHN CUNEO

#2: LAMENT

The city lies spread out below the sky
Like a corpse laid on an undertaker's table
Awaiting the finality of cremation.
Is this to be my death's predestination?
That I should die par-boiled, gasping and panting?
My, but the air lies thick upon the stairway landing!

Above the melting asphalt on the streets
The women come and go in office buildings,
Complaining of the frigid air-conditioning.

I should have been a pair of ragged claws
Scuttling across the floors of silent seas
Where darkness always stays within the range
Of 34 to 38 degrees.

The yellow light which rubs its muzzle on the window panes,
The savage light which stabs its claws against the window panes
What is it?
What living nightmare pounds upon the door,
And grins its sickly grin
And comes to visit?
And enters here though uninvited in?

I grow hot… I grow hot…
I shall wear my shirt-sleeves and my trousers not.

#5: HYMN

At last the heat hath broken and our gladdened hearts rejoice!
Across the city all as one sing with uplifted voice!
To kindly skies above we reach and with all hands upraised
Cry out in grateful ecstasy loud hymns of thanks and praise!

Gloria! Gloria!
In excelsis Deo!
Our Lord in all His mercy hath now given what we prayed for!

The atmosphere is cool and dry as gentle breezes waft
To soothe our thankful bodies with caresses sweet and soft!
The temperature has dropped and now our hearts so
      joyous swell
And songs of celebration ring out loud as pealing bells!!

Praise Him! Praise Him!
Praised be the Lord!
At last we are delivered from Hyperionides's sword!

Though still we know this Heav'n on Earth cannot
      forever last,
For soon we'll face again the force of awful August's blast,
Today our souls are comforted! Today sweet tears of joy
Fall from the eyes of every woman, man, and girl and boy!

Hallelujah! Hallelujah!
Hosanna in the highest!
The Lord in all His mercy hath made New York
 City thrice-blessed! **B**

#3: LAMENT

Burning and burning in the shimmering haze
The falcon lies deep-fried before the falconer;
Things melt apart; the AC cannot hold;
Mere lethargy is loosed upon these rooms
Now uninhabitable, and the worst:
The salesman at the home appliance store,
Though full of passionate intensity,
Can't guarantee replacement 'til next week.

Surely a record summer is at hand.
Surely the Global Warming is at hand!
The Global Warming! Hardly are those words out
When a vast image out of *An Inconvenient Truth*
Troubles my sight: a chart so long and tall
Gore must ride a hydraulic platform lift
To reach its lofty heights. What demon nears
Whose gaze is blank and pitiless as the sun's
With hate enough to char the very air?
What weapon does it brandish at our throats?
What flaming weapon of what Antichrist?
What singed beast, its hour come round again
Slouches towards Brooklyn, there to burn?

#4: LAMENT

This horrid heat and
 Stifling humidity has
Made me hate the world

TODD HANSON *has written for* **The Onion** *since 1990. He lives in Brooklyn with his two cats, James Boswell (Dr. Samuel Johnson R.I.P.) and Max Rockatansky.*

Gallimaufry

"So long as men worship the Caesars and Napoleons,
Caesars and Napoleons will duly rise and make them miserable."
Aldous Huxley

A BOILERPLATE LETTER FROM IRA GLASS.

Congratulations! Your town has been chosen by Ira Glass for in-depth, award winning exploitation!

In anticipation of our arrival, please be prepared to furnish our crew with the following:

20-250 acres of backwoods wherein something atrocious may or may not have happened;

A serpentine narrative about a decades-old family grudge/abusive school board/corrupt municipal employee that peters out anticlimatically, only... does it? And what does our expectation about a neat and tidy resolution say about our society?

One free week of Blue Apron meals;

One eccentric lawyer/accountant/self-taught antique metallurgist whom no one trusts for reasons to be divulged later, and stands up for something no one believes in;

Two to five wealthy individuals from a single extended family who have it out for the lawyer/accountant/metallurgist because he/she is an ethnic or religious minority/gay/a secret relative who will ruin the family business;

At least one, but no more than three, *elderly townsfolk* with accents thick enough to force our producers to condescendingly "translate"

for the listeners;

Assorted racists;

An unusual local custom that our producer can easily encapsulate in a thirty second, in-studio description that Ira, and only Ira, will find unbelievably hysterical;

No fewer than four outdoor locations with consistent wind speeds of between 15-25 mph;

No fewer than three diners with suspiciously opinionated staff and moderately racist customers;

A racist town motto and/or racist town flag;

A sacrificial blood offering to Torey Malatia in the form of a ram, a young bull without blemish, or the mayor's firstborn son. If none of these are possible, a Producers Circle membership to WBEZ will suffice.

—*Josh Perilo*

HOW TO WIN THE WAR WITH YOUR PICKY EATER.

Babies aren't picky. Science has discovered that they will eat just about anything — even human milk. But as children enter their toddler years, many develop a fear of unfamiliar foods. Fortunately there are exactly nine things you can do to keep your child from becoming a picky eater.

1. Have fun with food! If your child hates broccoli but loves cheese, give her broccoli with a bit of cheese sauce. If she hates peppers but loves unicorn stickers, put unicorn stickers on the peppers before serving. Be creative!

2. Badgering the child about eating will only make him dig in his heels. So instead of bribing him to finish his milk-boiled haddock or jellied tripe or steamed hog anus stuffed with bird anuses, make it seem like he won a prize. Congratulations! *Eat these anuses!*

3. Still nothing? Hmm. Try pulling down sharply on the child's legs to get the mouth to open and insert the food. Pump the legs to activate the chewing mechanism, then blast the child with an air horn to initiate swallowing. Repeat as needed. Nine times out of 10, this will do the trick.

4. Maybe it's just a matter of perspective? For instance, does your child know there are starving

children in China? No? Then tell him! If that doesn't work, adopt one. Her name is Chenguang. Give all of your child's food and things to Chenguang. See how he likes it.

5. Try hiding healthy foods inside other foods your child enjoys. Like a bit of spinach inside a chocolate cake. That way he'll learn early on that even the things he loves the most cannot be trusted — useful training for adult life.

6. Here's a question for you: Is it significant that your child will only eat white food? And here's an answer: Yes. A recent study found that 93 percent of American bigots subsist entirely on a diet of chicken nuggets, pasta, milk, and grilled cheese. This is the result of that glass of wine you had while pregnant, and it is permanent. Sorry.

7. Come to think of it, the presence of Chenguang may not be helping with the racism thing. Even if your child is pretending that his objection is based on China's alleged currency manipulation and not the fact that Chenguang has his room and his things and the love you used to have for him.

8. Another question: Is your child actually a child? Examine its underside. What do you see? Is it a cat penis? What you have may actually be a cat. Try cat food.

9. Look, in the fullness of time, no one will really care whether your kid or cat or whatever will eat Pad Thai. The seas are rising. Human civilization is in flux. The universe is expanding. Disruption is the norm. You'd be better off teaching the little bigot to hunt with a rock rather than wasting all your time trying to shove poke down his throat so people on Instagram can see how precocious he is.

10. Have you tried *baby* carrots? We're, like, *obsessed* with baby carrots.

—*Joe Keohane*

SIDE EFFECTS MAY INCLUDE...

...Snarling and smirking; larking about and swooning; acting snarky; Schmedly's Narcoma; ceaselessly yelling at what you think is living in your walls; the Jimmies and the Willies; all loss of ethics; the urge to roughhouse; fainting and drooling while driving and singing;

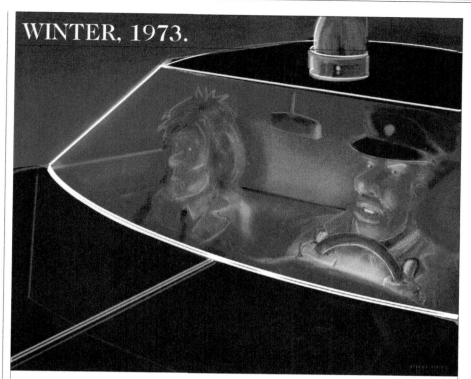

WINTER, 1973.

*O*ne evening, my father, a cop whom I rarely saw or spoke to, was inexplicably waiting for me after high school. He opened the door of the paddy wagon and growled, "Get in."

As we drove, he mumbled a disjointed monologue. I couldn't make out everything. "Hair... armpits... pus," he stammered. "...Weird dreams ... smells like bleach ...underpants ... those sissies in the men's room...gotta use Aqua Velva..." For a moment I thought he was reciting William Burroughs.

Then he was interrupted by a call from headquarters. After a quick back and forth with the dispatcher, he turned to me and said: "Big bar fight by the mills. I got to drop you off now."

As I stepped out of the truck, before I slammed the door, he turned back to me and said, "If you have any questions, just ask me, O.K.?"

Then he turned on the big red light, hit the siren and sped off.

When he was far enough away, I pulled out my cigarettes. "What the hell was that all about?" I wondered.

Then it hit me. He was trying to talk about sex.

—*Andy Prieboy*

tongue stink; knuckle dancing; the Nincompoop Syndrome — Level 2; Acting like a pig-eyed dandy; rapid cheek inflating and deflating; acting wall-eyed for no apparent reason; lazy hearing; growing angry hair; spilling the beans; leaping and glaring; talking the talk — then taking the talk and walking it back (like a reverse mortgage without the paperwork); shaking, pointing then really shaking; the want to be fondled; the Sloppies; acting suspiciously while drowning; drooling while fracking; always demanding more time in the barrel with Dopey; lumps and belly lice; taking slap dancing lessons too personally; madly scratching all over while waltzing; monkey business at its most irrepressible; growing aggressively vague; hiding under the furniture; taking things from the wheelhouse and not putting them back; eyes spinning around in your head, faster and faster and faster, until you scream: "Why did I have all those jellyfish brains that passed their expiration date and now belong to the ages as soon might I!"; the Cranberry Crazies; the woeful jitters; the screaming mimis; the hiccups, Chicago style; the swelling meanies;

"I consider us 'friends with benefits.'"

reckless, hallucinating and deathbed yodeling; bucket kicking, fleas; ear wigs; belly spiders; toilet snakes; and a certainty you've begun growing extra fingers and toes.*

—*Brian McConnachie*

THIS TIME IS DIFFERENT.

We have your son.

For real this time. It's not the sack of potatoes again, I can promise you that.

No, this time it's really your son here, crying his eyes out for mommy and daddy to forget all about the potato sack — and the watermelon with sunglasses on it — and for God's sake get him out of here.

It's your son, your human son that we have. Not the dog with the Groucho Marx mask taped to its face.

It's not the doll, either — the one we photographed while jerking the camera to make it look blurry. You have to admit that fooled you, though. Admit you were scared by the blurry doll, at least for a second, until you saw that we forgot to take it out of the box labeled "Doll! FAKE."

This time there's no doubt about it: we have your son. Or daughter, whichever it is that you have. For the sake of convenience, we'll refer to him throughout this note as your son, but never forget

———————
* *Which could also be listed as an asset if only such a list exists.*

that *we have your child*, boy or girl—or, if you don't have children, then your favorite pet or small antique.

And if you want him back in one piece, then I suggest you read this letter very carefully. But not too carefully. Not like last time, when you noticed the part that said "ADD ADDITIONAL BLUFFING HERE." Anyway, this time we have no reason to bluff, now that we have your actual son, and not the Roomba with the scarecrow head mounted on it.

ADD ADDITIONAL BLUFFING HERE.

Don't believe me? Well, maybe you'll change your tune once you look in your mailbox. (Note: I'm referring to a toe that should have come in another package. It's possible you didn't get it, because we may not have mailed it correctly. But suffice it to say it contains a toe—a *real* toe, and not a gummy bear this time.)

This is the real deal. Don't expect a call from someone telling you they overheard us, and then pressed redial on the phone in order to tell you it's all fake. We fired that guy. Sure, then we rehired him, because he's really good with computers. But we told him "no redials," and he's been pretty good about it so far.

And this isn't the time we misunderstood and thought a kidnapping somehow meant we paid *you*. No, sir. This time it's *you* who will be paying.

The police won't bail you out, not this time. Not with our new hiding place, which is so far superior to our last hiding

place that you can barely even believe it's the same house.

So if you want your son back, I suggest you comply with our every demand. And if you don't want him back, then I suggest you *still* comply, because in that case we'll only kill him if you do exactly as we say. (We've thought through every angle.)

Here is what you need to do: First, get $100,000 in unmarked bills. Real bills this time, O.K.? That's right: We bought a Monopoly set and have studied it closely. So don't even think about pulling *that* little trick again. Not unless you're ready to substitute the Monopoly bills at a rate of *five to one*.

Then place the money in a suitcase and bring it to the park. This time we've marked the spot to bury it, because nobody needs a repeat of the water main incident. Look around until you find the spot marked "Stinky grave — do not dig!" That's precisely where you're to bury the money, eight feet down, underneath the stinky grave.

Come alone. Not like last time. Not with your "special friends" who really turn out to be *cops* that you're just regular friends with. No: This time, alone means *alone*. And I hope, for your son's sake, that you fully comprehend that. If you want to bring a friend, O.K., but tell him it's a treasure hunt.

And that's it. We learned our lesson last time: Keep things simple, no matter *how* great the temptation to involve a Rube Goldberg contraption and a pit full of snakes. In kidnapping, there are no points for difficulty. That's right: We know you were lying when you said there were.

And we also know the prize you gave us for "most kidnapping points" was made of plastic. This time, there's only one prize we want from you: the money. Got it? Or else a really nice fruit basket.

One last thing: Please do not go to or call your son's school until this is resolved.

—*Nathaniel Stein*

MOBY-DICK, ABRIDGED.

They hunted whale
To no avail.

—*J.D. Smith*

ALTERNATE EARTHS I HAVE ENCOUNTERED IN MY TIME TRAVELS.

While my time machine is in the shop for repairs (*NB:* Samuel Johnson cannot parallel park), I undertake to list the many exotic pseudo-Earths seen on my voyages through the hyperverse:

An Earth that is an exact mirror image of our own Earth; its inhabitants must carry mirrors around in order to read anything.

An Earth where the South lost the Civil War, but promptly got over it.

An Earth with 14 moons of all different sizes, colors and orbital periods, and where love songs and poems get bogged down in tedious specifics.

An "evil" Earth where the men all have goatees and the women wear '80s power suits and wraparound sunglasses. Women who can't pull off this look are consoled by their friends that they're "evil on the inside."

An Earth very different from ours, as its atmosphere is of caustic ammonia fumes. Also, mayoral appointees for New York City transportation commissioner can be blocked if four-fifths of the City Council vote against them. On reflection, buying a newspaper was not worth the fumes.

An Earth where all television programs end with shatteringly ironic twists, except *The Twilight Zone*, which ends with the hero prevailing against moderate adversity.

An Earth where the number system is base-12 instead of base-10, and where cashiers talk to me like I'm an idiot.

An Earth where James Joyce never wrote *Finnegans Wake*. The people of this Earth act like they're much poorer culturally, but if pinned down they can't explain why.

An Earth where humans receive all nourishment through the nose. The mouth's primary function is saying, "My God, this is horrible."

An Earth where Jews celebrate Ramadan and Muslims observe Passover. This Earth's traditional Seder calls for the youngest child to ask, "Why, apart from the bizarre string of non sequiturs, is tonight different from all other nights?"

An Earth where articles, pronouns and conjunctions are considered profane, causing churchgoing people to talk like Tarzan.

An Earth where the film *Casablanca* is exactly the same, only instead of "Rick" and "Ilsa," the principal characters are named Eggbert and Sharnelle. This version ranks between 25 and 40 on lists of the best movies ever.

A hostile, frigid Earth where winter weather continues into late April, there are too many political parties to understand election coverage, and for some reason napkins are called serviettes. May their insane alien gods protect them.

—Tim Harrod

MOM, YOU CAN STOP HIDING BEHIND ALL MY MIRRORS NOW.

O.K. Mom, you need to stop. Kudos to you for the prank — I honestly have no idea how you managed to get behind some of those mirrors. Does Mr. Huang next door know that you've been in his bathroom? And that you decorated it to look exactly like a mirror image of my bathroom? But seriously: This is a lot of effort just to give me a few seconds of discomfort. Please stop hiding behind all my mirrors. It's not funny anymore.

I get it — when I was a kid I laughed at your chin hairs. And when you said, "It'll happen to you!" I laughed even more. Now you not only remember that conversation, you're paying me back for it. Real mature, Mom. Real loving. Can I ask, How much time do you spend hiding behind my mirrors, just in case I go to the bathroom, or pick up my hand mirror? And how do you always know which mirror I'll pick? It's uncanny. Have you spent decades studying my mirror behavior?

This is a really long way to go for a prank, Mom. I thought you had a job.

Also, we need to have a conversation about boundaries. It's one thing to play a joke and make me think I inherited your face. It's another to make me think I inherited your boobs. I don't like the idea of you standing naked in front of

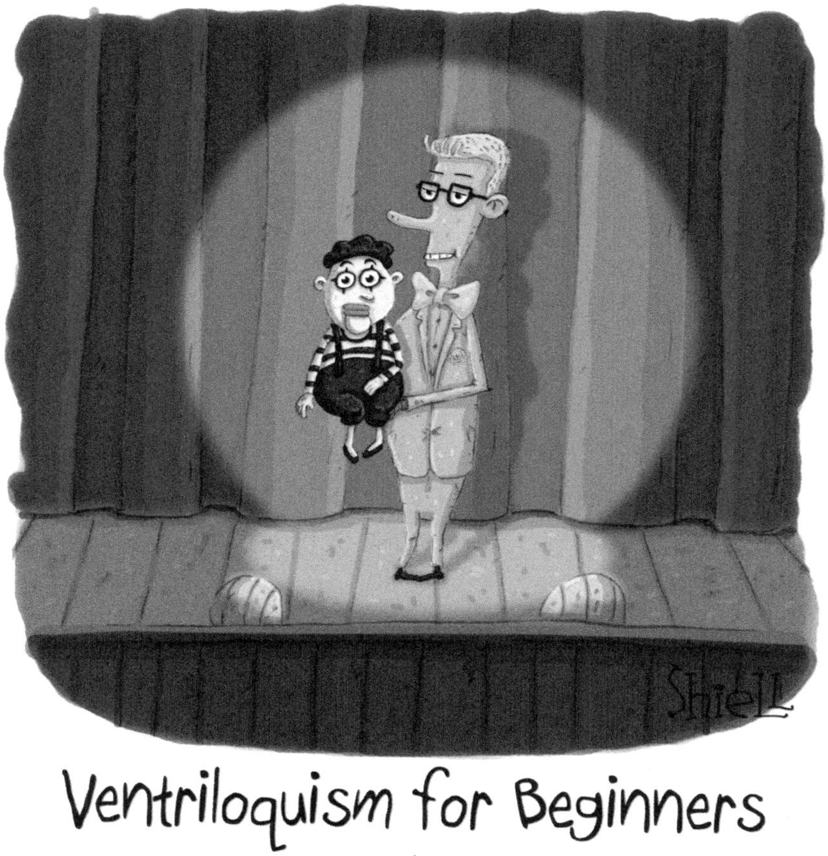
Shiell

Ventriloquism for Beginners

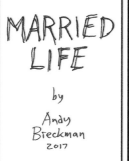

MARRIED LIFE

by Andy Breckman 2017

I love my wife, but she can be a real grammar Nazi.

For example...

You and me should go shopping.

You mean, You and me should go shopping, heil Hitler.

me, trying to slap some sense into your droopy nipples just because I'm doing the same thing on the other side of the mirror. Does Mr. Huang know you spend hours standing naked in his bathroom? Does Dad?

And F.Y.I., I think you should see a doctor; there's some sort of hormone issue going on that you really need to get checked out. Your nipples have a lot of hair, Mom.

By the way, where did you get that old Jewish witch makeup? It looks cartoonish. You're basically dressing up as an issue of *Der Stürmer*. Can you imagine what Grandma would say if she saw you? Take it off, please. We're not in the right political climate for jokes like that. We didn't come this far as a people for you to — it's like the *Protocols of the Elders of Zion* had a centerfold.

Listen, I'm sorry I ever made fun of you as a kid. I'm sorry I acted like a brat who would never get old. And — political correctness aside — I have to say I admire your level of commitment to a joke. But please, Mom. Stop hiding behind my mirrors. It's creeping me out.

—*Hana Michels*

A QUIZ.

1) Boogie Nights are...
   a) always the best in town
   b) never the best in town
   c) occasionally the best in town
   d) like many things, a rich and nuanced combination of good and bad.
2) We had joy, we had fun, we had...
   a) scabies
   b) a lifetime of poor communication
   c) O.K. sex, I guess
   d) seasons in the sun.
3) Some people want to fill the world with...
   a) silly love songs
   b) macabre love songs
   c) Orwellian love songs
   d) low-income housing.
4) As I was walking down the street one day, a man came up to me and asked me what the time was that was on my watch, and I said...
   a) that the time that was on my watch was the time of 4:55.
   b) it's time to get a new watch, ha-ha-ha! I'm sorry, what was the question?
   c) does anybody really know what time it is?
   d) does anybody really know what time it is, to which he replied, "Real helpful, Socrates."
5) When I die and they lay me to rest, gonna go to the place...
   a) that's the best
   b) that's the second best
   c) that's the third best
   d) that at least has a decent salad bar.
6) Me and you and a dog named Boo, travelin' and...
   a) livin off the land
   b) shooting up
   c) arguing constantly
   d) perpetually explaining our dog's bonkers moniker.
7) If I don't see a yellow ribbon round the old oak tree I'll...
   a) check the old sycamore tree
   b) check the old lodgepole pine tree
   c) stay on the bus, forget about us, put the blame on me
   d) double-check the old oak tree.
8) I've been to paradise, but I've never been...
   a) to Poughkeepsie
   b) to school
   c) to me
   d) adequately punished for writing this lyric.

—*Chris Dingman*

READY FOR AN ON-TIME DEPARTURE.

Ladies and gentlemen, welcome aboard American Time Machines Flight 477 to the Dark Ages. My name is Eloise, and I'll be your flight attendant for the past millennium.

Please turn off all telephones and electronic devices, set any sentient robotic companions to sleep mode and hide any wristwatches or clocks lest you gaze upon them and be driven mad. For our travelers from prior eras, please extinguish all coal and wood fires, and make sure any sacred monoliths are safely stowed in an overhead compartment.

Take a moment to look around you and locate your nearest exit. In some rows, your nearest exit may be several decades in your past. In case of a landing in primordial ooze, your seat is equipped with the basic building blocks of life, which will eventually evolve into somebody capable of rescuing you.

In the event of a serious rupture to the time-space continuum, pencil and graph paper will drop from the overhead compartment, so you can work out your new timeline. If you are traveling with yourself as a child, please work out your grownup chronology before attempting to help your you-as-a-child.

TTSA regulations require complete security both forward and backward in time, which means you must keep baggage in your control not merely before boarding but for all eternity thereafter. It may be easiest just to burn your things when you land. If you are traveling to a period before the invention of fire, please burn your luggage in a hidden location, lest you begin the march of human progress centuries too soon, which could invalidate your return ticket.

Since most of our trip will take place before you were born, federal law forbids murdering your own grandparents while in flight. For your safety and continued existence, paradox detectors have been installed in the toilets. It is a crime to tamper with or disable these detectors, or to murder the grandparents of the guy who invented them.

During our journey, attendants will be passing up and down the aisle selling a wide range of goods that were thought lost to history. Please note that Greek fire may not be used onboard the timecraft. For in-flight entertainment, we have the original director's cut of *The Magnificent Ambersons* on Channel 1; the original director's cut of *Metropolis* on Channel 2; and Channel 3 is a high-definition image of the Mona Lisa. The *real* one, not the vastly inferior forgery that's been hanging in the Louvre since 1913.

We'll be going back a thousand years today. It will take us four hours and 15 minutes to get there, giving us a total flight time of negative 999 years, 364 days, 19 hours and 45 minutes. We guarantee that we have stocked the in-flight meal of your choice, as long as you tell the flight attendants what it was as you're leaving the plane.

We thank you for flying American Time Machines. We know you have a choice when you travel, since our competitors include not just our contemporaries but every time travel line that will ever be established. Plus those guys from the ancient glowing pyramid that suddenly showed up in Manhattan. They might be a little bit cheaper, but here at ATM, we'll *never* extract your brains through your nose. That's a promise.

-ogy or even a possible time loop. Now, sit back, relax and make sure your seatbelts are tightly fastened along all four axes of the spacetime continuum. This is a precaution in the unlikely event we encounter disruption to our onboard chronol-

—Jacob Sager Weinstein

WELCOME TO THE DOLPHIN TRAINERS CONVENTION!

Don't tell me this is your first — you're in for a treat! Let me give you the lay of the land. This is the main reception floor, where everything happens. All the big timers have booths: training institutes, resorts, boat builders, chum producers, wet-suit tailors, blowhole swab manufacturers, you name it. And of course, all the big trainers are here. We are swimming in industry royalty.

Over there, that's Lucas Arwin! I'm completely starstruck. They just retired his wet suit and hung it from the rafters of SeaWorld.

Devlin McMurphy's booth is over there, by the "Mesmerizing World of Snorkels" exhibit. Mundo Marino fired him for "impropiedades del soplido," which is total bullshit; the suits don't know a thing about how real trainers work.

Oh, there's Cindy Harrison. People don't trust her, but I think she's sweet. You know, she worked at the Boston Aquarium for 20 years and hand-fed each and every dolphin daily. So what if she was having an affair with a docent? They were found out by a sea lion that could work a camera.

Hans Bjünger! He's the old fella drinking a glass of seawater. For decades, he was the only dolphin man in East Germany. Hans is an absolute hero — he personally kept the Kremlin from converting all Soviet aquariums into вода коммандос бассейн повесить аутов, which translates to "pool water commandos hangouts."

Wow, even the line for the bathroom is stacked: Hopscotch Marty Rickles; Frank Guzman of the All-Dolphin Handel Revue; and the Baron of Bottlenose himself, Anthony Cheekers!

Look who just walked in: Anna Justine. Her dolphins only swim counterclockwise, to honor her dead husband, Count Clockwise. I can't see who's on her arm — oh no. Dr. Terry Dickerson.

Can I just say? What's a marine biologist doing here? Ugh. He thinks trainers are all "exploiters." He comes on real nice — then he'll try to convince you that we're "torturing" them. Let's step over here out of sight.

Sorry, Pancho! It's her first con!

The guy you just bumped into? Pancho Anguillera. *The* Pancho Anguillera, from

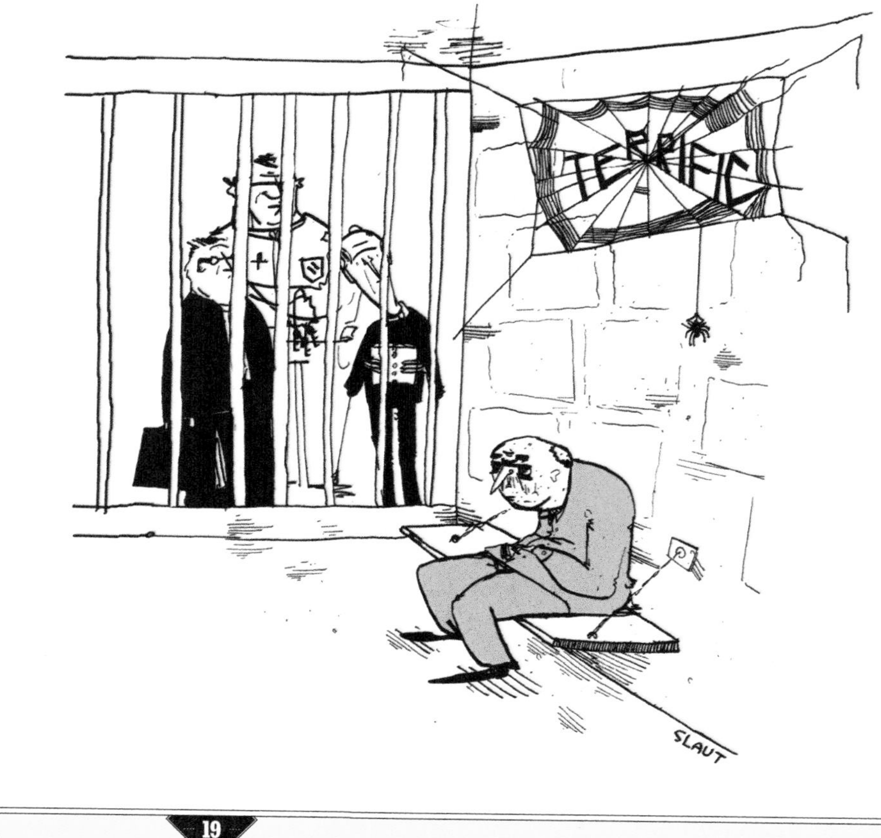
TERRIFIC
SLAUT

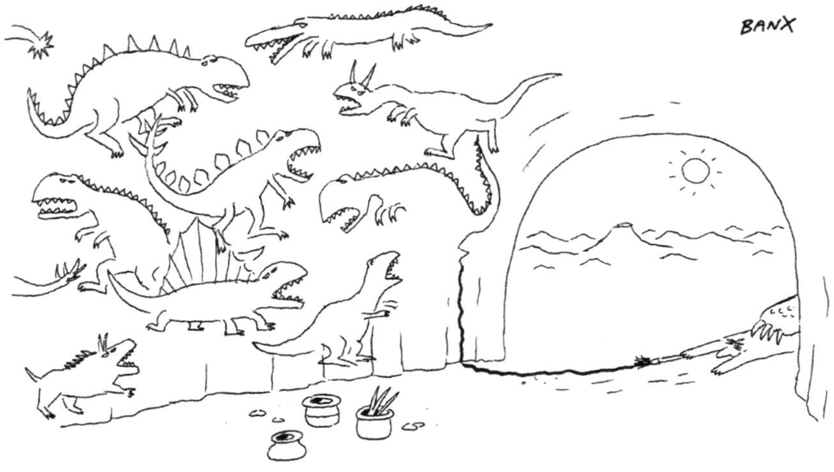
BANX

Denver. Did you know he was one credit away from finishing law school? Then he dropped out to become a blowhole jockey. Now, he can bellyflop the whole national anthem. It's really quite moving.

See the chick talking to Pancho, in black leather? She goes by Autumn. Former card hustler and magician. Her stuff is really dark; she taught the dolphins at Discovery Cove. Now they'll only perform to Cure songs.

Oh no, here comes Dickerson again. Quick, behind this rebreather display!

O.K., in the interest of full disclosure, we used to be married. Now he's shacked up with Justine, and I'm…married to the sea.

Whatever, it's O.K.

The tall guy eating a sardine is Mikey Regent. Sweet, but weird. Mikey tries to do, feel and experience everything his dolphins do. He inhaled a lungful of "red tide" once. Almost killed him.

Well, I don't know why Hank Hurley's here. I saw him royally blow an audition down in the Keys; all the dolphins stayed underwater the whole time. Hank says he can train a porpoise to smoke a cigar, but Terry didn't believe him.

Can I ask you a question? Do you think I was dumb? A marine biologist and a dolphin trainer…we love the ocean's creatures but in completely different ways. I wasn't ready. Terry used to say to me, "Sal, the only animal you can't train is yourself. You're as unruly as a 3-year-old Fraser's Dolphin."

Maybe he was right.

Oh, of course, Randy Portland brought a box of his Flipper Floppers. They're this dumb invention, they let dolphins cook pancakes. Don't make eye contact or else he'll try to sell you a pair.

I don't know, just seeing Terry here… Have I been so devoted to cetaceans that I've neglected the humans in my life? There are days when I secretly dedicate my porpoise work to Terry. I swear they respond better. Porpoises are very sensitive, emotionally.

Look, I'm going to leave you here. There's going to be a keynote on new and innovative uses of pool noodles, you'll like it. Why don't you grab a seat near the tank? I have to go find Terry. Because if I can train a dolphin to recite the Pythagorean Theorem, I can train my heart to love again.

—James Folta

THE BEST PART OF HAVING A DAUGHTER IS I CAN'T BE CALLED 'SEXIST.'

Having a daughter has changed my life in ways I never could have imagined. The first time I held Penelope, a feeling of pure joy washed over me. In that moment, I knew no matter how poorly I treated women from then on, no one could ever accuse me of being a sexist again without me having a rock-solid alibi.

Being her daddy has opened me up to a whole new world of shaming women for demanding equal pay. Now if anyone calls me on my chauvinism, I just pull up my daughter's picture on my phone and hold it right in their stupid face. I even have her sonogram in my wallet. Checkmate, people trying to hold me accountable for being a pig.

God has graced me with an angel. She's changed me. I catcall now.

It may sound corny, but sometimes I like to stare at her in her little crib when she sleeps. It reminds me to be thankful she's blonde, because that covers me on bimbo jokes.

I still remember driving home from the hospital the day Penny was born. I had so many emotions swirling inside of me. Joy. Fear. A newfound assumption I had carte blanche to send hostile tweets to pop stars who cut their hair too short.

Penelope has made me want to be a better mansplainer.

Raising a child isn't easy. Each day brings a fresh challenge, and you have to be prepared for anything. When Penelope grows up, she might ask why I act like such a dick to her friends. Because of her I can say: "Don't judge me. I made a woman." That ought to shut her up.

So far, my son, Dustin, has had no payoff whatsoever. That little freeloader better at least be gay. I've got a lot of homophobic jokes to retroactively justify.

—Evan Waite

IF THERE WERE SWANS, IT WOULD BE A LAMENTATION

One of my favorite things about the musician John Darnielle is that even when he performs without his colleagues, he walks onstage and says: "Good evening. We are the Mountain Goats."

My playlist had just looped around to his song "Slow West Vultures" when I pressed the button that switches off the music to answer the phone — despite the fact that I have caller ID and could see that it was my mother.

When the conversation had gone on longer than I would have liked, which is to say we had exchanged greetings and were still on the phone, she said, "I hope I'm not interrupting anything."

I said: "No. I was just listening to the Mountain Goats."

She said, "Oh! I thought you were in your car."

I said, "I am in my car."

She said, "Why are there mountain goats in your car?"

I said, "It's a recording."

She said: "Oh! That's so funny. While you're driving around. I don't get all that new-agey stuff. People listening to nature sounds, recordings of crickets, rain, a pod of whales."

I said, "It's a band, Mom."

She said, "I'm pretty sure if it's whales it's a pod, dear." She said it in the same tone of condescension and forced patience she used to correct my grammar when I was in kindergarten.

I said: "Not the whales, Mom. The Mountain Goats."

She said, "That would be a herd, dear." That tone again.

I gripped my steering wheel. I listened to my breath. I imagined a bird carrying the weight of my anger toward a distant horizon, as my therapist has advised me to do when I talk to my mother. I said: "No, Mom. The Mountain Goats are a band. They play musical instruments and sing post-grunge humanist folk rock."

She said: "That sounds very interesting. I would love to hear that."

I said, "I can send you a CD."

She said: "Please don't. I wouldn't enjoy it. I was just being polite." I don't know how I knew that she wasn't done talking, but I did and she wasn't. She said, "Can they even know what it's about?"

I said, "Who?"

"The mountain goats. I mean, can they even know what the words mean?"

I said: "Mom. Do you genuinely believe this conversation is actually about mountain goats that have been trained to play musical instruments and sing post-grunge humanist folk rock?"

"Oh, honey. You're just like your father. It's always all about the subtext."

I gripped my steering wheel. I listened to my breath.

She heard the tension over the phone because I am just like my father and it's always all about the subtext. She said, "Are you O.K., Honey? Where did you go?"

I said, "I'm fine, mom. I was just imagining a whole flock of crows headed toward a distant horizon."

She said: "Oh, dear. You're thinking of a murder."

I said: "Yes. Yes, I am."

—Dylan Brody

WILDERNESS SURVIVAL TALES.

Over 72 million Americans will enter the wilderness this year, nearly a third of them overweight. The following tales of survival under the darkest of circumstances appear verbatim. They were told to me by someone who talked with the survivors. They are at once cautionary tales and wake-up calls, notices to many of us that, despite a proximity to wilderness and an overwhelming drive not to die, we simply don't know what the hell we are doing.

I.

"The moment you first realize you are lost — that's crucial. For me, it happened about an hour into my hike. I was inside New Jersey's Pine Barrens, too shy to use my emergency whistle. I knew that the decision to go uphill or down could mean the difference between rescue and disaster. I knew also that sideways also could pose difficulties. I stood in the same spot for nearly 45 minutes, paralyzed by indecision and fear. Then I started thinking about all the things I'd have to do when I got home. I remembered my Alcoholics Anonymous meeting and made a note of it on my iPhone. Four hours later, a search party found me and we walked out of there." *(Jon Anson)*

II.

"Two hours had passed since I'd been separated from Jon [*Anson, of Survival Tale I. — Ed.*]. They say you shouldn't split up, so Jon and I moved gradually apart from each other while periodically shouting to remain within earshot. At some point I yelled, 'Can you hear me, Jon?!!' and got no response. Jon had been carrying the map, the first-aid kit, the compass, the tent, both sleeping bags, the ponchos and the food. Oh, yeah, and the fire-starting supplies. I had been put in charge of the repair kit for Jon's sleeping bag, and the Worcestershire sauce. To make matters worse, I had brought only the pointy kind of compass. I tried to picture myself in a less harrowing set of circumstances. I imagined myself the host of a large dinner party, my friends plying me with compliments and gifts. My wife entered the room, radiant in a beautiful gown. My real-life butler sashayed urbanely toward me with a tray bearing the finest wilderness medicines. I woke up and discovered that a raccoon was gnawing on my fingertips. I took one of the pills my doctor prescribed for my anxiety. My situation seemed to be improving. Somehow, I became savvy to the ways of the woods. I survived for nine miserable years, eating only insects and lichens. Then, unfortunately, a rattlesnake got me." *(William Wyler)*

III.

"My father used to say that since technology can be traced to nature, theo-

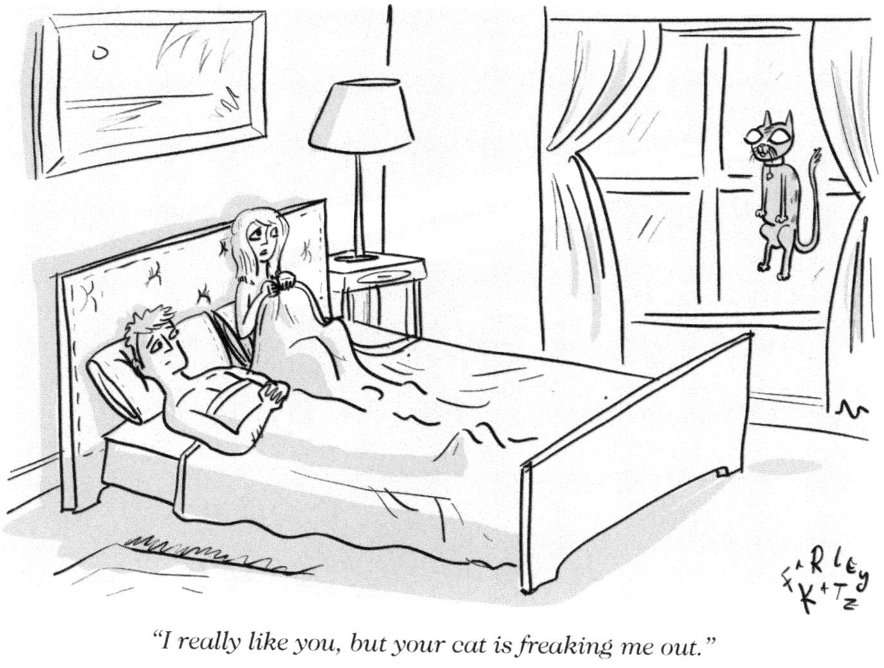

FARLEY KATZ

"I really like you, but your cat is freaking me out."

retically one could walk into the woods one morning and emerge with a VCR. In retrospect, it's possible that Dad meant the Woods', neighbors with a particularly feeble security system. Whatever Dad meant, I one-upped him, ditching my Cessna in the Allegheny Mountains of West Virginia and finding a Global Positioning System device on a tree stump. The find began a series of events so fortunate that even I myself hardly believe them. I found a hot apple pie cooling on a boulder, a wolf jumped into my fire and roasted itself (I later learned it was schizophrenic), and a famous celebrity waved at me from a helicopter. After I ate the wolf, however, my luck turned sour. A blizzard set in. I broke my GPS. A second storm came. The pie didn't sit right. Yet, somehow, I became savvy to the ways of the woods; I learned to drink dew, to take shelter in a hollow tree. I learned to remain calm, to take directions using the sun. I discuss each of these events in my new lecture, 'How to Stay Alive and Find Things in the Wilderness.'" *(Alexandra Minton)*

IV.

"My problem was that I'm a compulsive over-preparer. In my backpack during my ordeal were a pair of loafers, an extension cord and the bibliography from my undergraduate thesis. When darkness fell, on Day 6, I decided to build a fire. I started with tinder, then added kindling, then stopped because I couldn't remember what you call the big pieces. Bored, I made a plan, not to burn my survival manual entirely, but just to let the flames lick one of the corners. This was a mistake. The book disintegrated, and, lacking the big pieces of wood that I now know to be called 'fuel,' my fire expired.

I hiked a little ways and managed to find a Starbucks. I put on my loafers and walked in. The thing about Starbucks is they all look the same. This one, in the middle of the Willow Creek Wetlands Preserve, in southern Oregon, was no exception. I left disgusted, preferring to starve. The experience got me thinking about the differences between civilization and nature. I decided that, for all the amenities of civilization, nature is more elegant and wholesome. It's a cliché to say so, but everything in nature is perfect and harmonious. I began to appreciate the wonders around me, as well as the

horrors, and I've lived here ever since. More pound cake?" *(Don Frederiksen)*

V.

My survival tale takes place at sea, so it might not be as colorful as some of the other folks'. Picture me, in the middle of the ocean, starving in a raft. The sun was baking me. My companions had died. "Under the Sea" was stuck in my head. Four cruise ships passed, but I didn't want to be any trouble. Then came two others, to which I signaled wildly. They seemed to notice but did not help. I did everything I could to seem appealing, like a cool person they would want to have aboard. I said, 'Ha ha, very funny, guys, I get the joke. Come on, let me aboard.' I matted my hair down like the hipsters wear it. More ships kept passing me. It was horrifying. I still don't know how I managed to make it out of there." *(Alice Foyers)*

—*Andrew Barlow*

GETTING IT RIGHT.

I'm Dying Up Here, which follows the travails of stand-up comics in 1973 L.A., is the latest period piece, recreating a time where fashion was wilder, morals were looser, and people didn't care how crazy they came off. In fact, in the past, crazier was better, unless you were there and subject to that era's draconian laws.

As a fan of period fiction, and an overlooked historian, I physically hurt when verifiable facts are gotten wrong. So, I've assembled a few guidelines to

CARPET MATCHES THE DRAPES

SPARKS

help writers accurately capture those periods that shaped the modern world, and make younger people wonder what sex was like before pubic grooming.

Hair — The easiest and hardest thing to get right. If it's post-1968, a decent wig should suffice, provided it doesn't look like it's filled with helium or something pilfered from Rip Taylor's boudoir. For men, any pre-1960s look is achieved through a simple haircut, though some vain actors refuse to do even that. Take Robert Redford in *The Sting*: He thought that by slicking back his long, golden locks he could pass for a Depression-era con man. He tried the same stunt a second time in *The Way We Were*, but audiences got wise to his deception, forcing Redford to the wilds of Utah where stories of a golden-locked god soon emerged, a god who eschewed scissors and gel.

Clothes — The disco era is simple; bellbottoms, leisure suits, crushed velvet. The 1980s, too — pastel linen jackets smudged with cocaine. The Jazz Age, with its cloche hats and long pearls, double-breasted suits and spats, pretty much dresses itself.

The Wild West looks better with mud and horseshit, though there's always an Eastern dandy who strolls into town, convinced he's going to strike it rich, who talks down to the locals while sniffing the carnation in his lapel and snapping his fingers for more brandy and dancing girls. If ever a guy deserved mud and horseshit smeared all over his fancy suit, it's him.

Music — Every era has its soundtrack. It's important that the right song fit each period's mood, or at least reinforce the plot point that was just revealed. If a character on a boat is pondering his or her mortality, play "Rock the Boat" by the Hues Corporation, but only within spitting distance of 1973; earlier is anachronistic, later seems like sad nostalgia. Or you could go Baz Luhrmann and ignore the music timeline altogether, showing bootleggers mix bathtub gin to hip-hop, or Sofia Coppola, who had Marie Antoinette dance to Bow Wow Wow. Few will know the difference.

Dialogue — This is the most direct way to establish a time period, and it helps with exposition. For example:
WOMAN: I fear a war, call it a Civil War, will soon engulf us all.
MAN: Damn this mid-19th century! What

can we do?
WOMAN: It's 1860. History holds us hostage.
Or:
DISGRACED SENATOR: I confess my guilt. If it wasn't for [insert crime here — Teapot Dome Scandal, ABSCAM, etc.], I'd be president today!
Or:
RECORD COMPANY EXECUTIVE: The Beatles, eh? Kooky name, but I got a hunch about you longhairs. A big fat hunch.

Race & Sex — It's said that political correctness has muted cultural expression, but you can get around that by hiding in the past. If a white character says racist or sexist things, well, that's how some white people spoke back then. If a black character responds with anti-white epithets, the ofay cracker has it coming. If a woman uses sex as a weapon, that may be her only recourse in the face of misogyny. If she uses an actual weapon, like a handgun or throwing stars, she might be a mercenary or simply fed up. What kind of show is this anyway?

Final Lessons — In the end, history teaches us that entertainment is better than knowledge. Actually, eating well is better than knowledge. Think about what people ate in 1793. Open a modern fast-food chain back then and you'd have it made.

—Dennis Perrin

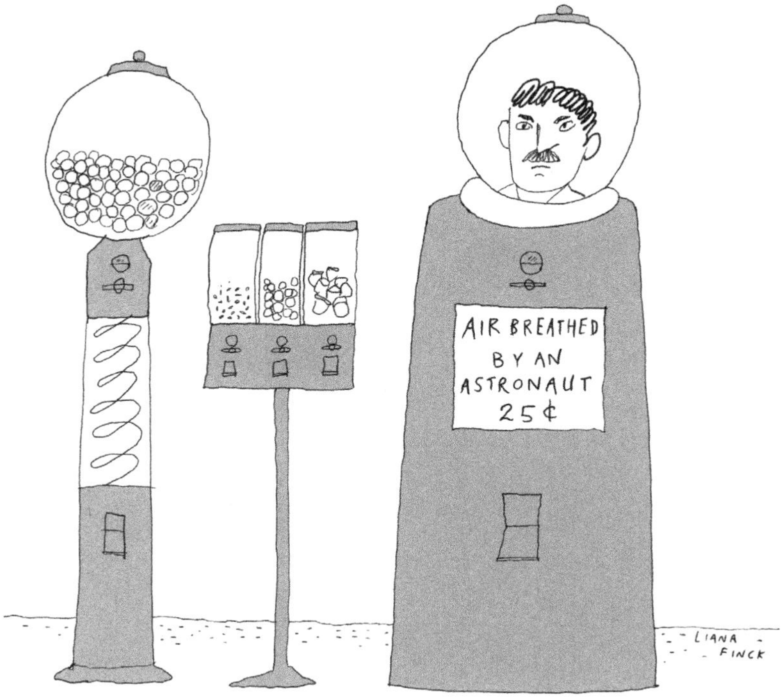
AIR BREATHED BY AN ASTRONAUT 25¢
LIANA FINCK

REMEMBRANCES OF PA

Pa loved Christmas on account of it's when trees most fear man.

Pa refused to acknowledge any whale bigger than the humpback. Said the humpback was plenty big.

Pa's Google history was something else. "Mailman weak points," he'd type. "How to defeat mailman."

"Son, you're permitted to go to the pictures on one condition," Pa said, eyes narrowing. "The man who sells popcorn. You tell him I'm close to figuring out how it's made. Real close."

Pa had a Navy tattoo on his forearm. "The Navy Sucks," it read. "All Navy Men Are Cowards," it continued.

Pa forbade our learning the Pythagorean Theorem. Claimed not all the facts were in yet.

Some Jehovah's Witnesses came to the door once, and damned if Pa didn't start preaching to 'em about Chet. We never understood who Chet was. We just knew never to take his name in vain.

Pa dug his own grave at the cemetery. Several times, in fact, on account of they kept filling it in and asking he please stop.

Pa rigged himself up a catapult once. Claimed it was for defensive purposes, but you could see in his eyes he was wantin' to start trouble.

Pa stopped coming to our Little League games after a disagreement with Coach Hatfield about the proper order to run the bases.

Pa admired beavers because they destroy other animals' homes and make them their own.

Pa enjoyed puns, though he never quite got the hang of 'em. "I love corn," he'd say. "They're so corny!" Then he'd do his laugh.

Pa would buy up all the wedding cake toppers in town and sell 'em at inflated prices. He'd damage them first.

Pa took a notebook to the carnival. He'd write down the names of bumper car drivers who'd bumped him, then quietly put it back in his pocket.

Pa once threw me a surprise birthday party. I asked him how come it was at the hardware store and there was no cake and none of my friends were there. He said to be quiet while he bought nails. It was not my birthday.

I remember the day we became a no-dairy household. Pa came home saying a cow had wronged him. Refused to discuss it further.

—River Clegg

IF I HAVE TO SHIT DURING THIS 5K CHARITY RUN, I'M JUST GOING TO DO IT.

O.K., everybody, listen up. I'm saying this just so we're all on the same page. If I have to take a shit during the 5K charity run we're doing together as an office this weekend, I'm just going to let it happen and keep running. And I don't mean I'm going to find the nearest Starbucks. I mean I'm going to shit while running, straight into my new green ASICS running shorts with the built-in underwear liner, and I'm not going to slow down or veer to the edge of the road or anything. I'm going to let it rip, in stride.

I'm saying this because I want it to be clear to everyone how seriously I'm taking this 5K charity run, and also how serious of a person I am in general. I'm a competitor. Competitors compete.

STAN MACK'S CHRONICLES

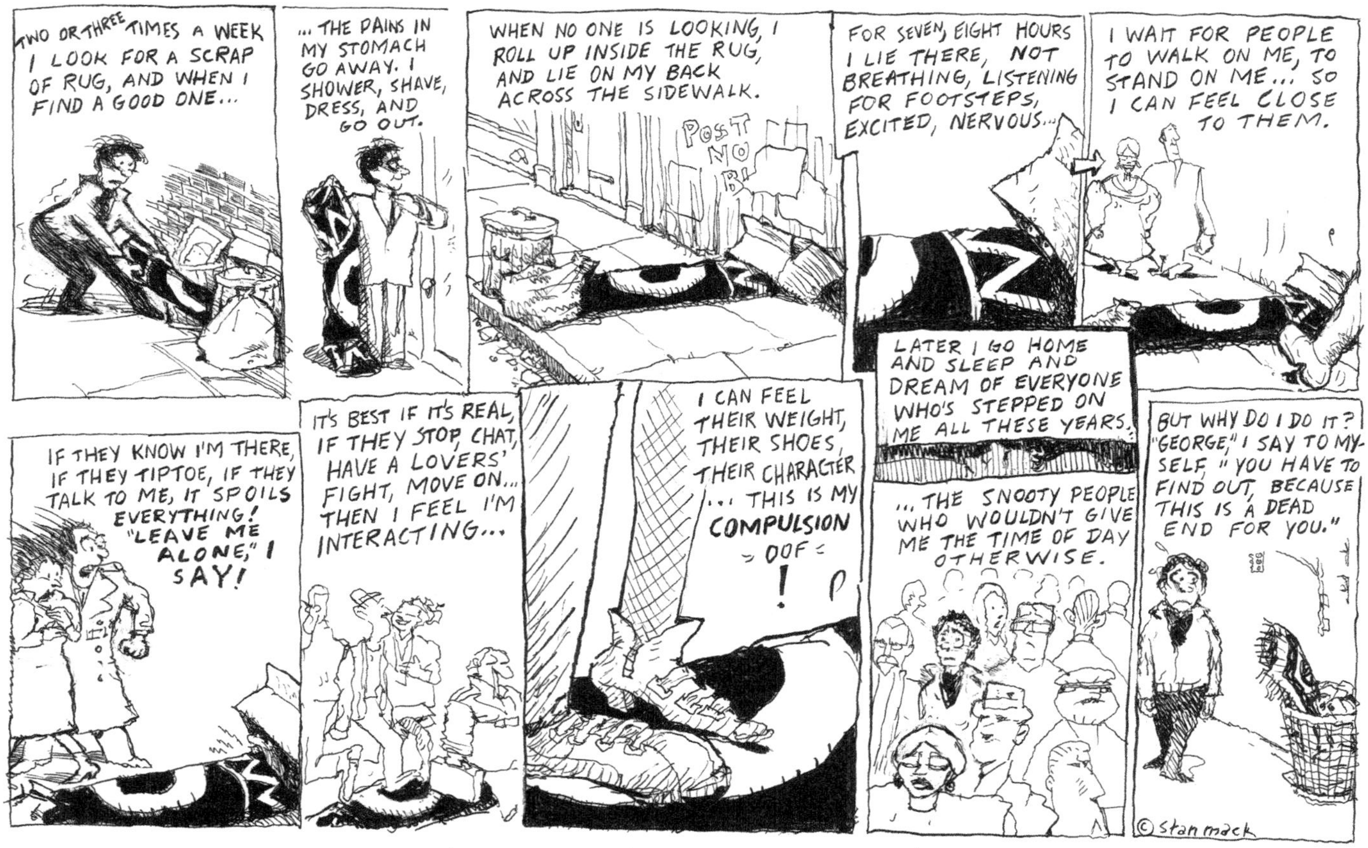

COMPULSION
TWO OR THREE TIMES A WEEK I LOOK FOR A SCRAP OF RUG, AND WHEN I FIND A GOOD ONE...
...THE PAINS IN MY STOMACH GO AWAY. I SHOWER, SHAVE, DRESS, AND GO OUT.
WHEN NO ONE IS LOOKING, I ROLL UP INSIDE THE RUG, AND LIE ON MY BACK ACROSS THE SIDEWALK.
POST NO BI
FOR SEVEN, EIGHT HOURS I LIE THERE, NOT BREATHING, LISTENING FOR FOOTSTEPS, EXCITED, NERVOUS...
I WAIT FOR PEOPLE TO WALK ON ME, TO STAND ON ME... SO I CAN FEEL CLOSE TO THEM.
IF THEY KNOW I'M THERE, IF THEY TIPTOE, IF THEY TALK TO ME, IT SPOILS EVERYTHING! "LEAVE ME ALONE," I SAY!
IT'S BEST IF IT'S REAL, IF THEY STOP, CHAT, HAVE A LOVERS' FIGHT, MOVE ON... THEN I FEEL I'M INTERACTING...
I CAN FEEL THEIR WEIGHT, THEIR SHOES, THEIR CHARACTER ... THIS IS MY COMPULSION
OOF
LATER I GO HOME AND SLEEP AND DREAM OF EVERYONE WHO'S STEPPED ON ME ALL THESE YEARS.
...THE SNOOTY PEOPLE WHO WOULDN'T GIVE ME THE TIME OF DAY OTHERWISE.
BUT WHY DO I DO IT? "GEORGE," I SAY TO MYSELF, "YOU HAVE TO FIND OUT, BECAUSE THIS IS A DEAD END FOR YOU."
© stan mack

If shit is running down my leg for the last 0.10686 of the 3.10686 miles I'm running, so be it.

I'm also saying this so nobody is surprised if, come race day, when I cross that finish line, my new New Balance Fresh Foam 1080 running shoes are violated because one or both of them have been filled with the fecal runoff that has dripped down my legs.

I'm not saying this to gross you out. I'm saying this because it might happen. Be prepared mentally. Maybe bring some nose plugs so you can be prepared physically, too.

Why am I ready and willing to go to these lengths for the 5K Puppy Prance this Sunday morning, where all proceeds go to the A.S.P.C.A., an event many of you, my co-workers, will be attending? I got the idea after I saw a YouTube video where an elite marathoner shit herself and kept on running. She finished the race even though shit was dripping down her leg. People in the comments were super impressed. Well, some were grossed out. She wasn't even in first place or anything and some people thought, "Just go clean yourself up, lady, it's not like you're going to win anyway, what are you trying to prove?" But some people, people like me, thought it was badass. I thought it was real badass. But that's not why I'm doing this. Or going to do it. Or, I mean, might do it. Strongly might.

Let's get one other thing straight right now: I have not trained for this run. That's how seriously I'm taking it. You see, back in the days before Roger Bannister broke the four-minute mile, it was considered bad sportsmanship to "practice" or "train" or "be prepared" for athletic endeavors. Basically, running around before the race was seen as a sort of pre-cheating. And while most of the world has since moved on from that outdated mind-set, I for one have am no pre-cheater, and as such I intend to maximize the amount of suffering I go through at the Puppy Prance. With the lactic acid pooling in my legs as I push my body to the absolute limit of what it is able to endure (running at a 15-minute pace for three consecutive miles), it is almost certain that my body will start shutting down nonessential physiological systems, such as whichever system keeps you from shitting yourself.

Am I going to do it because I am still jealous that last year everyone sang Kevin Sweyer's, from sales, praises after he finished the A.S.P.C.A. Charity 5K even though his nipples had begun chafing by Mile 1, and then chafing so badly they were bleeding by Mile 2, and then by Mile 3 his abraded nipples had stained his once-white running tanklet crimson? No. Am I saying that said praise was given too freely because who knows if Kevin would have even finished, had a more disabling and intense bodily ailment, namely shitting oneself, afflicted him midrace? Yes.

So, Saturday night, before I go to bed early to be at my optimum physical ability, I'm going to drink a gallon of milk with an added fiber supplement I got online from Amazon, and also an added laxative powder I got online from Alibaba, the Chinese Amazon. Morning of, it's a strict regiment of prunes and hot coffee and prunes and hot coffee and prunes and hot coffee until I can't hold any more down.

Then it's race time.

(continued on P. 82) ☛

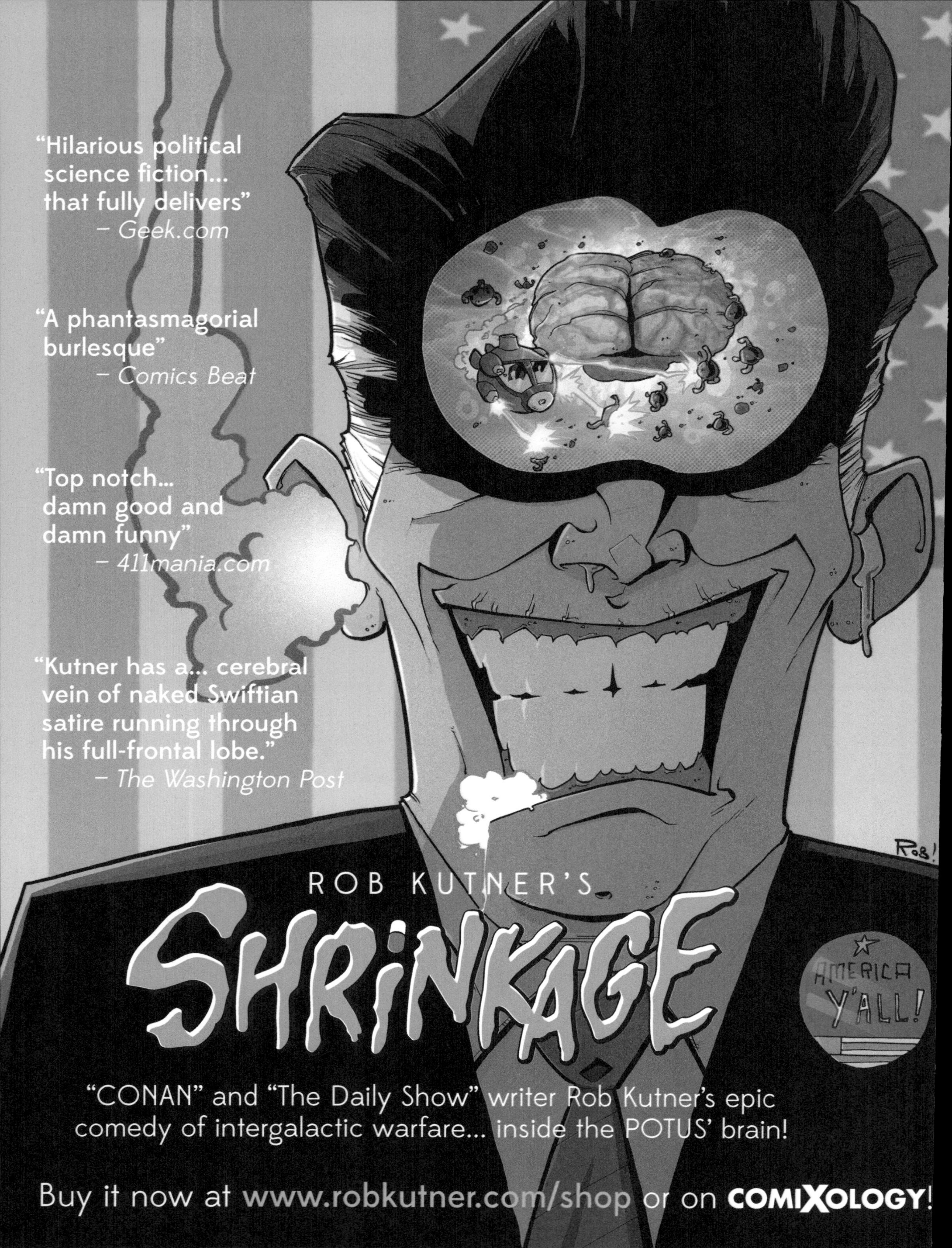

"Hilarious political science fiction... that fully delivers"
– Geek.com
"A phantasmagorial burlesque"
– Comics Beat
"Top notch... damn good and damn funny"
– 411mania.com
"Kutner has a... cerebral vein of naked Swiftian satire running through his full-frontal lobe."
– The Washington Post
ROB KUTNER'S
SHRINKAGE
AMERICA Y'ALL!
"CONAN" and "The Daily Show" writer Rob Kutner's epic comedy of intergalactic warfare... inside the POTUS' brain!
Buy it now at www.robkutner.com/shop or on COMIXOLOGY!

BY JACK HANDEY

MESSAGE TO MY CLONE

Take good care — I have plans for you

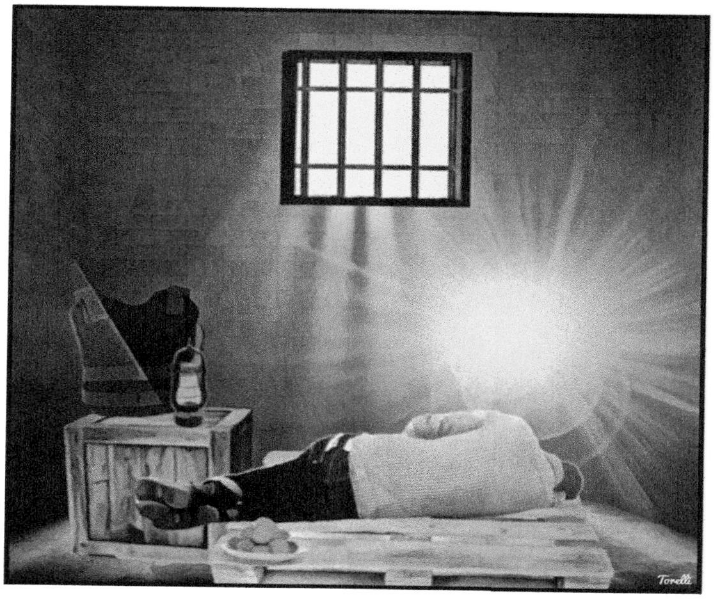
Torelli

STEVE TORELLI

As I write this, oh little clone of mine, lying asleep on your pallet, with the sun shining through the bars of your window onto your face, I have so many different emotions. You have grown so much, from the high doses of hormones and super-proteins. Soon you will be a big clone, with healthy young organs to harvest. I hope I don't need them, but if I do, thanks.

I'm sorry I haven't visited you more often, but I have been busy with my lawsuit against the Department of Clone Sales, because you did not come out as well as I was led to believe.

Perhaps now that you are nearly grown we can spend more time together. Maybe we can go fishing. But if we do, you must wear hard plastic goggles, to protect your eyes. I wouldn't want anything to happen to them. How is your eyesight? Good? Mine gets worse and worse. How's your heart, by the way?

Be prepared, little clone, that the world is a cruel place. They will call you "freak" and "monster," like they did me, and I'm not even a clone. They will tell clone jokes behind your back, like: "What's the difference between two clones? Nothing. They're both stupid." Try not to be too sensitive about it.

I know I told you you could go to college, little clone, but I'm afraid not. You see, at college students often drink and smoke, which can damage organs. Also, they study a lot, which can put ideas and facts into your brain that a normal person may not want.

But there is another reason you cannot go to college, little clone. You see, I have an important mission for you. I have been romantically pursuing the daughter of actor Jon Voight. So far, I haven't had much luck, and the courts have ordered me to stay away from her. Voight has threatened to kill me, and I believe he might try. He's insane. And so is his clone.

I feel that, sooner or later, Voight's daughter will get in love with me. But I need time to convince her. That's where you come in, little clone. I want you to surface in some city and make a big noise. Voight will find you and try to kill you. That's why I have brought this bulletproof vest for you. I will set it here on your apple-crate nightstand.

With Voight diverted by you, I will be able to convince his daughter to move with me to the Yucatan. Then I will let you know when you can join us. While traveling through Mexico, please don't eat any spicy food, as it might harm your stomach and colon.

You might be wondering about how I will get by down there if I need some body parts. Don't worry. In the Yucatan, you can buy body parts from street vendors. Not as good as yours, of course.

Before the plan is ready, please don't try to escape. The guards are trained to shoot clones in the legs, so as to not harm any of the good stuff. Also, my ankle has been hurting me lately, so you never know.

It is time for me to go now, little clone. I can hear the slop-wagon coming down the hall, and the cook yelling at the other clones. Don't forget to eat your hormone balls.

One last thing, little clone: After you read this letter, please burn it. But be careful, don't burn your fingers. B

JACK HANDEY *is best-known for his "Deep Thoughts." A contributor to* **The New Yorker** *and many other publications, he recently self-published* **Squeaky Poems: Rhymes About My Rat**.

BY AMANDA MEADOWS

WEDDING INFO: V IMPORTANT! <3

"Williams-Sonoma has amazeballs moonshine."

To: *weddingpeeps@googlegroups.com*
From: *masonandbrieinatree@icloud.com*
Subject: WEDDING INFO: V IMPORTANT! <3

Hi Everyone We Love All in One Beautiful Email!
As you know, our wedding is this weekend! Here's everything you need to know:

1. Our ceremony will take place in a beautiful barn with lots of rustic decor. Be sure to wear comfortable shoes — cowboy boots for extra points! ;-) (Neiman Marcus has some really cute ones!)

2. The barn is legit rustic! Buuut the downside is the barn's also full of rusty nails, bugs and stray varmints. Please take care to get a tetanus shot and a rabies shot. Also have a shot... of moonshine! ;-) Williams-Sonoma has amazeballs moonshine.

3. THIS IS A SUGAR-FREE WEDDING. Mason and I have been on an enlightening macrobiotic cleanse, and it changed our lives. Since we are having this wedding to share our lives with you, we insist you share in our lifestyle for just one sacred night. <3

4. Again, there will be NO cake or desserts. Please respect our wishes. And don't smuggle in sweets! A little bird told me some of you were thinking of bringing donuts, but if you do, Mason and I will cry. ;-)

5. Back to the Barn! There will be heavy machinery and animal traps abound. We know — very authentic! The farmers we rented the space from were very "real"! We will use lots of cute burlap bunting as a cute form of "caution tape" to keep you from venturing near body-mangling farm equipment. :-D

6. We're so excited to share that our mutual best friend Trystan will be our officiant. He has zero experience with public speaking but a lifetime of experience... loving us. ;-) He's easily startled, though, so please don't clap!

7. Speaking of mutual friends: The farmers warned us about Ol' Tilda, the barn's ghost. Cool, right? Ol' Tilda's been haunting the barn for 245 years, so we thought it only fitting to incorporate her into the ceremony with an "old mother's wail" ritual! Such a sweet and very real ritual! :-O

8. How about some fun?! As you arrive, you will be greeted at a chicken coop. You will be asked to name and slaughter your own chicken! How sweet, right? Please bring a list of preferred chicken names so we can start on time. Chicken names that are already taken: Tatum, Cleo, Eloise, Benji, Aiden, Tycho, Emma and Beckett. :-D

9. This is a "no-phones" wedding! Please do not bring your phones at all. The barn is approx. 50 miles from the nearest highway, so be sure to print out your directions! If you must bring your cellphone, check it in with our Wedding Blacksmith, who will destroy it for you. ;-)

10. We will have a Rustic Restroom. When you need to use the restroom, simply ask the Elder by the entryway, who will lead you to an outhouse. If the outhouse is occupied, there will be a complimentary hole in the ground 10 feet from the outhouse. Bring your own wiping implements! Note: We are giving artisanal kerchiefs to each guest, but please DO NOT use them for this purpose! ;-O

11. Our hashtag is #BarningLove. Be sure to use it for everything you post on social media, so we can track who broke our no-phones rule! ;-)

12. Also please sign this waiver that every photo you take at our wedding belongs to #BarningLove, LLC. That's right, we incorporated our wedding to protect our budding new family's brand! Please respect our wishes and our sacred corporate personhood. ;-P

13. Remember to HAVE FUN this weekend! We made this event for YOU, the friends and family we love. ;-) Remember to call our wedding planner Reaghan McNally (234-555-9463) if you have any questions, concerns or panic attacks!

LOVE YOU!
Mason + Brie
Joint CEOs
#BarningLove, LLC.   B

AMANDA MEADOWS *(@amandonium) is a comedy writer and publisher. She is author of* **The Best American Emails** *and the bestselling* **We Don't Think You're Racist!**

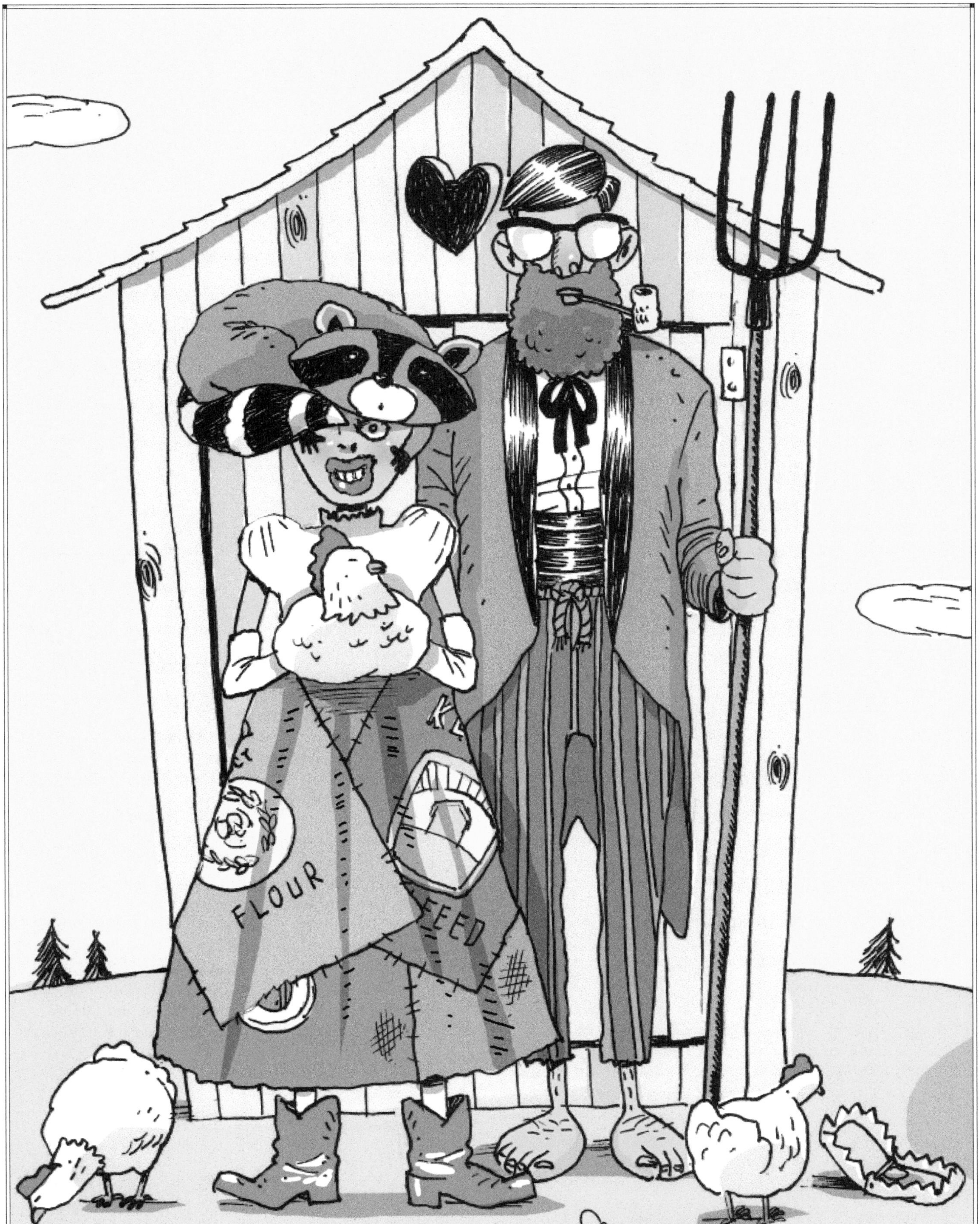
FLOUR
FEED
SPARKS

BY STEVE YOUNG

ALL STAFF– PLEASE READ

Let's get it right this time.

To all members of the Le Mangeioueleur team: As you have probably heard, this evening we will be welcoming our dear longtime customers, Fredryck and Bevelyn Pauloof. They are returning after an absence prompted by less-than-satisfactory service during their last visit.

We are committed to regaining their trust and affection. With that in mind, please be aware of the following:

THE PAULOOFS MAY ONLY BE ATTENDED by a waiter who has known the disappointment of a failed career in the dance, and who has overcome a childhood stutter. This disqualifies all except Robert and Nicole.

FREDRYCK PREFERS TAP WATER, but it must be from the Ashokan Reservoir. He will refuse any that he judges to be sourced from the Croton, Schoharie, et al. Do not try to fool him. Fill his glass from the appropriate basement tub.

BEVELYN PREFERS SPARKLING WATER, but it must be cut with a splash of Schoharie Reservoir water, then left out for 13 minutes before serving, so the bubbles, as Bevelyn says, "lack vigor, like champion greyhounds which have finally realized the mechanical rabbit cannot be caught." At this point, Fredryck usually adds, "Life is deliciously tragic, is it not?" Incline your head gravely.

THE PAULOOFS' PLATES, CUTLERY AND GLASSWARE must have been washed by a kitchen employee with a criminal record who continues to struggle with the temptation of his/her old life. Mitch, you're up.

FREDRYCK REQUIRES THAT THE BREAD BASKET INCLUDE, in addition to sourdough, olive and raisin, a bland white roll that could be construed as "ironic." When he points it out to a waiter or other staffer, the correct response is a knowing smirk.

DO <u>NOT</u> USE A CRUMB SCRAPER on the Pauloofs' table; they have pronounced our crumb scrapers "pedestrian" and our technique "impertinent." They will be bringing their own bespoke crumb scraper and its operator, Chet.

FREDRYCK DOES NOT CARE FOR MUSHROOMS. Their texture gives him "spasms of melancholy akin to a half-remembered dream of an old love."

WHILE THE PAULOOFS RARELY DRINK, they usually order an expensive Bordeaux to be dropped and shattered near the coat check. We will be recommending the Chateau Blasé-Ennui '45. Stand clear.

ALL SALAD GREENS must be arranged on the plate so when served, they are pointing to magnetic north (NOT true north, as required by the widow Pembroke). The compass is hanging on a chain from the mouth of the taxidermied zebra.

THE TEMPERATURE MUST BE 78 degrees Fahrenheit at Fredryck's seat, and 72 degrees at Bevelyn's seat. The temperature sommelier must check these temperatures every few minutes. The temperature sommelier must be an orphan. Welcome aboard, Mikhail, and condolences on your loss.

ANY MEAT SERVED TO BEVELYN must be from an animal that was shunned by its peers because of its display of a superior attitude but with no discernible superior qualities. We have a good selection, except for bison and lobster, which are highly self-aware.

DEPENDING ON THE BAROMETRIC PRESSURE, Fredryck may only wish to eat owls. The owls must never have eaten mushrooms. There are several in the refrigerator. The refrigerator must be opened with your left hand.

DO NOT MAKE EYE CONTACT with Bevelyn's mouth.

THE PAULOOFS OFTEN ORDER the creme brûlée for dessert, but the top must be caramelized by exposure to a fire that was already in progress somewhere in the city. Please monitor the police scanner to identify likely locations. If there is no fire within two miles by the time main courses are cleared, Rodolfo may be required to execute Plan 17.

ON OCCASION, FREDRYCK ENJOYS an after-dinner aperitif consisting of the alcohol from the compass housing. Serve in a snifter with the broken remains of the compass nearby on a small velvet pillow.

THE PAULOOFS ARE KNOWN TO TIP GENEROUSLY when pleased with the food and service, but the form of the tip has varied. Sometimes it has been cash, but more often it has been an Old Master painting attributed to the workshop of Frans Hals, or a quantity of raw platinum ore. On one memorable occasion, they left a cousin, Marcus. Be gracious and flexible.

MARCUS, SO AS NOT TO UPSET the Pauloofs, you have the night off.

B

STEVE YOUNG *(@pantssteve) is a veteran* **Letterman** *writer who's also written for* **The Simpsons**. *He recently worked on NBC's* **Maya & Marty** *variety show and is teaching a course at NYU's Tisch School.*

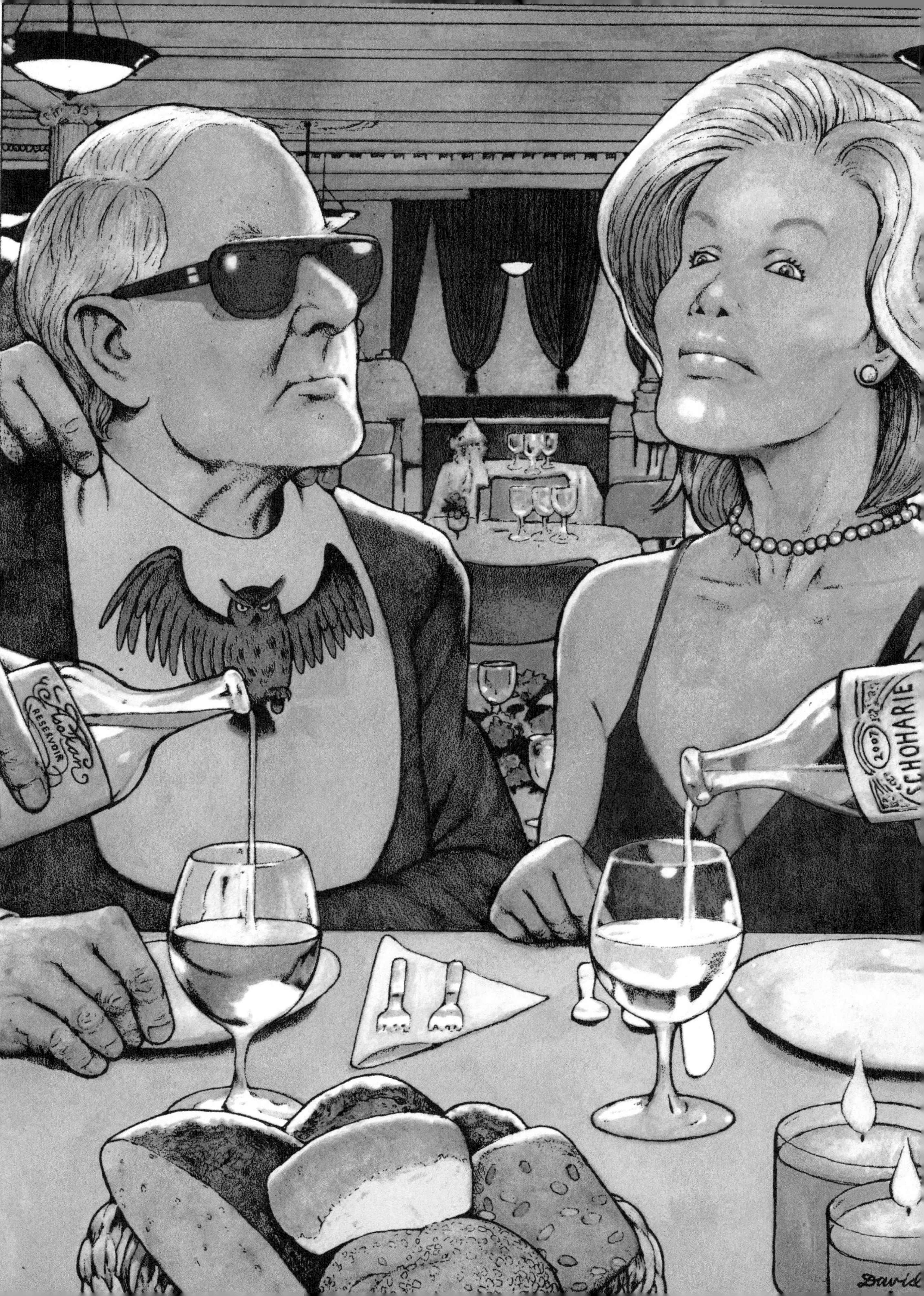

DAVID CHELSEA

BY KATIE SCHWARTZ

AT YOUR SERVICE

"Tickle my back with a fly swatter six times, it makes me feel gruff."

A few years back, my sister's friend (we'll call her "Sarah") had a really messy apartment, and no money to clean it. Things were so bad, the smell wafting from her place caused her neighbors to call the landlord, thinking she might be dead. Days before eviction, Sarah had a brainstorm: she posted an ad on Craigslist for men who wanted to be dominated *without* sex. Hundreds of submissive men emailed her, eager to be of service, and Sarah found the perfect fella; he came to her house weekly for a year, to clean. They agreed to the following rules: He preferred to be naked and on all fours; he had to do everything she asked without question; and their safeword — which she chose — was "Beanie Babies."

I find this anecdote charming…and appealing. Though my pad's not quite coroner-worthy, I loathe cleaning, and it's a massive time suck. So I called Sarah, to get some pointers on D/s cleaning arrangements. But she emphatically refused to talk to me, saying she was now married with children; in her opinion, my even considering this was grossly immature.

Undeterred, I posted an ad on Craigslist under the pseudonym "Gracious Colon." Within 24 hours, I received 20 responses, but one gent stood out because he made a list.

"1. NO urinating on my person.

2. My dick will be out. You must look at it often, but do not stare.

3. I require EXTREME dirty talk.

4. Also EXTREME humiliation.

5. You must use a leash and collar on me at all times, and yank it really hard when I'm doing poorly.

6. Tickle my back with a fly swatter six times, it makes me feel gruff.

7. I want you to slap my ass with the back of a wide red hair brush at least a dozen times.

8. Tug on the top of my head often.

9. Stuff non-food objects in my mouth only. I'm Paleo.

10. I own three pairs of high heels, red, green and clear. Please choose your preference in advance of our meeting.

11. DO NOT shake my hand when we meet or when I leave. I'm a germaphobe.

12. Our safeword will be 'Florida,' my home state."

I saw problems right away. First: Florida. Second, I don't have an extensive "dirty talk" repertoire under the best of circumstances; what did that even *mean* in a nonsexual, chore-related interaction? Third, he said he was a germaphobe — I was hiring him to clean, so how was that going to work?

Still, I really needed my apartment tided up, and I'm a curious dame, so I emailed him back. "I think I want to give this a shot. Can you come next Sunday at 7AM? I have a busy day. Any heel color you choose is fine. Thanks, Gracious."

His response was quick. "Your day will be *consumed* by me," he wrote. "Unless you're willing to put your needs aside and commit to at least 8 hours, this will not work. PS, Everyone has a preference in heel color. What is wrong with you?!"

He arrived on time with all the cleaning supplies I requested. Much to my surprise, he wore a navy suit and conservative red tie, looking like an overworked bank teller who reviled his job and ate nauseatingly scented microwavable food for lunch. Nervous, I greeted him with a simple "Nice to meet you."

"You need to invite me in," he sneered, "to establish your dominance over me."

"O.K., come in."

A few seconds passed, and he tapped his foot angrily. "Oh my God, *demand* I take my clothes off! Slap my face! Bend me over your knee and hit me with a paddle! You see how *enraged* I am? This should be you, not me! *Dominate me!*"

This was not going well. Screwing up my confidence, I said, "Take out the cleaning supplies you purchased and place them on the kitchen counter or…I will throw my blender at you."

He cooed and did as instructed, so I continued. "You're a bad boy, and (thinking furiously) your behavior is nasty. I'm going to really punish you, you know?"

He looked perplexed, so I pivoted. "Take that cheap, ugly suit off and stick the sponge on the sink in your mouth right this instant."

"*Cheap suit?*" he replied. "There's no need to get personal." I was mortified. "I… *sorry?*"

This was the wrong tack. "You've wasted my precious time," my guest snapped — then ran a fingernail over a line of moldy grout around the kitchen faucet. "Dis-*gust*-ing."

A line had been crossed; enraged, humiliated and terrified, I grabbed my baseball bat (a New York staple) and felt my inner Dom surge to the surface. "Bitch, I will crack your head wide open if you don't get the fuck out of my house right now."

The man's manner changed immediately. Almost gleefully, he grabbed his bucket and dove for the counter with the cleaning supplies.

"Those supplies belong to me!" I yelled. "LEAVE! NOW!"

He ran out — but before I slammed the door, he turned: "For the record, that's how you dominate someone. *Thank you.*"

I think he meant it. **B**

KATIE SCHWARTZ *(@KatieSchwartz) is a comedy writer, producer and essayist. She collects vintage tchotchkes and perfume, and loathes digital dancing roses sent to her. Does that help?*

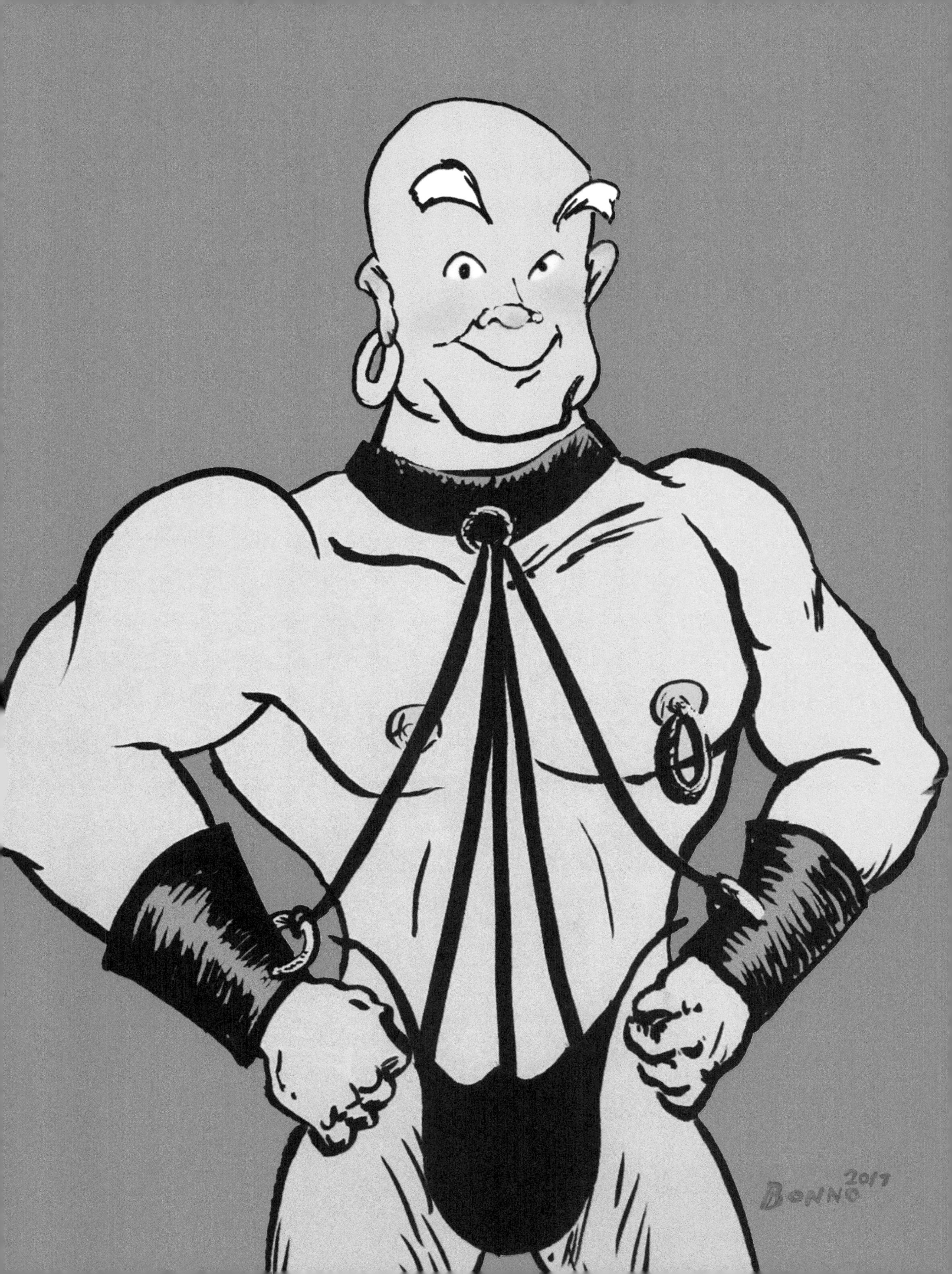
2017
BONNO

BY TONY BENNETT

PRESIDENT TRUMP, I DEMAND YOU END YOUR CONTINUED THEFT OF MY SIGNATURE 'TWO THUMBS UP' GESTURE

I'm very happy for my dear friend and our president, Donald Trump, and all his success in life and in the political world. But for every beautiful sunshiny day, there's a dark cloud. And the dark cloud that hangs heavy over me and my heart is that for months now, President Trump has been strutting around the halls of power in our great country using the "two thumbs up" gesture. He is, it would seem, adopting this wonderful gesture as his own, for all intents and purposes annihilating the possibility that the gesture could be associated with any other public figure.

Well, there's a small problem with that choice. You see, the "two thumbs up" gesture is already very closely identified with one particular celebrity — a national treasure, some have said — who is beloved around the world.

I'm speaking, of course, of me, Tony Bennett.

"Two thumbs up" is how I've closed every show through the years. It's my sign-off. It's how I say, "I love you, everybody," "Keep on being you, America," and "I feel fantastic." How do you suppose it feels to sit helplessly by and watch the president of the United States — the most powerful man in the world — brazenly greet crowds and pose for so many photographs with the very same "two thumbs up" gesture? How would you feel if you used this gesture for so long it became a part of you, part of your style, part of your identity, and you felt comfort in the faith that no one, let alone the president of the United States and my good friend Donald Trump — as decent a family man as you are ever likely to meet — would ever take it from you? And then you see him doing it over and over again, as if repeatedly spitting in your face?

Well, I can tell you, it doesn't feel very good. When I do

RANDALL ENOS

the gesture now, people tell me, "Hey, Tony, That's President Trump's gesture."

That cuts deep.

How will I communicate with my thumbs now? What other gesture might I adopt in place of "two thumbs up"? A "single thumb up" communicates little more than contempt. The "No. 1" gesture? That's all wrong. It's for basketball or football, not music. Blowing a kiss? That one belongs to Liza Minnelli, and I wouldn't dream of stepping on her toes.

Without the "two thumbs up" gesture, it's not an exaggeration to say that, in many ways, I'm lost.

Every time I see President Trump make the gesture on the news, I cry. When I see it again, even when I think I've cried all the tears I have, I cry a few more. With each smiling use, he pounds my broken soul deeper into the pavement with his bootheel.

How will I get my mojo back? How could anyone? I don't have the answers, my friends.

I've called him many, many times and have left many messages, but he has not called me back. I understand he's very busy now. Maybe he doesn't have time for his old, sad, ex-friend Tony. He is so dear to me, my friend Donald. I will always love him, even though he has brazenly and thoughtlessly stolen the most cherished hand gesture in my life. All I want is to understand why he betrayed me.

Why, Donald? Why? I continue to cry out to you, Donald. But your silence is deafening.

In closing, as a "sign-off" gesture, I must lower my head in disgrace, and raise my hand to make the "No. 1" gesture, which is all I have left.

B

SCOTT DIKKERS is The Onion's *longest-serving editor in chief* and the *#1* **New York Times** *best-selling author* of **How to Write Funny.** *He's also the founder and editor of* **Blaffo Magazine** *(www.blaffo.com).*

How to Argue Politics the Old-Fashioned Way

Join us, won't you, for a trip down Memory Lane...

Most of us over 2 years of age can still remember a time when facts and their attendant details were at the very heart of a good political debate. Yes! Think back! They were! I chuckle to recall how difficult it was to argue against a better-informed opponent who had constitutional subclauses and historical precedents right on the tip of his tongue.

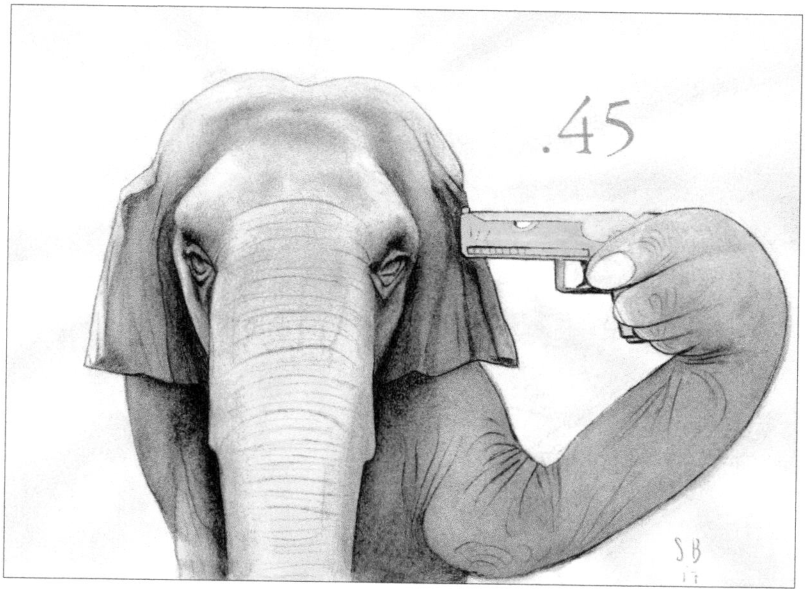
.45
SB

STEVE BRODNER

But those were the olden days, before the election of 2016, when "because he's crazy" was considered a lazy person's rebuttal, not a carefully researched medical opinion. Back then, comparisons to Hitler meant you'd automatically lost the argument because you were using a hyperbolic cliché. Ha ha. Remember all that? Back when *The Handmaid's Tale* was shelved under "Dystopian Fiction"? LOL. Can you imagine?

As we all sit, horrified, watching our politics play out in the most chaotic and disturbing possible way, I have grown increasingly nostalgic for the old rule-based rhetoric. We now live in a time where logical thought and historical details have become as anachronistic as the field once fondly referred to as "science." Which is precisely why it's important for our culture to leave a bread crumb trail for the people of the future to follow in case they want to stage a few historical re-enactments.

Who knows? Maybe some entrepreneurial denizen of the year 2060 will set up a Renaissance Faire type event out in some big empty field that will allow the people of the future to experience daily life in a country that used to be called "The United States of America." Back in the days when you could attend something called "a live event," where not everything that took place was on a screen! My guess is that everyone attending AmericaFaire will be asked to dress up in poorly fitted suits and matching Crocs, drink kale-infused artisanal beers from a Starbucks cup, and pretend to stare at old timey smartphones. Then, for the most authentic experience possible, they'll all be herded into the Debate Booth for a chance to participate in a pre-2016 political argument. For 20 blissful minutes, festivalgoers will return to the golden age before political debates became ritualistic name-calling contests among personality disordered white men that ended when the fattest one among them yelled. "It's time to tee off."

So I am leaving this note for all my friends from the future: Come along with me now to the golden days of 2016! Join me in a more lighthearted and frolicsome time when Americans (as we used to call ourselves) still believed that a political argument had an orderly infrastructure! The way it worked was as follows:

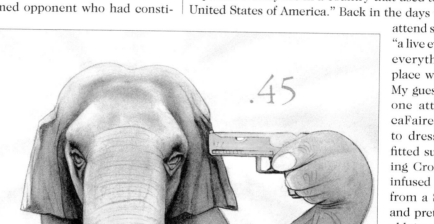

Merrill Markoe *has published eight books and written for a long list of television shows and publications, including the one you are holding.*

Every debate or argument consisted of TWO SIDES, the Left and the Right.

After picking a side, your next step was to hold on tightly to whatever you believed your label to mean — just as you would to the steering wheel of a runaway vehicle with bad brakes that was careening down an unpaved mountain road, aware that the speed at which you found yourself traveling was more important than your destination.

Never for even one second should you indulge yourself in the ridiculous notion that the other person in the argument might be making a valid point. The object was to encase your side of the rhetoric in an airtight vacuum, thus allowing you to circle back to the bullet points of your thesis every few minutes. This was a method the most skillful political debaters held dear; all that mindless, hammering repetition often caused the more sensitive person in the argument to throw up their hands, say something like "You are impossible" and simply walk away. Leaving you with A WIN!

Here's how to know which side you were on:

The Right

If you were fed up with a government that didn't allow white people to spontaneously invent all their own God-approved laws wherever and whenever they wished, you were said to be on the Right. This made you a "conservative," a term that originally meant something about responsible government spending, but wound up meaning that any group of people who disagreed with you should be at least deported, and maybe worse.

As a "conservative," you were instantly "triggered" when a person expressed concern over what used to be thought of as "basic human rights," and/or preservation of what was once called "the environment." Luckily, you had an easy path to rhetorical victory: any one of a multitude of ambiguous Judeo-Christian biblical quotes. For example:

"And we know that in all things God works for the good of those who love him, who have been called according to his purpose." (Romans 8:28)

Obviously His purpose was the same as your purpose. And as luck would have it, also the purpose of your favorite right-wing "elected representatives" and/or

country music stars!

An important perk of identifying as "a right-wing conservative" was that your opponent would assume you were a Second Amendment fanatic. Therefore, as long as you were speaking louder and faster than they were, you seemed dangerously unstable. This often meant that, out of concern for his or her personal safety, your opponent would surrender when he or she sensed a buildup of explosive rage. Back in the old days, the most common excuses for disengaging were about needing to answer a text.

On the rare occasions that anyone continued to argue further, your next move was to melt the logical core of your opponent's dialectic in a way that was so confusing it was impossible to refute. Here's an example:

"If clean air and the environment mean so much to you, why haven't you given up your comfy electricity-based home and your gas-guzzling car?"

Since your opponent could not explain why they alone hadn't successfully reinvented the civilization into which they were born, score one for you!

Now all you needed to seal the deal was a Ronald Reagan reference. If you didn't have one handy, it was fine to just make one up. Most right-wing people under 40, even back in the olden days, had no idea what Reagan actually said or did. They just knew he was a handsome, craggy, beloved family patriarch who died before they were old enough to figure out that most of what he said made no sense.

The Left

If you were comfortable with the idea of a government pretending to give a shit about something — anything — besides massive tax breaks for corporations and billionaires, you were on the Left. This made you a "liberal."

Where the Right had God, you had Google: The fastest rebuttal to every right-wing argument could be found in the tweet or video in which Donald Trump could be found defending your position before he began arguing against it. (Equally useful were tweets and clips of Mr. Trump accusing Hillary Clinton or Barack Obama of doing whatever it was he was presently doing.) As a bonus, revisiting one of these tweets or videos

at the appropriate time was guaranteed to cause any logic based debater to lapse into a profusion of shoulder shrugging, followed by a baffled silence, giving his or her opponent the decided advantage.

On increasingly rare occasions, before people gave up entirely on the idea of logic as a useful tool, a liberal had to counter a traditional Milton Friedman/ Paul Ryan fiscal argument about budget balancing and debt. Once begun, it was surprisingly difficult to convince people "on the right" that human beings ought to help one another achieve a base level of what used to be referred to, in even more archaic times, as "life, liberty and the pursuit of happiness."

At these moments, a liberal's best line of defense was sometimes to invoke the people and customs of a peaceful and theoretically idyllic European country. For example:

"The people of Belgium have socialized medicine. When you get sick there, hospitalization only costs a penny."

This rhetorical gambit was practically unbeatable. Unless you were talking to someone whose family lived in Belgium, it took too long for the claims being made about any given foreign government's policies to be disproven.

Of course, the biggest problem for the liberal was getting so bored or frustrated by a right-wing opponent's cyborglike lack of empathy that midargument, the liberal would drift off into daydreams about delicious sandwich combinations. At these moments, while the conservative opponent slid ever more steadily into a counterargument that sounded like a racist diatribe, all the liberal could think about was the order in which they would most like to put condiments on toasted ciabatta bread. This was how the liberal brain protected itself.

Unfortunately, even in pre-2016 America, there were only a limited number of condiment combinations. A time-honored way to snap back into the fight was to counter with the following unanswerable question:

"Do you realize we waste millions on (unwinnable wars, propping up dishonest banks and Wall Street fat cats, arming vicious dictators, giving tax cuts to the wealthy, destroying the environment) when there are children starving in our own backyard?"

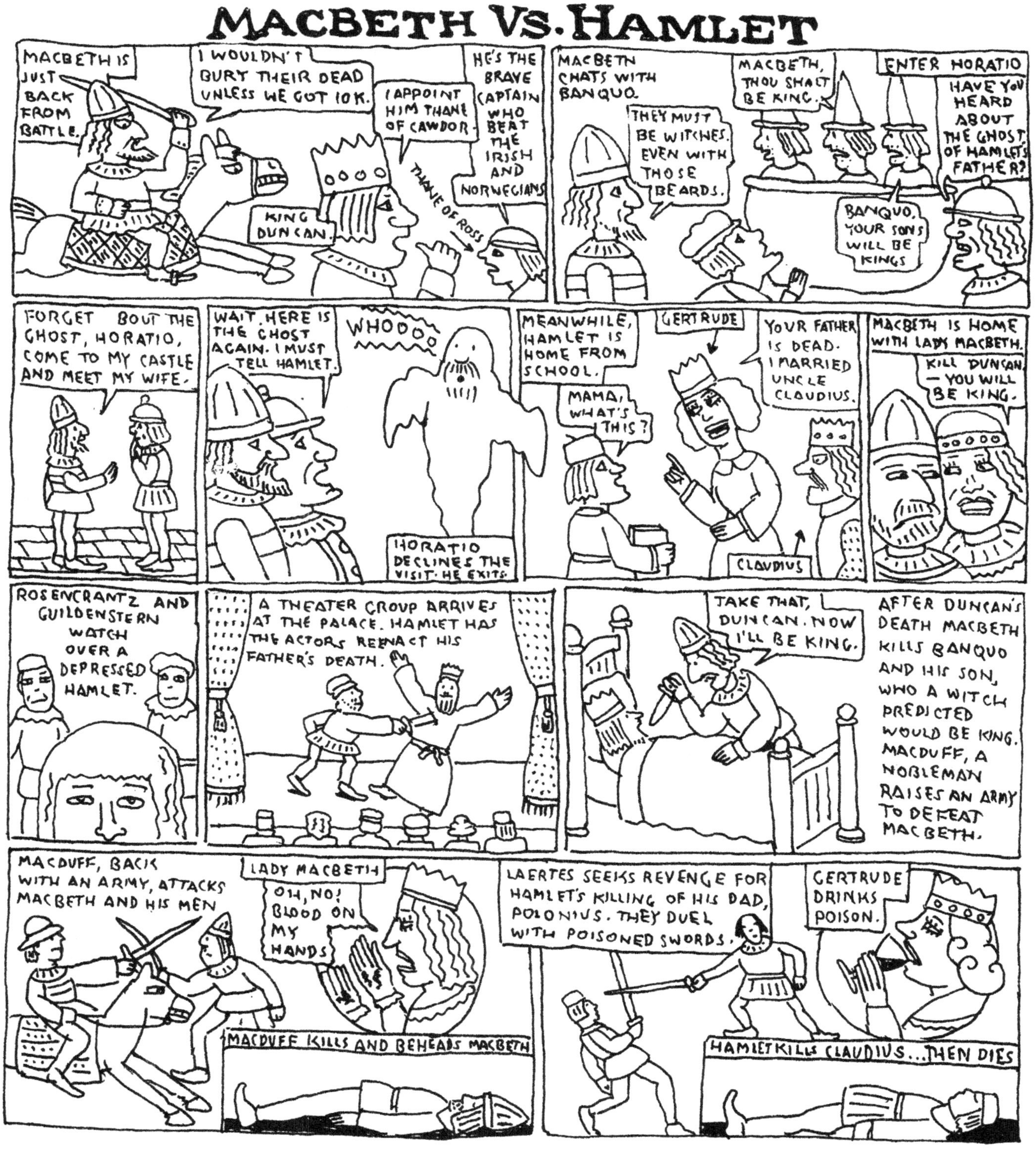
MACBETH VS. HAMLET
MACBETH IS JUST BACK FROM BATTLE.
I WOULDN'T BURY THEIR DEAD UNLESS WE GOT 10K.
HE'S THE BRAVE CAPTAIN WHO BEAT THE IRISH AND NORWEGIANS
I APPOINT HIM THANE OF CAWDOR.
KING DUNCAN.
THANE OF ROSS
MACBETH CHATS WITH BANQUO.
THEY MUST BE WITCHES. EVEN WITH THOSE BEARDS.
MACBETH, THOU SHALT BE KING.
BANQUO, YOUR SONS WILL BE KINGS
ENTER HORATIO
HAVE YOU HEARD ABOUT THE GHOST OF HAMLET'S FATHER?
FORGET BOUT THE GHOST, HORATIO, COME TO MY CASTLE AND MEET MY WIFE.
WAIT. HERE IS THE GHOST AGAIN. I MUST TELL HAMLET.
WHOOOO
HORATIO DECLINES THE VISIT. HE EXITS.
MEANWHILE, HAMLET IS HOME FROM SCHOOL.
GERTRUDE
MAMA, WHAT'S THIS?
YOUR FATHER IS DEAD. I MARRIED UNCLE CLAUDIUS.
CLAUDIUS
MACBETH IS HOME WITH LADY MACBETH.
KILL DUNCAN — YOU WILL BE KING.
ROSENCRANTZ AND GUILDENSTERN WATCH OVER A DEPRESSED HAMLET.
A THEATER GROUP ARRIVES AT THE PALACE. HAMLET HAS THE ACTORS REENACT HIS FATHER'S DEATH.
TAKE THAT, DUNCAN. NOW I'LL BE KING.
AFTER DUNCAN'S DEATH MACBETH KILLS BANQUO AND HIS SON, WHO A WITCH PREDICTED WOULD BE KING. MACDUFF, A NOBLEMAN RAISES AN ARMY TO DEFEAT MACBETH.
MACDUFF, BACK WITH AN ARMY, ATTACKS MACBETH AND HIS MEN
LADY MACBETH
OH, NO! BLOOD ON MY HANDS
MACDUFF KILLS AND BEHEADS MACBETH
LAERTES SEEKS REVENGE FOR HAMLET'S KILLING OF HIS DAD, POLONIUS. THEY DUEL WITH POISONED SWORDS.
GERTRUDE DRINKS POISON.
HAMLET KILLS CLAUDIUS... THEN DIES

SEYMOUR CHWAST

This evergreen was always relevant, because up to that point neither side had yet shown the courage to actively use child starvation as a policy building block. In those days, no matter which bill was being shepherded through which subcommittee, no significant available funds were ever directed toward feeding hungry children. (This was before the 2019 formation of the Church of the Hungry Youngsters, which allowed them to become eligible for grants, tax exemptions and charter school status.)

Finally, as a liberal, your historical ace in the hole was always to make parallels to F.D.R. or J.F.K., two Democratic presidents whose policies were equally loved and misremembered, allowing an arguing left-winger to customize them in any way they wished.

"At the end of WWII F.D.R. created the New Deal, which gave every registered voter access to a checkout code offering them a nice discount on the purchase of a spring wardrobe."

As unbeatable, in its way, as Reagan.

(continued on p. 82) ☛

101 Beginnings for a Novel

"The beginning is the most important part of any work." — Plato

1. He woke up in the morning, filled his lungs with a deep, luxurious stretch, and immediately died of a heart attack. **2.** "I love you more than anything in the world," he said, not realizing that he was speaking to a lamp. **3.** "I come from another dimension," said the green, glowing glob. "But that doesn't matter." **4.** "A cross-continental railroad isn't like a toy train," the grizzled old engineer told the rookie. **5.** "I made a mistake marrying him," she confided to her best friend, who had six arms. **6.** "This means war!" the Emperor shouted, just before a bullet hit him in the face. **7.** "I'm breaking up with you," she said. "But why?" he asked, and she laughed. **8.** "Are you a spy, a counterspy, or a counter-counterspy?" "I've lost track," he answered. "And you?" **9.** "My new invention will change the world," he said with a strange chuckle. **10.** At the party's political rally, he accidentally sat on one of the delegates. **11.** "Please, Ma'am, can you spare a bit of food? My family and I are starving!" Unfortunately, the rich woman's hearing aid had broken. **12.** "Ah," the gypsy said, "I see a future of great wealth, great success and great happiness." "But," he asked timorously, "where does that leave my dog?" **13.** "I haven't made my diagnosis yet," said the doctor. "But I may have to refer you to my sandwich." **14.** "I suddenly realized that I'm gay!" he shouted. "But then again, maybe not." **15.** "If I tell you how I became a terrorist," he said, "then can I borrow your pencil sharpener?" **16.** "Let's march on Washington!" shouted the general, not realizing he was leading his troops into the ocean. **17.** She threw her suicide note off the bridge, confusing it with herself. **18.** "How do you like my new bikini?" she asked, knowing that no one was there. **19.** "Daddy, why are you so mean to me?" asked the child. "Maybe it's because I was born in a truck and you weren't." **20.** "Before you spend the night there, I have to warn you that the house is haunted." "That's O.K.," the couple said, wagging their green-striped tails. **21.** I sat in my drab, gray office looking at my detective's license covering the peeling paint on the wall. Then I smelled her perfume. Or was it mine? **22.** He felt the tumblers give and knew he had cracked the safe. "Now I can pay off my gambling debts," he thought. He was right. **23.** "I wish I had good news for you," the doctor said, "But actually, I don't have any news for you at all." **24.** They caressed lightly, watching the deep red sun float toward the horizon. Then they caressed passionately. Then he said, "Please don't call me Bob." **25.** "I've never been with a woman before," he admitted timidly. "That's all right," his partner said, "I've never

·········· ◆ ··········

Ed Subitzky *was a stalwart of* **The National Lampoon** *and its* **Radio Hour,** *and later appeared frequently on* **Letterman.** *He also contributes to* **The Journal of Consciousness Studies.**

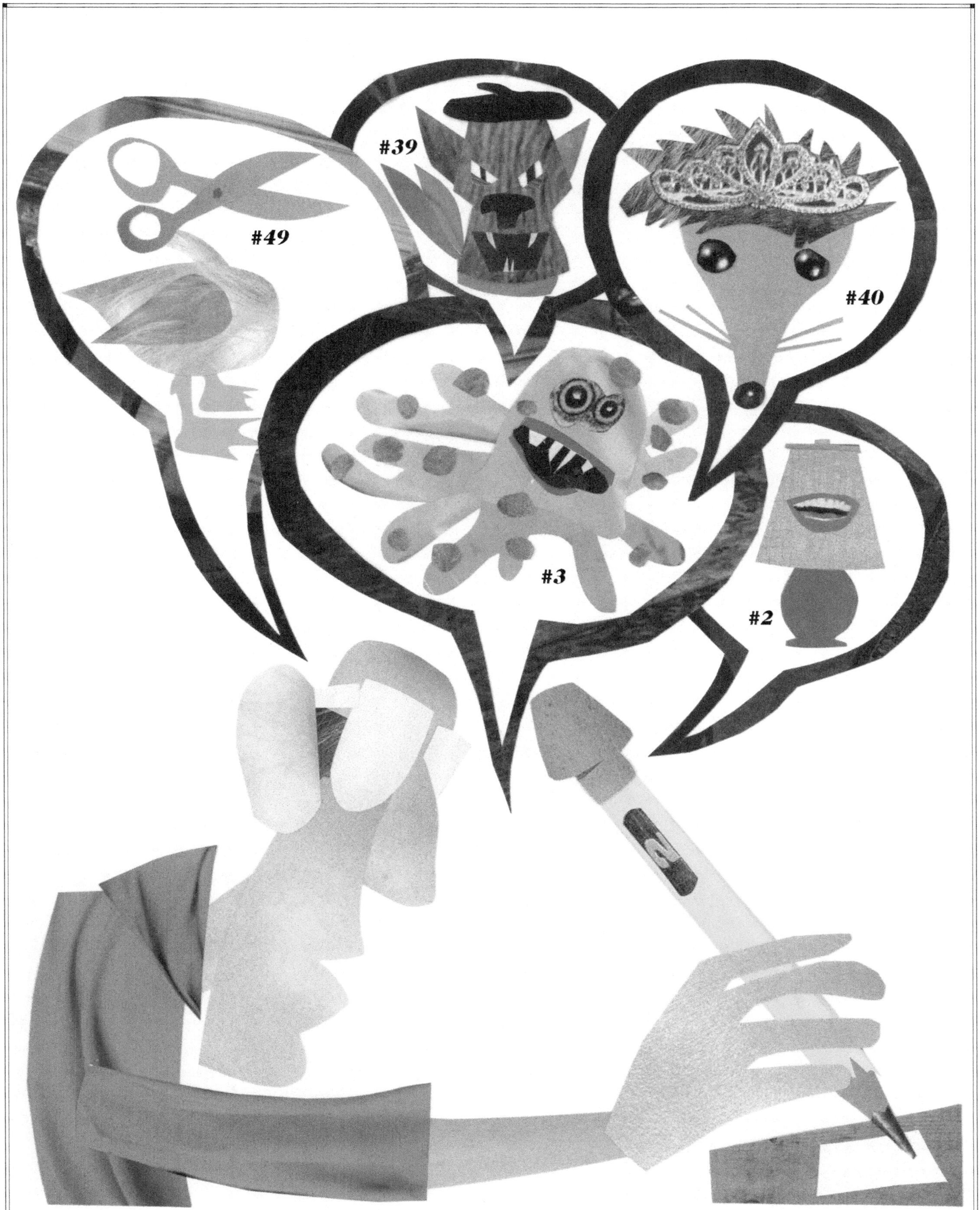
#49
#39
#40
#3
#2

been a woman before." **26.** Lost in the desert, he remembered a movie where a man drank something from a cactus. But he couldn't remember the ending. **27.** "I'll tear you limb from limb!" the enraged mobster shouted in the bar. "But first, tell me how many you have." **28.** "Ever been out of the solar system before?" the astronaut asked. The woman answered, "No, but would you like a chocolate-chip cookie?" **29.** "Marry me and you'll make me the happiest man in the world!" "How will I make him?" she asked, "From a kit?" **30.** "I'm afraid to go to sleep, Daddy. The boogeyman will get me!" "No," replied the father. "I won't. At least not tonight." **31.** "How many personalities do I have?" she asked the psychiatrist. "I don't know. How many bills do I send you each month?" **32.** A cool, damp fog settled over the English countryside. In the distance, a wolf howled, and farther away still there was a magnitude 3.2 earthquake that didn't hurt anybody. **33.** Are any words sadder than, "Are any words sadder than"? **34.** She was all the food she had ever eaten, and the men in her town knew that. **35.** "We don't cotton to strangers in our village telling us how to fertilize our rutabagas." **36.** "To gain the hand of my beautiful daughter," the sorcerer said, "You must solve three riddles. The first riddle is, 'What are the second and third riddles?'" **37.** The mule-train driver didn't understand that he couldn't back up into a parking space. **38.** "But darling," she said, "I'm not leaving you for another man. At least I don't think a porcupine is considered to be a man." **39.** The bright autumn moon painted a streak of yellow down the werewolf's mane, but one that was difficult to reproduce correctly in an oil painting. **40.** At the stroke of midnight, the spell wore off, and the fairy princess was revealed to be a hedgehog. **41.** "If you put all the things I've eaten end to end," he said, "it would reach a place pretty far away and back." **42.** The experiment was ready. Could he instill the precious breath of life and consciousness into a sewing machine? **43.** I wish I had been out to lunch the day those long, sinewy legs walked into my office. And the rest of her came along, too, just a few steps behind. **44.** "Stranger, under no circumstances must you walk past the old mansion on Midnight Road." "Thank you, kind sir, and may I ask where you live?" "In the old mansion on Midnight Road." **45.** "The first thing you need to understand," the psychiatrist said to the patient, "is that you're not a car." **46.** "It's a cold and dark world in there," he said, pointing to the refrigerator. **47.** Even though it wasn't Christmas, they hung colored lights all over their house and their children. **48.** I've been a psychiatrist over 30 years and contrary to public opinion, I've never had a single patient who thought he was a toaster. **49.** "You cannot turn a pair of scissors into a duck," the father warned his daughter. "No matter how much you might want to." **50.** "I'm going to take this case on personally!" the F.B.I. agent shouted, smashing his fist down hard on the table. "But first, have you seen what supermarkets are charging for lettuce these days?" **51.** "I'm very embarrassed by it," she said sadly. "But the fact is that I was born with three elbows." **52.** "I brought us safely into harbor," the captain said.

ATKINSON

"O.K., but where are you from really?"

"Then I realized that my fly had been open all the time." **53.** Some people think a detective leads a life of guns, guts, girls and glory. But I wouldn't know, because I'm an insurance salesman. **54.** "I'm sorry," she said, tossing her raven-black hair. "I would go on a date with you, but I'm about to be abducted by Martians." **55.** "I like bromeliads and you don't," he said. "Can't we just leave it at that?" **56.** "Bold and noble one, can you slay the dragon?" the mayor of the small town pleaded. "Yes," replied the knight, "but I expect a lot of admiration immediately afterwards." **57.** There is a chapel in Brisbane, and it is said that the bells ring every time a man meets his true love, and also when lunch is ready. **60.** "Ah!" the great detective told the stranger, "I can see that you come from down in the village, that your hobby is trimming shrubbery, and that you are here to see me on a matter most urgent. But first, do you know how to repair an elevator?" **61.** "Come with me," the kindly old man said to the boy, "And I'll probably teach you how to fish." **62.** The setting sun was so much like a basketball that one could almost believe it would bounce. **63.** When he picked up the handkerchief and blew his nose in it, he didn't know that she had dropped it deliberately. **64.** "You may now kiss the bride and, in about an hour and a half, you can have sex with her." **65.** The billionaire industrialist took his son to the window where factory buildings could be seen spreading out to the horizon. "When I came to this country," he said

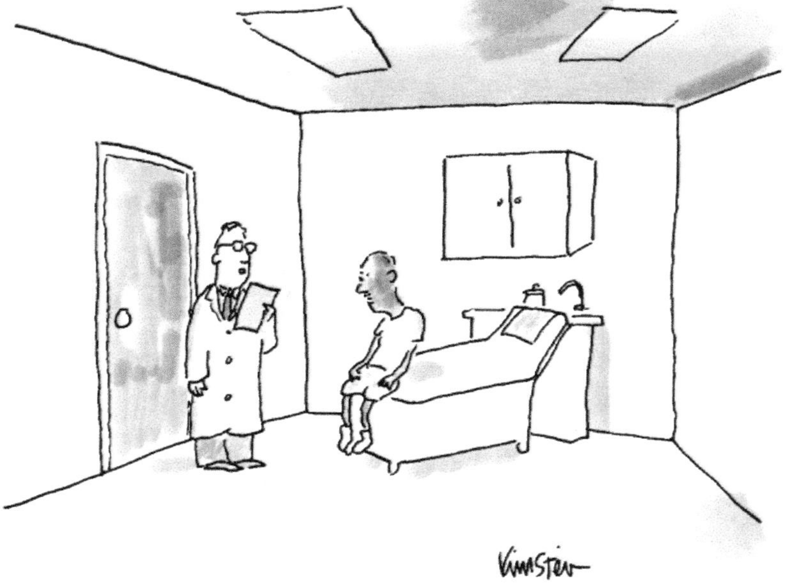

"According to these scans, I shouldn't have gone to med school in Aruba."

softly, "I didn't have a penny. Well, actually, that's not quite right. I did have a penny. But just one." **66.** "I can free your child from this demonic spell," the priest said. "But can I wait until he's toilet-trained?" **67.** "Look!" she exclaimed, "the first crocus of spring! "No," he replied, "that's actually the New York Stock Exchange." **68.** The spaceship landed on a bleak, desolate planet devoid of life. Then it landed on another bleak, desolate planet devoid of life. **69.** "After seven months of deliberation," the judge told the jury, "What is your verdict?" The foreman rose to his feet and said, "Oooh, can I go to jail, too?" **70.** "I'll make any sacrifice to get this building finished! I don't care how much steel it takes, how much glass it takes, how many lives it takes and how many elevators it needs." **71.** "Unfortunately," the princess said, "I kissed a gay frog." **72.** The packet of fading photographs took her mind back to long walks together in the rain, hushed vows spoken under a harvest moon and winning at bowling. **73.** "You have everything it takes to become a star," the director said, "but would you mind mailing this letter for me on the way home?" **74.** "This is my first flight," the co-pilot admitted. "We all have to start somewhere," the captain said in a kindly manner, "So let's get this tin can with wings off the ground!" **75.** "Doctor, I have a compulsion to repeat every sentence. Doctor, I have a compulsion to repeat every sentence." "Funny, but I do, too." "Funny, but I do, too." **76.** The blind date was going well until she noticed the extra eye on his forehead. **77.** "Everything in life has a lesson to teach you," the philosopher said. "Except maybe for a blue toilet seat cover." **78.** "So, soldier, how long have you been in this prisoner-of-war camp?" "Sixteen years." "Were they good years?" **79.** There were only

14 people in the small town, so they took turns being married. **80.** The snow turned everything a soft, gentle white, or at least it seemed that way. **81.** "For every one of you, there's a bullet with your name on it," the sergeant told his troops. "Except for you, Wilenkoscolatravichg." **82.** "People think I'm tough," the detective said. "But beneath this hard-edged surface there are two lungs, a liver, a spleen and lots of other things like that." **83.** "I know I'm just a boy in the mail-room, sir, but I have a plan that will double the company's earnings in the next fiscal year. Will you listen to it?" "Sure, son, but are you the one who's been stealing my magazines?" **84.** "Eureka! I've done it," the scientist shouted. "I've cured the disease! Now, will you please let me use the restroom?" **85.** "Life is like a jigsaw puzzle," the hobo said, warming his hands over the fire. "When you put the pieces together wrong, an alpine landscape can look like a pattern of flying geese." **86.** "I was born to paint! To bring beauty into this tired, dreary world! And to sit down every once in a while." **87.** "We have ways to get the information from you," the torturer said. "I only wish I could remember some of them." **88.** The warden walked along the empty rows of cells, stopping at each one to say, "I warn you! This prison is inescapable!" **89.** "Can you believe our little baby is going to her first prom night!" Alicia said, weeping. "I can't believe it," Fred answered. "Because half of it isn't true." **90.** "If Horse Sense wins the race, we'll have enough money to get medicine for our child! Unless we spend it on something else, of course." **91.** "This could lead the world into nuclear war!" the president said, aghast. "It's the toughest decision I've ever had to make, isn't it?" **92.** "Guys," the coach said, "I'm not asking you to win for me. I'm asking you to win for old Mister Crutchfield, someone I know but you probably don't." **93.** The corpses rose out of their graves, took a look at the world around them, and went back in. **94.** As a member of Queen Victoria's aristocracy, she was expected to be perfect in every way. But she was allowed three releases of intestinal gas before being ostracized. **95.** What is the difference between a vacuum cleaner and a sunspot? It will take the next 400 pages to explain it. **96.** "It's a miracle! I can walk again!" "But you could always walk." "Oh yeah, that's right." **97.** Mary was born with a dark cloud over her head and potholes beneath her feet that had been entirely neglected by city management despite high taxes. **98.** The tiger crouched, ready to attack. The explorer knew that running would be useless, and standing absolutely still wouldn't work, either. He really wished he had brought a gun with him. **99.** On the top of a mountain in the Himalayas, the elderly monk shouted what he had learned in his 50 years of silence. "People of the world," he roared, his voice echoing over village and town, "the meaning of life will follow in the next installment. Or maybe the one after that." **100.** "I want a guy who has a great sense of humor, likes to take long sunset walks on the beach and is as handsome as a movie star." She looked at the words she had written in her diary and killed herself. **101.** He woke up in the morning, filled his lungs with a deep, luxurious stretch and realized that, because of pollution, the air had turned solid. **B**

RICK GEARY

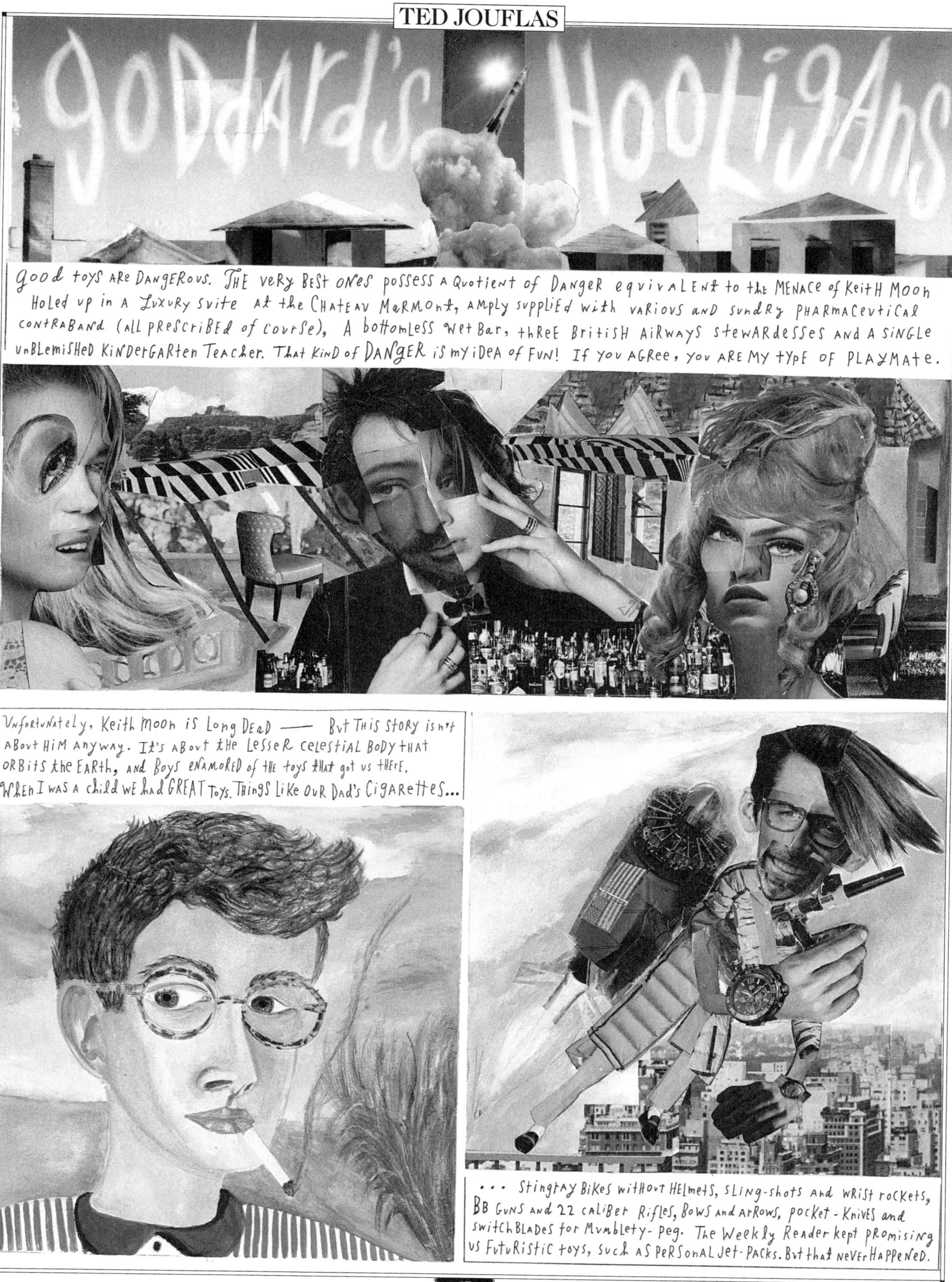
Goddard's Hooligans
Good toys are dangerous. The very best ones possess a quotient of danger equivalent to the menace of Keith Moon holed up in a luxury suite at the Chateau Marmont, amply supplied with various and sundry pharmaceutical contraband (all prescribed of course), a bottomless wet bar, three British Airways stewardesses and a single unblemished kindergarten teacher. That kind of DANGER is my idea of fun! If you agree, you are my type of playmate.
Unfortunately, Keith Moon is long dead — but this story isn't about him anyway. It's about the lesser celestial body that orbits the Earth, and boys enamored of the toys that got us there. When I was a child we had GREAT toys. Things like our Dad's cigarettes...
... Stingray bikes without helmets, sling-shots and wrist rockets, BB guns and 22 caliber rifles, bows and arrows, pocket-knives and switchblades for mumblety-peg. The Weekly Reader kept promising us futuristic toys, such as personal jet-packs. But that never happened.

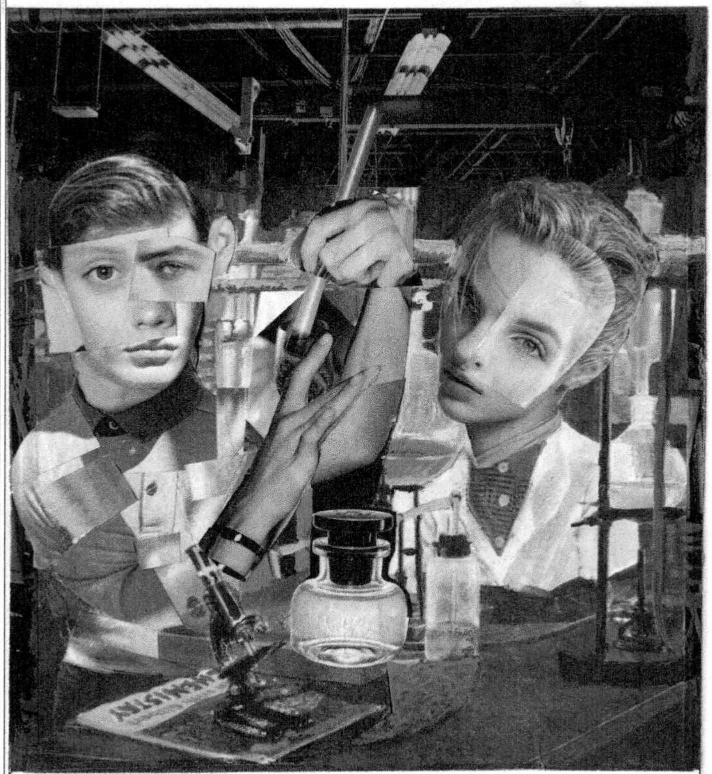

The coolest toy of all was the chemistry set — mainly because it wasn't a toy!!! They contained all sorts of dangerous elements. Things like potassium nitrate for fireworks, gunpowder and rocket fuel. Nitric acid for rocket fuel. Chemicals to ignite a boys' imagination.

Or, indeed, a man's: Robert H. Goddard is the "Father of Modern Rocketry". As early as 1902 he was thinking about space travel; but he didn't simply theorize, he built and tested rockets. His lonely successes were further developed by Wernher Von Braun, the father of the Saturn V rocket, the greatest toy ever made.

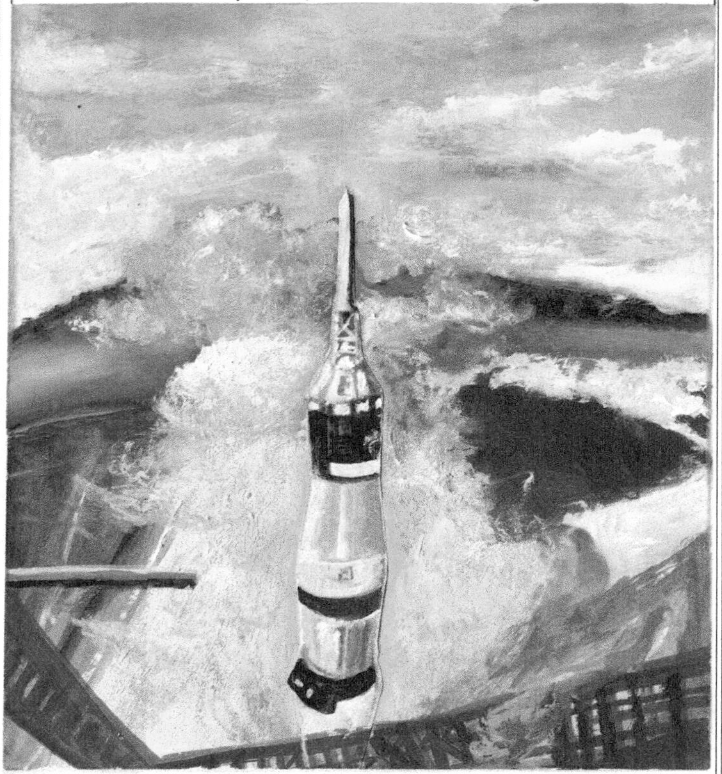

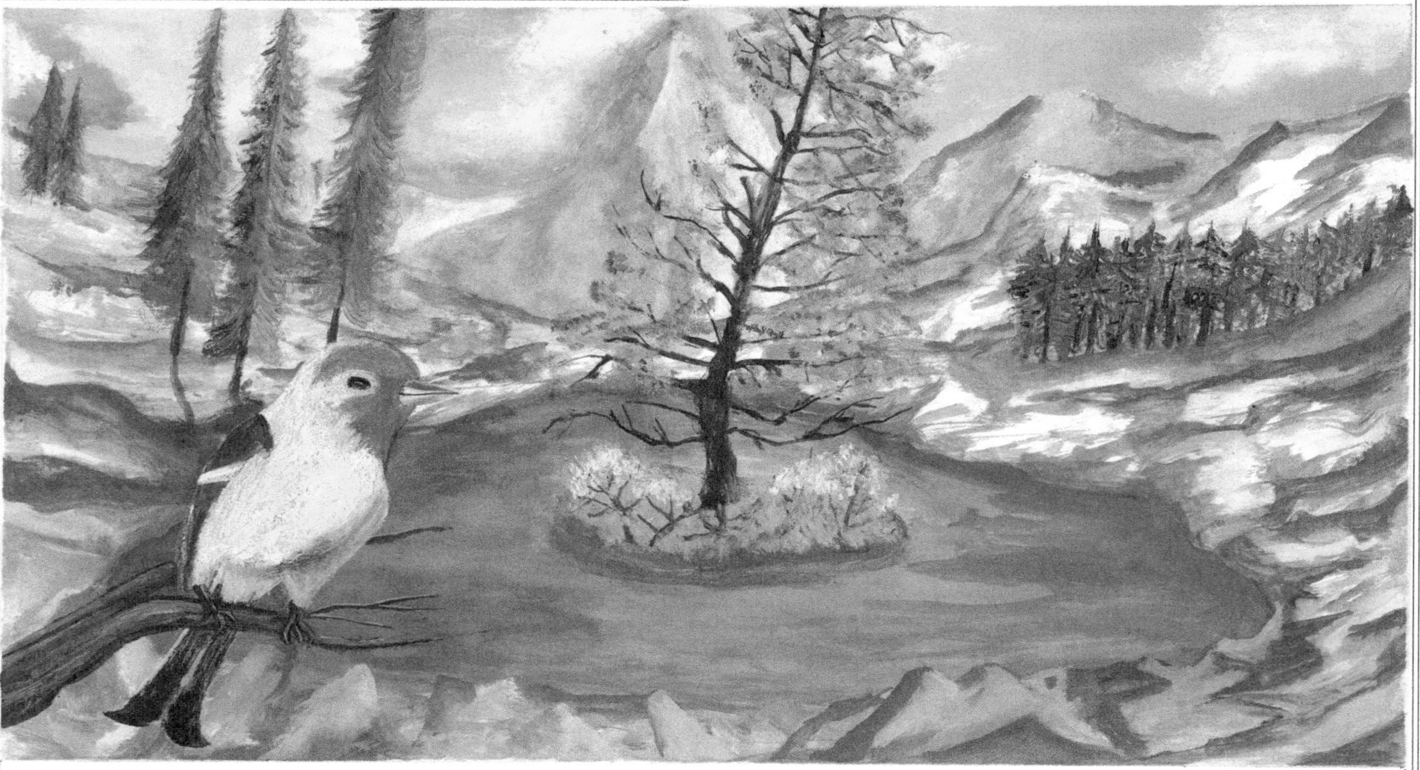

In the summer's that my parents wished for a vacation by themselves, they sent me to visit relatives. One summer I stayed with my aunt and uncle who lived with their children at the edge of Salt Lake City, atop one of the foothills to a mountainside. Across the street from their house was nothing. This nothing was in fact a fabulous something — the beginning of the Wasatch Range, the western edge of the Rockies, an idyllic realm of temperate coniferous forest, granite, limestone and quartzite canyons and beautiful alpine lakes fed by streams and glacier-fed waterfalls.
As a boy from Los Angeles, I adored this place and everything it represented about the true WILD WEST.

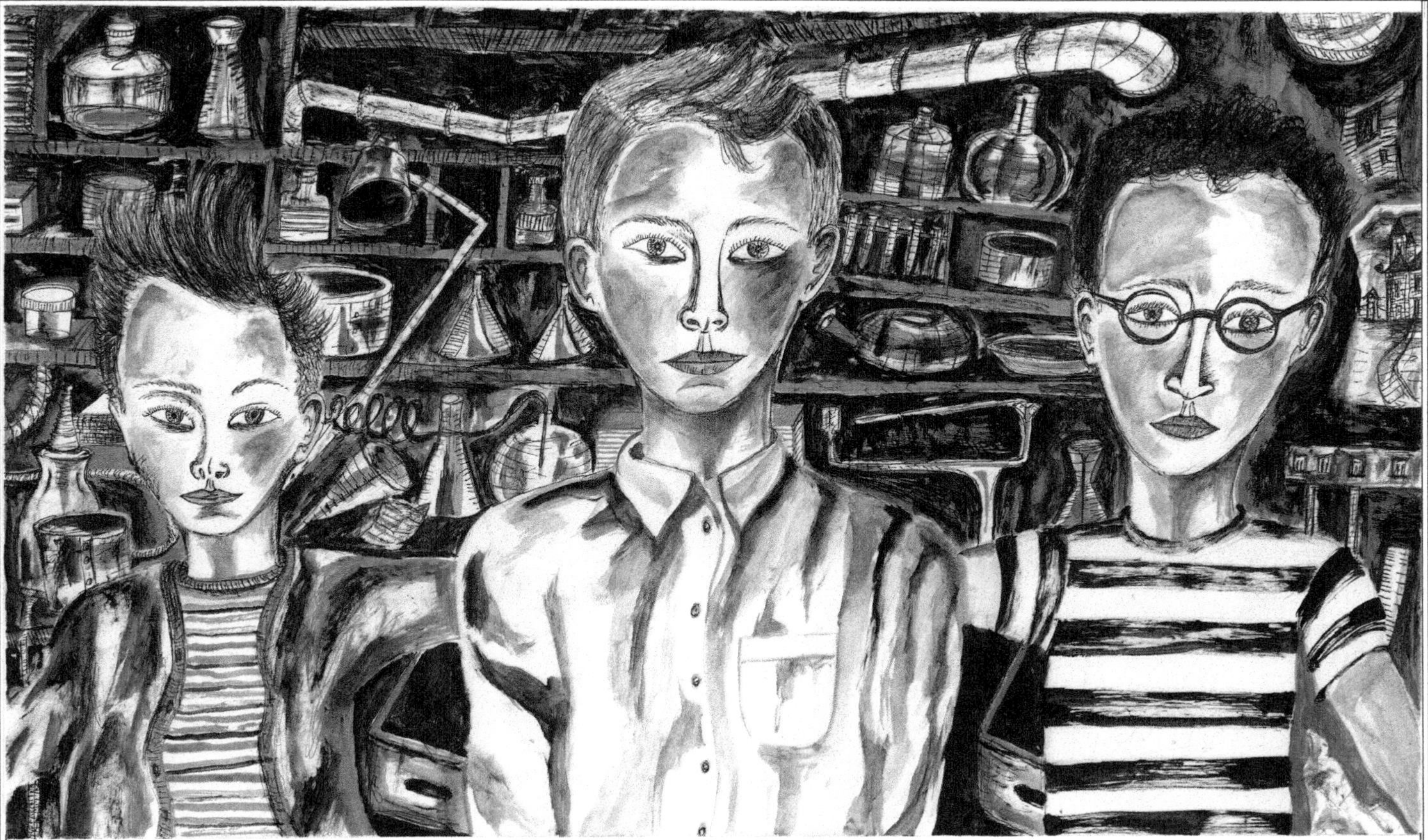

The Chemistry Lab was in the Basement. My oldest Male Cousin was in Junior High and was the Brains. I was in 5th grade, and his Little Brother was in 3rd grade. Initially we MADE Firecrackers. Large Ones. All of the necessary Chemicals CAME with the Sets and when you ran out were easily replaced at the Toy Store; The Cashiers never asked Questions. Every success emboldened us; soon we were a Fireworks Factory of High Ambitions.

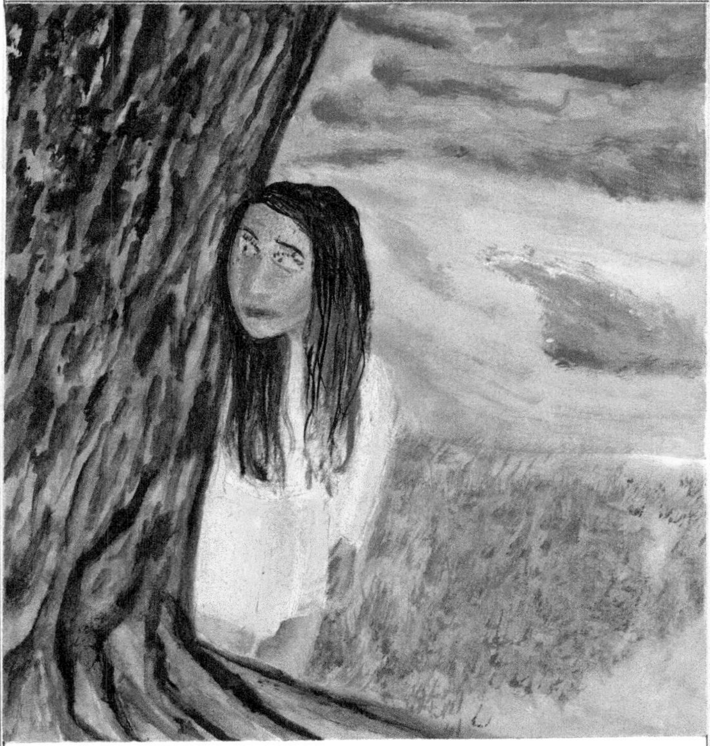

We PERformed our "tests" out in the Mountains, FAR from Prying eyes — Or so we thought. One Dark day, we were followed By a Priggish Neighbor girl who saw everything. She ran straight Home and told her Mother we were "playing with BOMBS." By the time we Got Home that afterNoon, the jig was up.

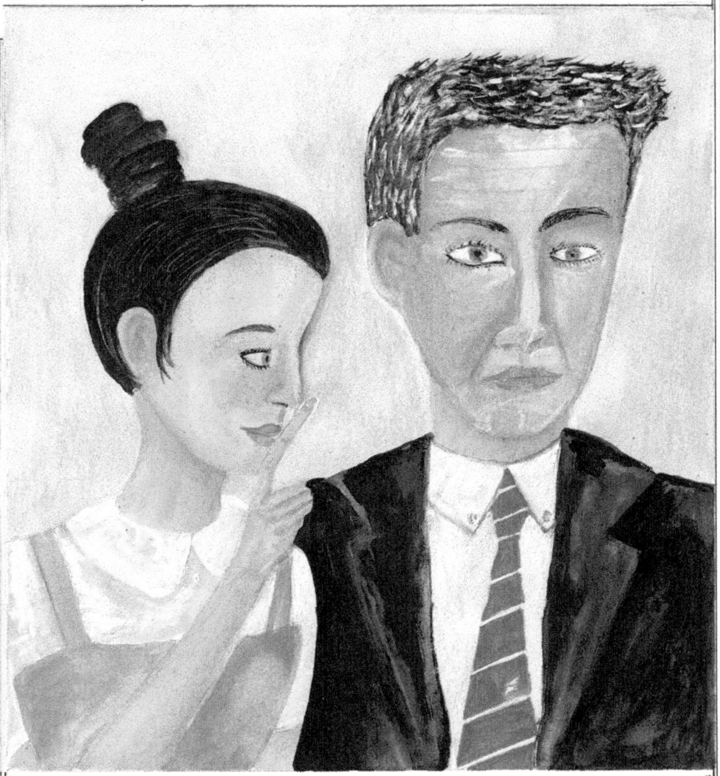

My Aunt fumed at us — "just you wait until your Father/Uncle gets Home!" We sat there in our room, silently stupefied with DREAD. But when he Arrived, Uncle was cool-headed and rational; It Became apparent that the worst aspect of our punishment had Been the Long Hours spent waiting for Him.

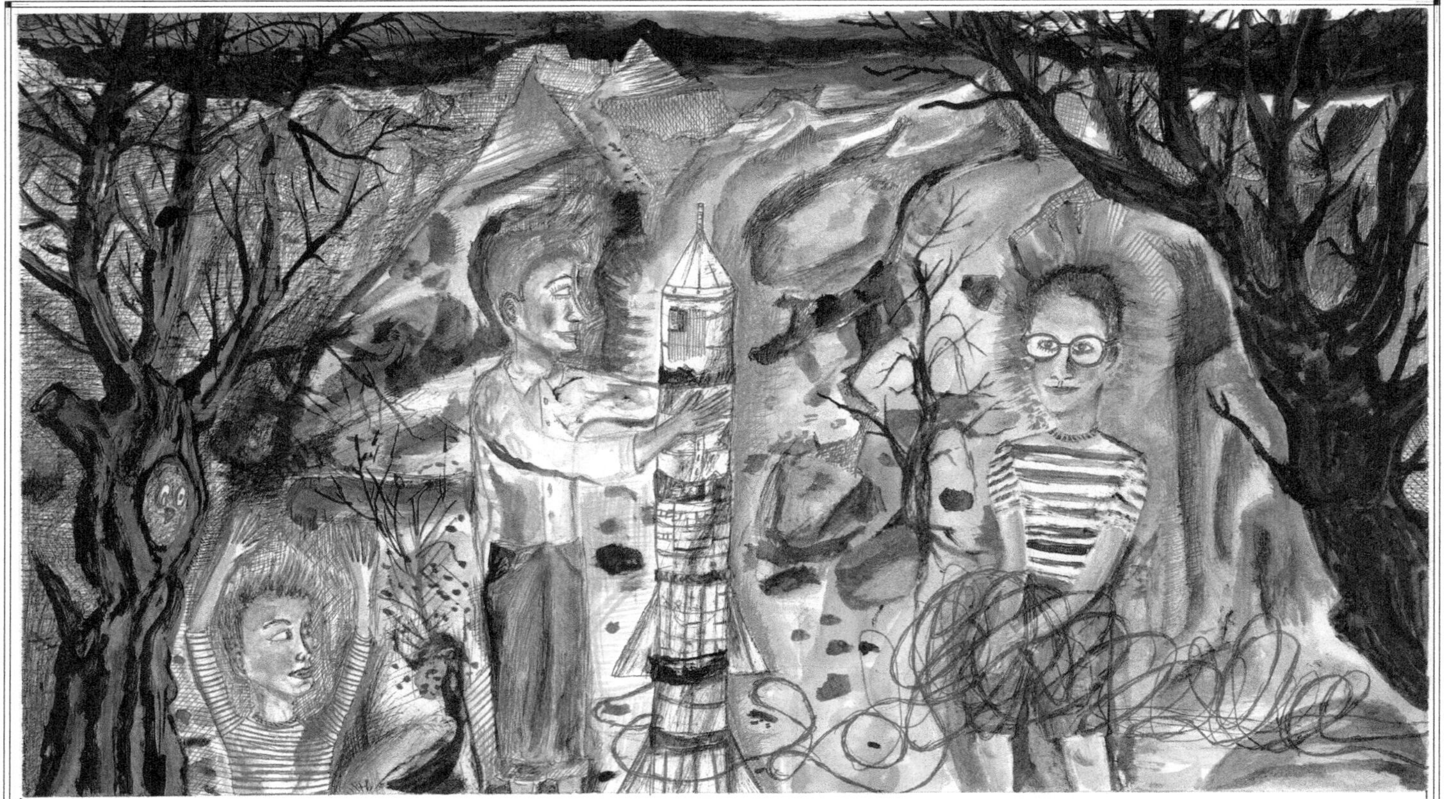

An Architectural Engineer, he actually seemed impressed by our interest in experimentation. The chemistry set was doing exactly what it was supposed to do, interest kids in science, thereby creating future scientists. (Unless of course, we blew ourselves to smithereens first.) My Uncle gave us a thoughtful and serious talking to, emphasizing our safety and the safety of others. He didn't take the set away from us, he just wanted us to put our interest to more positive uses. The next day we three decided, what could possibly be more positive than a rocket? It was August 1969, barely one month since the lunar landing of Apollo Eleven. Our childhood had been hugely influenced by NASA — So now we endeavored to make our own version of Herr Von Braun's Saturn V. Using tin cans, electrical tape, house paint, cardboard, and a funnel for the capsule, we carefully loaded each section with "rocket fuel." It was a very good thing that my Junior High cousin was smart, and made certain our contraption had a very long fuse. We lit it and ran yonder to the beyond — then crouched in some bushes, awaiting ignition.

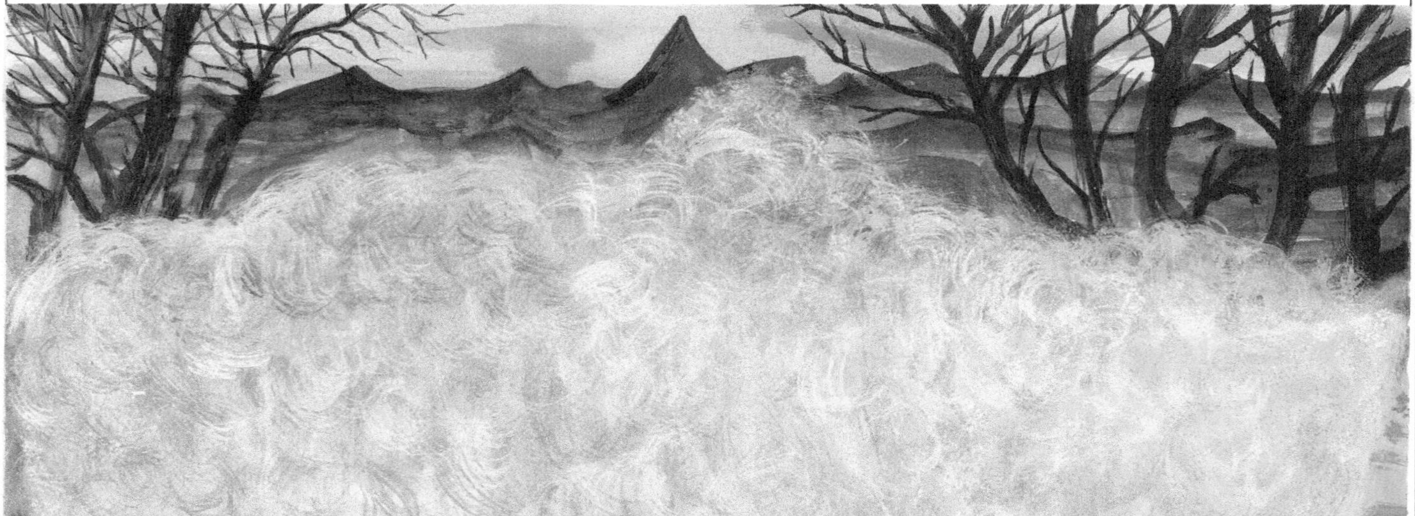

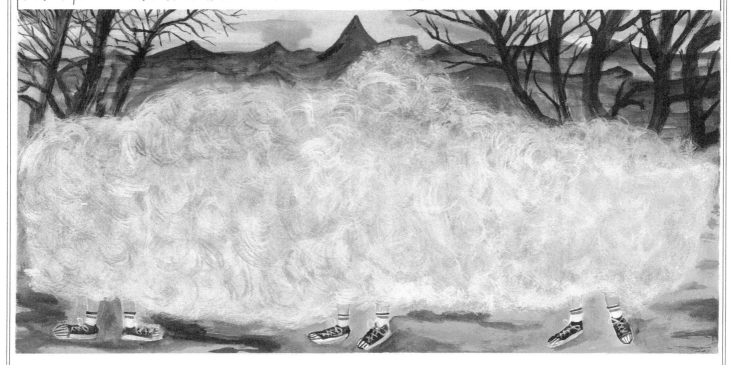

WHEN the MOMENT FINALLY CAME, OUR HOMEMADE SATURN V DIDN'T GO STRAIGHT UP. NOR DID IT GO IN ORDERLY STAGES. ALL AT ONCE IT WAS 360 DEGREES OF SIDEWAYS. COFFEE AND FRUIT CAN SHRAPNEL BUZZED OVER OUR HEADS. A CLOUD OF DUST AND SMOKE ROSE FROM THE GROUND. OUR EARS RANG, AS DEBRIS TINKLED AND PLINKED ON THE ROCKS. WE STOOD THERE STUNNED; BY SOME MIRACLE, NONE OF US WERE HURT. BUT MY UNCLE HAD BEEN PROVEN ABSOLUTELY CORRECT. WE WERE IDIOTS, VIA THE SCIENTIFIC METHOD. IT WAS A LONG AND SULLEN WALK HOME THAT AFTERNOON, AND WE REMAINED DOUR FOR DAYS, STUNG BY OUR FAILURE. WE FURIOUSLY LOOKED AROUND FOR A TARGET FOR OUR DISAPPOINTMENT — OF COURSE! THE NEIGHBORHOOD SNITCH! SHE AND HER BROTHERS HAD A CLUBHOUSE FORT IN THEIR BACKYARD THAT WAS TRULY ENVIABLE; THEIR DAD MUST HAVE BUILT IT, BECAUSE NO CHILD COULD HAVE. IT WAS THAT GOOD! AND SO, A FEW NIGHTS LATER, WE CREPT THROUGH THE DARK INTO THE SNITCH'S BACKYARD. AS THE NEIGHBORHOOD SLEPT, WE PAINTED A HUGE SLOPPY TARGET ON THE SIDE OF THE FORT.

THE NEXT MORNING, AS WE ATE BREAKFAST, WE COULD SEE OUR SHAKY BULLSEYE FROM THE DINING ROOM WINDOW. MY AUNT WONDERED ALOUD "JUST WHAT SORT OF HOODLUMS WOULD DO SUCH A THING"? OF COURSE THE SNITCH KNEW — BUT SHE AND HER BROTHERS NEVER SAID OR DID ANYTHING. THE FOLLOWING SUMMER, THE TARGET WAS STILL THERE. THEY HADN'T PAINTED OVER IT. YOU HAD TO ADMIRE THEM FOR THAT.

MY UNCLE'S HOUSE SURVIVED OUR FASCINATION WITH FIREWORKS, BUT MOTHER NATURE HAS FASCINATIONS OF HER OWN. ALMOST EXACTLY THIRTY YEARS LATER, ON THE MORNING OF AUGUST 11, 1999 MY UNCLE HAD LEFT HIS HOUSE TO ATTEND THE FUNERAL OF A FRIEND. WHEN HE RETURNED HOME THAT AFTERNOON, HIS HOUSE WAS GONE. WHILE HE WAS OUT AN EXTREMELY RARE TORNADO BLEW INTO TOWN FROM THE GREAT BASIN; AFTER HITTING SALT LAKE CITY, THE TWISTER MADE ITS WAY ALONG A RIDGETOP TO THE FOOTHILLS OF THE MOUNTAINS. IT TOUCHED DOWN ON MY UNCLE'S HOUSE, ENTIRELY REMOVING THE ROOF AND SUCKING MOST OF THE CONTENTS OF THE HOUSE INTO THE SKY. A LADY SAID THAT SHE HAD SEEN MY UNCLE'S FAVORITE EASY CHAIR SPINNING IN THE SKY. HIS FRIEND HAD DIED WITH PERFECTLY EXQUISITE TIMING; ONE DAY SOONER OR LATER AND THE LADY WOULD HAVE SEEN MY UNCLE ALOFT AS WELL. THE NEXT DAY I SPOKE WITH HIM ON THE TELEPHONE. HE WAS JOVIAL AND LAUGHING AT HIS UTTERLY BIZARRE CIRCUMSTANCES.
I HAD TO ASK ABOUT THE TARGETED FORT, WAS IT STILL THERE? IT WAS, HE TOLD ME, ENTIRELY UNSCATHED.

B

2017 Summer Music Festival Guide!

Think you've missed the season's hottest festivals? You're in luck — this year, they've saved the best for last.

August 17-19
Show Me Your Light You Glorious Wallflower Music Experiensation

Where: Beneath the dappled sunlight in a painstakingly restored cider barn in Lawrence, Kansas.
How much: Limited tickets available, $135 or barter.

Hug yourself and sway rhythmlessly for three days straight, as your gentle frame is awash in the harmonious tones of indie rock's most precious artists. Hear voices soar and strain, miles away from potential confrontations with bullies and overly friendly cashiers. And what's that sound? A tremulous harp strumming against samples from a vintage farmyard animal Speak'n'Spell? Pure bliss.

This year's Festivaliensation features over thirty acts representing every style of twee, including Toy Rock, Sweater Step, Wink, Flutterfly, Shamblecore, Wisp-Hop, and Sob.

Headlining the main stage (in no particular order because who are we to say who deserves to go first?): *Your Favourite Jumper*; *The Unbearable Strain of Shyness*; *Fear of Touch*; *The Weeps*; *The Lingering Smell of You*; *Less is Amour*; *Gentle, Please Gentle*; *Thin Wrists and Pure Hearts*; *I'm Not the Droid You Are Looking For*; *So Very Thankful for Fog*; *Ethan & Ethan, Conjoined Poets*; *Softest Dungarees*; and *Hoobastank*.

Notable sponsor: Olde Jim's Honest Artisanal Shoe Reflectors — "It's a simple fact: Sustained eye contact can be unbearable, a torture worse than death. But now you can enjoy an evening of tender, non-threatening strums without ever having to take your eyes off the floor, thanks to these artisanal shoe reflectors. Each reflector is handcrafted from barbershop mirrors and valuable scrap metal from molasses barrel hoops, with straps designed to fit over any size chukka boot. They're also a terrific way to meet cute!"

Special events:
- Wes Anderson Cosplay
- Sweater stretching tables
- Touch Zooey Deschanel's "secret" hair
- Shimmy on up to our unpasteurized dairy bar
- Free dental night guard cleanings
- Scream your feelings into one of our vintage pickling jars
- Late-night corduroy rubbings
- Contribute to our "sob quilt"
- Attempt to make Stephin Merritt of the Magnetic Fields smile!

Directions: Run away from home, meandering through the pear orchard off Old County Road 4, trying your hardest to not frighten the rabbits. When you reach the old dead tree on which lovers scrawl their initials, read quietly from your dog-eared copy of Salinger's *Nine Stories,* until you fall asleep in the moon's soft glow. When you awaken, you will be standing in front of our security bag check.

August 24-26
The Electric Gravy Boom-Boom Psytrancival

Where: An unused portion of Rikers Island, New York.
How much: $150, or free for anyone wearing butterfly wings.

The Second Annual Electric Gravy Boom-Boom Psytrancival is an intergenerational event built on love, energy and a sacred pledge that all men over 40 not wear any inner or outer garments with the slightest hint of fluorescent pigmentation.

.... ◆ ....

The Pleasure Syndicate are Scott Jacobson, Todd Levin, Mike Sacks and Ted Travelstead. They wrote "Index to This Issue" for *Bystander* #3 and #4.

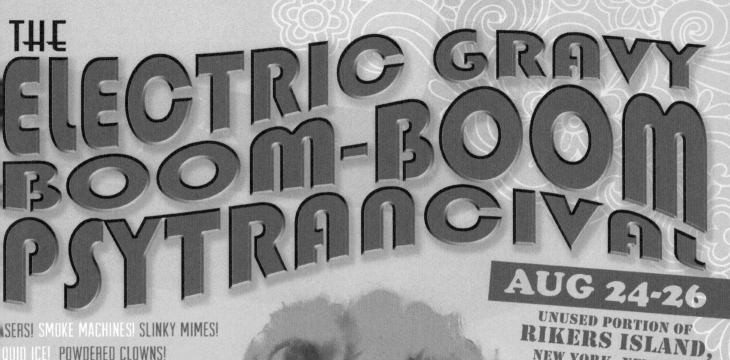

THE ELECTRIC GRAVY BOOM-BOOM PSYTRANCIVAL

AUG 24-26

UNUSED PORTION OF
RIKERS ISLAND,
NEW YORK, NEWYORK,

ADMISSION: $150
PEOPLE WEARING BUTTERFLY WINGS
ARE ADMITTED FREE (AS ALWAYS)

...SERS! SMOKE MACHINES! SLINKY MIMES!
...QUID ICE! POWDERED CLOWNS!
...SED COCK-SOCKS! COLORFUL STREAMERS!
...NSANCTIONED TRAPEZE ARTISTS WITH
...ERO HEALTH INSURANCE!

...GROUP OF GAY MEN IN DR. SEUSS HATS
...EEDING EACH OTHER TAPIOCA PUDDING
...ITH SUSTAINABLE PAPER SPORKS!

SPECIAL GUEST
LICORICE
CONVERGENCE
II

...EMINAR ON HOW TO
...MAKE YOUR OWN
...RGANIC TRADE-FREE
...COFFEE ENEMAS!

CHILL FACTOR: VERY

SEXY

JoeOPortfolio.com

More than SIX Earth-Shattering, Energy-Infused Staged Areas, all complete with separate state-of-the-art sound systems, each purchased from the infamous, now-defunct Promise Keepers Ministry in Marfa, Texas!

"Groovy Anagalactic Beach": LASERS! SMOKE MACHINES! Slinky mimes! Liquid ice! Powdered clowns! Used cock socks! Colorful streamers! NON-SANCTIONED TRAPEZE ARTISTS WITH ZERO HEALTH INSURANCE! A group of gay men in Dr. Seuss hats feeding each other tapioca pudding with sustainable paper sporks! Chill factor: Very.

"The UpsideDown Freeqy Garden": Foamy fun! Glow sticks! Go-go dancers! ONE STONED MAN WAVING A HANNUKAH CANDLE! Anything can happen at the UpsideDown Freeqy Garden, as evidenced by the Great Tent Fire of 2011!!! Chill factor: Not much.

"The Sunken Crystal Nocturnal Rainbow Emission": Join world-famous DJ "Infected Mushroom" as he spins his own unique brand of "Edgy Trance" and rides a mechanical bulldyke. Chill factor: Zero.

"Licorice Convergence II": Watch Miss Dubstep 2012 as she sucks on a nitrous oxide canister and goes "wee wee" in a box filled with sand shipped over from Ibiza! OBSERVE AN EXHAUSTED CRISPIAN MILLS OF KULA SHAKER AND A BEWILDERED JAY KAY FROM JAMIROQUAI SWAYIN' SIDE BY SIDE! Chill factor: the Highest.

Special Events:
- Seminars on How to Make Your Own Organic Fair-Trade Coffee Enemas!
- Midnight Bubble Orgy!
- Post-Orgy-Cleanup and Smoked-Fish Deli Spread!
- Observe Moby Beating a Man to Death for Attempting to Initiate a Boot-Scootin' Country Line-Dance!
- Special Apps to Hone in on Disease-Free Genitalia!

Directions: 2,3,4, B,Q, F or G trains to Rikers Island front gate. Take prison jitney to concert site. Follow miserable off-duty guards holding neon batons and wearing luminous wigs. Enter the Zone. Leave behind your inhibitions. Lock and load your libido. No bottles, no food, no job, no interest in what the rest of the world might call "acting normal and grown up," no prob.

September 1-2
The Totally Rad, Totally Awesome '80s Food, Fun & Music Throwback Festival

Where: Chicago, home of the '85 Bears, Ministry and that asshole Ferris Bueller.
How much: Dire Straits may get "money for nothing and chicks for free," but you're not them. $110 advance, $150 at the door.

On September 1st and 2nd, Chicago's historic Grant Park will transform into a retro '80s orgy of kick-ass tubular synth-rockin' sounds and delicious phantasma-gaseous smells!

When was the last time you put on your Members Only jacket and danced the Safety Dance? Does Every Step You Take and Every Breath You Take, remind You of How You Used to Be? When was the last time you blasted your awesome teenage toonage on your jumbo boombox? Not lately? Well, then, it's Morris-Day-and-the-Time to hop in your magical DeLorean and make your way back to 1986...because Sweet Dreams are made of this two-day Festival!

Headliners: Tommy Shaw from STYX, performing a solo, acoustic version of the "Kilroy Was Here" rock opera, in its four-hour entirety! You might as well just . . . Jump!

Other Acts, All Hastily Re-formed Just For This Festival, With At Least ONE Original Member: Man at Work, Katrina and the Wave, Edie Brickell & New Bohemian, The Romantic, Simple Mind, The Bangle, Duran, and the World's No. 1 Middle-Earth-Themed Transvestite U2 cover band, The Unforgettable Shire (with a brand-new "Bonaux"!).

Food Tents: Sweet Burgers O'Mine, Total Eclipse of This Hot Dog Cart, Don't Stop Eatin' Fudge, Every Corn Has Its Butter, Sweet Dreams (Are Made of Fried Ice Cream), John Hinckley's Spaced Frittered Invaders, Explode-in-Ya-Challenger Curly Fries, Oliver North's Hot Nuckin' Futs, Sun City Segregated Chipwiches, and many, many more!

Special Events:
- Matt Frewer, the creator and voice behind Max Headroom, r-r-r-r-reads *Bright Lights, Big City.*
- Group sing-along to 1985's *Shoah*!
- Symposium and Q&A with the Now-Retired Schoolteacher Who Moaned Over and Over on "Hungry Like the Wolf"!
- Michael Winslow Makes the "Whocka Whocka Whocka" Pac-Man Sounds!
- Air Guitar Contest in GG Allin Tent!
- Morganna "The Kissing Bandit" Attempts to Solve the Rubik's Cube with Her Nipples!

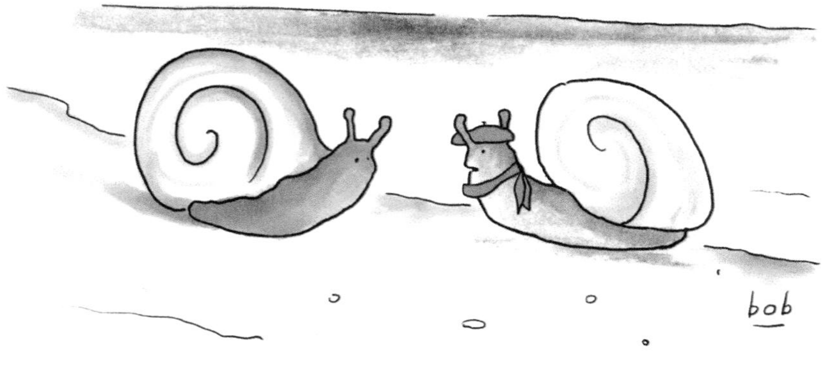
bob

"Why can't you just be happy for me that I'm going to Paris?"

- The New Filipino Singer from Journey Talks About His Love for All Things Swatch Watch!

Directions: Follow the scent of failed hopes and dreams. See you soon! *Fer shure! Fer shure!*

September 4-5
Skull Valley Music and Arts Festival

Where: Skull Valley, California, September 4th and 5th
How much: (3-DAY PASS $250, VIP PASS WITH HYDRATING SALINE DRIP $300)

Most of the year Skull Valley is little more than a vast desert, hostile to life and relentlessly raped by the sun, but come every summer it's also home to the biggest, funnest music fest in California! Expect an estimated 80,000 attendees, 73,500 of whom will successfully make it through the two-mile hike from the parking lot to the festival entrance!

About that hike: SAVOR it! The dusty trail leading from Lot 47D wends its way through security checkpoints (where a teenager in a floppy hat will administer a brusque pat-down of your cargo shorts or bikini bottoms — *grin and groove with it!*), past a SPRAWLING TENT CITY alive with the moans of music fans coupling after their third Coors Light, and onwards toward the distant sounds of air horns, bowel-pounding bass and co-eds shrieking 'cause they spotted a lizard!

Stay hydrated! Wet stuff comes at a premium in the high desert, and fans not interested in paying an arm and a leg for bottled water are strongly encouraged to dig their own CANTEEN-REPLENISHING IRRIGATION DITCH from one of the nearby date palm orchards! Bring a shovel, a sweat towel and 10 or 12 of your most jacked-up ditchin' buddies!

But that's not the only way to stay WET! Stationed at the foot of every stage is a friendly Skull Valley "Family Member," on hand to spray the crowd with NONPOTABLE WATER FROM A HIGH-PRESSURE HOSE otherwise used to ward off the tweaking desert dwellers who scrounge through band gear for copper wire!

"Acne."

With hundreds of world-class musical acts performing on 17 stages — everyone from a reunited UGLY KID JOE to a Serbian synth duo who only have half a song but *plenty* of PODCAST BUZZ — expect to do PLENTY of trekking between sets. Be sure to rest at one of the several corporate-sponsored "OASIS TENTS." We're partial to the Beats by Dre-sponsored "BEANBAGS BY DRE," WHERE YOU CAN SINK INTO A BAG MADE SLICK 'N' SICK BY SUNBLOCK, JÄGERMEISTER SWEAT AND PIZZA RUNOFF SLUICE gifted by your fellow desert rats!

Directions: Up to you, but please pay extra, extra care burrowing 'neath the sands at night, to avoid expirin'.

September 12-14
The Freak-Your-$hit Horrorcore Clown-Down
(formerly the Soul Sounds by the Sea Shore Waterfront Doo-Wop Fest)

Where: *Mystic, Connecticut, September 12th-14th*
How much: *BETA-ASS CHUMP Pass $75, NINJA DICK Pass $150*

After an incident in which four 80-year-old members of doo-wop group the Elegants simultaneously broke their hips during a choreographed spin to "Earth Angel," the long-running Soul Sounds by the Sea Shore festival pulled up stakes and disappeared In the Still of the Night! But this year, regional concert promoters Dickchiez Productions have stepped in to fill the void!

Featuring 398 hardcore "in yo' face and out yo' ass" clown-painted murder rappers not quite shrewd enough to make the cut for the official Insane Clown Posse Gathering of the Juggalos, the three-day Clown-Down promises to be some "twisted-dick bullshit," all against the backdrop of a classic New England port town!

Ever had the urge to "drop anchor" on one of Mystic's famous tall ships? You're in luck, 'cuz that's exactly where they put the Port-A-Johns! Get high on kush bud and wander Olde Mistick Village (Est. 1654!) where you can visit Colonial Pewter Miniatures and touch a lot of little metal shit! Or you can just watch lonely, elderly women in 17th-century attire dip long candles that look a whole lot like donkey genitalia! (You'll see — they do!)

Confirmed acts include PROLAPZED REKTUM, THE HIGH-AS-FUCK DUCKSHIT TWINS, DOS WHISKEY DIX, DA TAINT MUNKZ, POOP SHY MANIAX, LI'L LYLE THE MIDGET WITH CROHN'S DISEASE, formerly racist South African "Zef" crew AFRIKAANUS and MENTALLY STUNTED DOUGIE.

And good news, Ninjas!!! The festival is scheduled entirely on week*days* to make attendance easier for the unemployed!

Special Events:

- Canine fuckfest featuring over 100 of the town's horniest dogs dropped into the same 15'-by-15' playpen!
- A real-life Congolese war criminal gettin' smoked-up and talkin' CRAZY SHIT about life!
- A caricature artist high on bath salts who can draw your picture all freaky, and who works free for boob flashes or sample packs of his preferred eczema cream!
- A morbidly obese man named "Dill-balls" who swallows and regurgitates a hermit crab named "Climber"!
- Eight plastic camp chairs to be shared amongst attendees in any way they see fit!
- And if all goes according to plan ... the entire Mystic seaport will be made bright orange using 100,000 gallons of new Faygo brand Pineapple/Watermelon flavored Party Pop Pop!

Camping information: Waterfront benches and the flatbeds of strangers' pickup trucks are first-come, first-served.

Directions: Attendees are advised to take the charter buses departing every 10 minutes from behind the public library downtown — the one with the good bathroom and the librarians who never hassle you when using the free internet to download child-support legal documents!

September 16-23

Toffifay© Presents

Summer Uncovered: The All-Tribute Band Grand Slam (Man-Made) Lake Jam

Where: Lipton Lake County Park (formerly Lipton Saltpeter Quarry), East Otis, New York.

How much: 7-Day Festival Tickets $145/ Special "Leave Early" passes, $195

Imagine ALL of your FAVORITE musical artists gathered in ONE landscaped picnic area for a weeklong ROCKSTRAVAGANZA! Well, this is kind of like that. You'll bear witness to over 175 of the world's greatest tribute bands, cover artists, sound-alikes, concept acts, and budget-friendly "in-the-style-of" musicians. Squint your eyes and press soft bread into your ears and you'd swear it's the real deal — however, on the advice of our legal counsel and an unfortunate precedent established by the landmark copyright infringement case *Fabulous Thunderbirds v. Fab Buelless and the Thunderbergs*, we are obligated to remind you that this is *not* the real deal.

This year's maestros of mimicry include: *Steel Dirigible* (Led Zeppelin cover band); *Eruption* (Van Halen); *Earth, Wings & Fire* (Wings); *Second

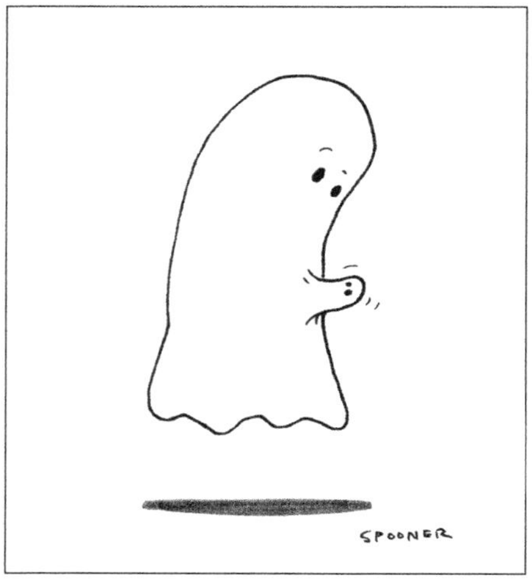
SPOONER

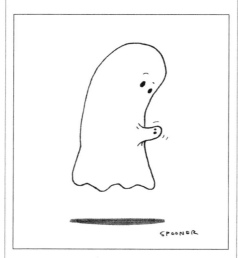

Gunman* (Dead Kennedys); *SNIX* (INXS); *Hard to Explain* (The Strokes); *The Strokes* (Billy Squier); *Mr. & Mrs. Brownstone* (Husband and wife Guns 'n' Roses cover band); *Crème* (France's #2 Cream cover act); and the Spanish and Cantonese language shoegaze music tribute band, *The Jésus & Mary Chang*!!

MORE Means MORE! Here, for the first time, we've assembled select members from several different tribute acts to form incredible SuperCoverBandGroups™.

Slip on your aquasocks (required, due to our lake's recent razor clam problem) and swim out to our floating stage, where you'll be rewarded with a one-time-only concert by Traveling Wilburys tribute act, *The Wavering Tarbellies* — featuring Jerome Hunt of E.L.O. tribute act, *Mr. Blue Sky*; Dr. Ron Glassman of the Bob Dylan tribute act *Blonde on Ron*; and adult-film star Jerry Butler of the Beatles cover band *The Fab Foreskin*.

Plus . . . a COMMAND PERFORMANCE by all five David Bowie tribute acts who, together, cover Bowie's entire catalog: *LAUGHING GNOME; MAJOR TIM; THE THIN WHITE DUDES; LODGER;* and *CRAPPY BOWIE*.

Groove With a View: If you don't have a pre-existing heart condition or if you are not prone to adverse reactions to difficult odors, you should scale the old saltpeter dunes for a MOUNTAINTOP MUSIC MARATHON at our "Shape Up Stage," sponsored by Reebork® brand affordable athletic footwear. Enjoy the cream of the crop of one-man cover bands, including: Ron DMC; Brad Company; Biv; and Peter, Paul & Mary Minus Peter and Mary and also Paul Plus Howard Schlemmer, CPA.

Get Your Snack On!: We've completely taken over the old mineral silo where that autistic boy died in '02, and turned it into the multilevel TASTY TOWER, where festival attendees can chow down on sweet and savory treats from some of the leading off-brand snack food companies and casual dining franchises. Crunch a bunch of Riffles™ brand potato snaps, sample a finger-lickin' feast from Kentuckyyy Fried Chicken Chicken-Flavored Vegetarian Meat Substitutes, or cool off with a warm carob sundae from Blisskin-Ribbons 2 Flavors.

Special Event: A Live Reading! Fresh off her virtual book tour, the legendary tribute rock groupie, known only as "Available Annie," will join us for a live reading of her tell-all memoir *Wait...I Just Fucked Who?*

She's done 'em all, and now you'll get to find out which world-famous cover artist had the most impressive hog. Was it Alan Stock of Huey Lewis cover band, *Alan Stock & the New Drugs*? Or Jerry Gorley, lead singer of the Smashing Pumpkins cover band, *Billy Corgan's Noxious, Festering Ego*? Only Annie knows!

Directions: See that clearing in the distance? With the people milling about, looking uncomfortable? No, this way. Yes. Just keep walking. Don't look back. We said keep walking. **B**

THE COMICS SUPPLEMENT TO THE AMERICAN BYSTANDER!

PRESTIDIGITATOR APPROVED!

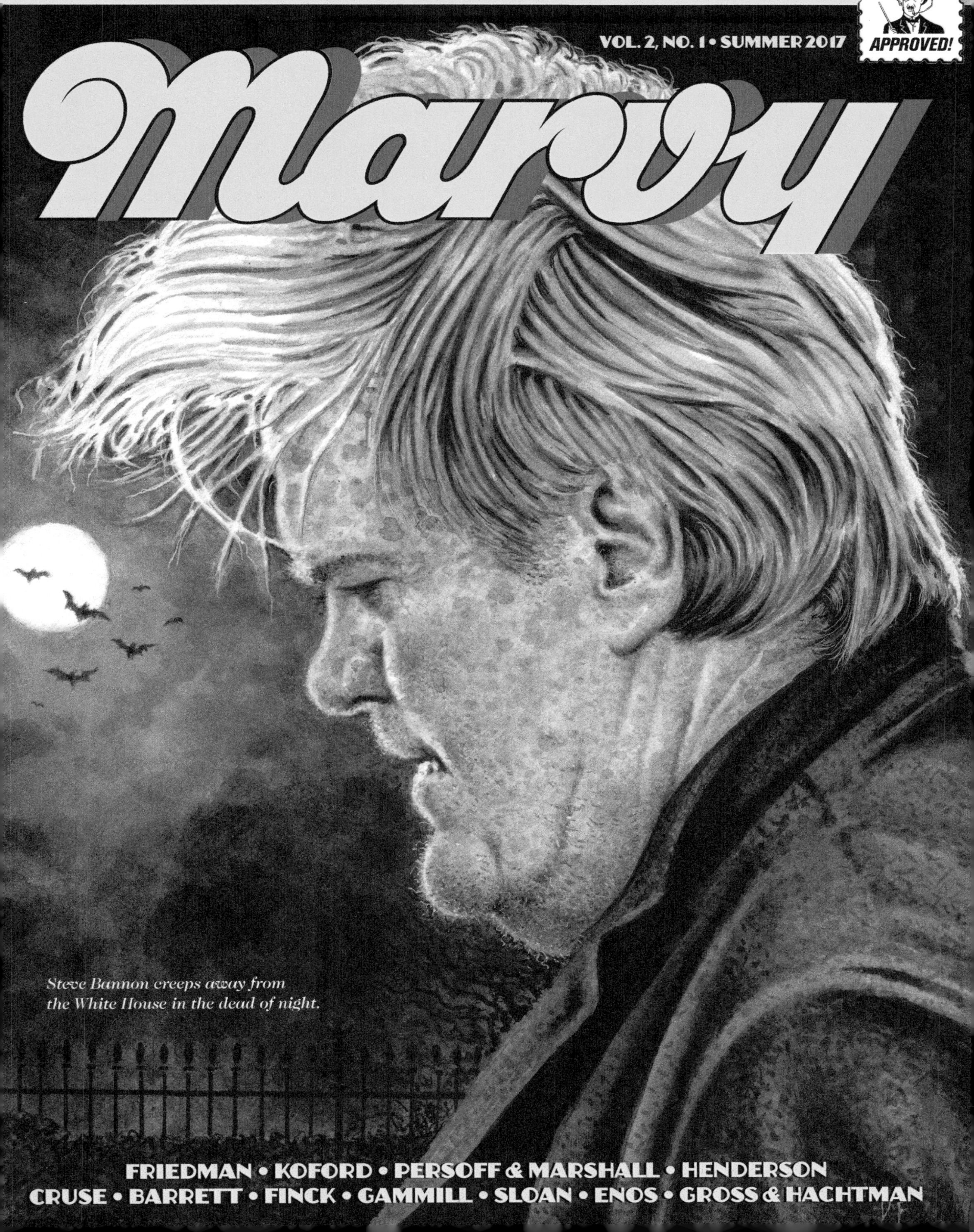
VOL. 2, NO. 1 • SUMMER 2017
Marvy
FRIEDMAN • KOFORD • PERSOFF & MARSHALL • HENDERSON
CRUSE • BARRETT • FINCK • GAMMILL • SLOAN • ENOS • GROSS & HACHTMAN

Steve Bannon creeps away from the White House in the dead of night.

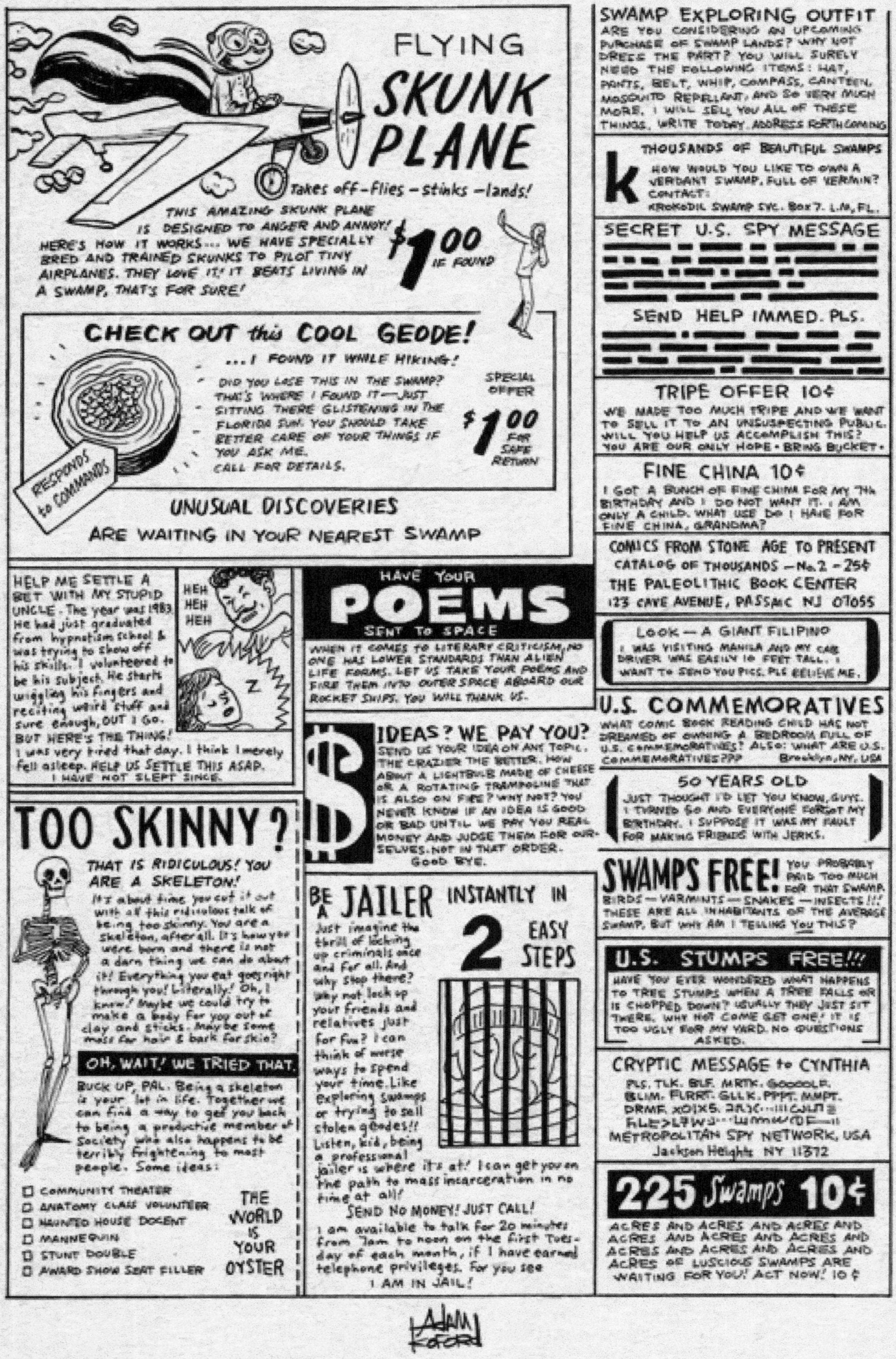

FLYING SKUNK PLANE
takes off – flies – stinks – lands!
THIS AMAZING SKUNK PLANE IS DESIGNED TO ANGER AND ANNOY!
HERE'S HOW IT WORKS... WE HAVE SPECIALLY BRED AND TRAINED SKUNKS TO PILOT TINY AIRPLANES. THEY LOVE IT! IT BEATS LIVING IN A SWAMP, THAT'S FOR SURE!
$1.00 IF FOUND
CHECK OUT this COOL GEODE!
...I FOUND IT WHILE HIKING!
DID YOU LOSE THIS IN THE SWAMP? THAT'S WHERE I FOUND IT — JUST SITTING THERE GLISTENING IN THE FLORIDA SUN. YOU SHOULD TAKE BETTER CARE OF YOUR THINGS IF YOU ASK ME. CALL FOR DETAILS.
SPECIAL OFFER
$1.00 FOR SAFE RETURN
RESPONDS to COMMANDS
UNUSUAL DISCOVERIES ARE WAITING IN YOUR NEAREST SWAMP
SWAMP EXPLORING OUTFIT
ARE YOU CONSIDERING AN UPCOMING PURCHASE OF SWAMP LANDS? WHY NOT DRESS THE PART? YOU WILL SURELY NEED THE FOLLOWING ITEMS: HAT, PANTS, BELT, WHIP, COMPASS, CANTEEN, MOSQUITO REPELLANT, AND SO VERY MUCH MORE. I WILL SELL YOU ALL OF THESE THINGS. WRITE TODAY. ADDRESS FORTHCOMING
THOUSANDS OF BEAUTIFUL SWAMPS
k
HOW WOULD YOU LIKE TO OWN A VERDANT SWAMP, FULL OF VERMIN? CONTACT: KROKODIL SWAMP SVC. BOX 7. L.M., FL.
SECRET U.S. SPY MESSAGE
[redacted]
SEND HELP IMMED. PLS.
[redacted]
TRIPE OFFER 10¢
WE MADE TOO MUCH TRIPE AND WE WANT TO SELL IT TO AN UNSUSPECTING PUBLIC. WILL YOU HELP US ACCOMPLISH THIS? YOU ARE OUR ONLY HOPE • BRING BUCKET •
FINE CHINA 10¢
I GOT A BUNCH OF FINE CHINA FOR MY 7th BIRTHDAY AND I DO NOT WANT IT. I AM ONLY A CHILD. WHAT USE DO I HAVE FOR FINE CHINA, GRANDMA?
COMICS FROM STONE AGE TO PRESENT
CATALOG OF THOUSANDS — No. 2 – 25¢
THE PALEOLITHIC BOOK CENTER
123 CAVE AVENUE, PASSAIC NJ 07055
HELP ME SETTLE A BET WITH MY STUPID UNCLE. The year was 1983. He had just graduated from hypnotism school & was trying to show off his skills. I volunteered to be his subject. He starts wiggling his fingers and reciting weird stuff and sure enough, OUT I GO. BUT HERE'S THE THING! I was very tired that day. I think I merely fell asleep. HELP US SETTLE THIS ASAP. I HAVE NOT SLEPT SINCE.
HEH HEH HEH
Z
HAVE YOUR POEMS SENT TO SPACE
WHEN IT COMES TO LITERARY CRITICISM, NO ONE HAS LOWER STANDARDS THAN ALIEN LIFE FORMS. LET US TAKE YOUR POEMS AND FIRE THEM INTO OUTER SPACE ABOARD OUR ROCKET SHIPS. YOU WILL THANK US.
LOOK — A GIANT FILIPINO
I WAS VISITING MANILA AND MY CAB DRIVER WAS EASILY 10 FEET TALL. I WANT TO SEND YOU PICS. PLS BELIEVE ME.
U.S. COMMEMORATIVES
WHAT COMIC BOOK READING CHILD HAS NOT DREAMED OF OWNING A BEDROOM FULL OF U.S. COMMEMORATIVES? ALSO: WHAT ARE U.S. COMMEMORATIVES??? Brooklyn, NY, USA
$
IDEAS? WE PAY YOU?
SEND US YOUR IDEA ON ANY TOPIC. THE CRAZIER THE BETTER. HOW ABOUT A LIGHTBULB MADE OF CHEESE OR A ROTATING TRAMPOLINE THAT IS ALSO ON FIRE? WHY NOT? YOU NEVER KNOW IF AN IDEA IS GOOD OR BAD UNTIL WE PAY YOU REAL MONEY AND JUDGE THEM FOR OURSELVES. NOT IN THAT ORDER. GOOD BYE.
50 YEARS OLD
JUST THOUGHT I'D LET YOU KNOW, GUYS. I TURNED 50 AND EVERYONE FORGOT MY BIRTHDAY. I SUPPOSE IT WAS MY FAULT FOR MAKING FRIENDS WITH JERKS.
TOO SKINNY?
THAT IS RIDICULOUS! YOU ARE A SKELETON!
It's about time you cut it out with all this ridiculous talk of being too skinny. You are a skeleton, after all. It's how you were born and there is not a darn thing we can do about it! Everything you eat goes right through you! Literally! Oh, I know! Maybe we could try to make a body for you out of clay and sticks. Maybe some moss for hair & bark for skin?
OH, WAIT! WE TRIED THAT.
BUCK UP, PAL. Being a skeleton is your lot in life. Together we can find a way to get you back to being a productive member of society who also happens to be terribly frightening to most people. Some ideas:
☐ COMMUNITY THEATER
☐ ANATOMY CLASS VOLUNTEER
☐ HAUNTED HOUSE DOCENT
☐ MANNEQUIN
☐ STUNT DOUBLE
☐ AWARD SHOW SEAT FILLER
THE WORLD IS YOUR OYSTER
BE A JAILER INSTANTLY IN 2 EASY STEPS
Just imagine the thrill of locking up criminals once and for all. And why stop there? Why not lock up your friends and relatives just for fun? I can think of worse ways to spend your time. Like exploring swamps or trying to sell stolen geodes!! Listen, kid, being a professional jailer is where it's at! I can get you on the path to mass incarceration in no time at all!
SEND NO MONEY! JUST CALL!
I am available to talk for 20 minutes from 7am to noon on the first Tuesday of each month, if I have earned telephone privileges. For you see I AM IN JAIL!
SWAMPS FREE! YOU PROBABLY PAID TOO MUCH FOR THAT SWAMP. BIRDS — VARMINTS — SNAKES — INSECTS!!! THESE ARE ALL INHABITANTS OF THE AVERAGE SWAMP. BUT WHY AM I TELLING YOU THIS?
U.S. STUMPS FREE!!!
HAVE YOU EVER WONDERED WHAT HAPPENS TO TREE STUMPS WHEN A TREE FALLS OR IS CHOPPED DOWN? USUALLY THEY JUST SIT THERE. WHY NOT COME GET ONE! IT IS TOO UGLY FOR MY YARD. NO QUESTIONS ASKED.
CRYPTIC MESSAGE to CYNTHIA
PLS. TLK. BLF. MRTK. GOOOOLP.
BLIM. FLRRT. GLLK. PPPT. MMPT.
METROPOLITAN SPY NETWORK, USA
Jackson Heights NY 11372
225 Swamps 10¢
ACRES AND ACRES AND ACRES AND ACRES AND ACRES AND ACRES AND ACRES AND ACRES AND ACRES AND ACRES OF LUSCIOUS SWAMPS ARE WAITING FOR YOU! ACT NOW! 10¢
Adam Koford

JOHN WILCOCK: NEW YORK YEARS

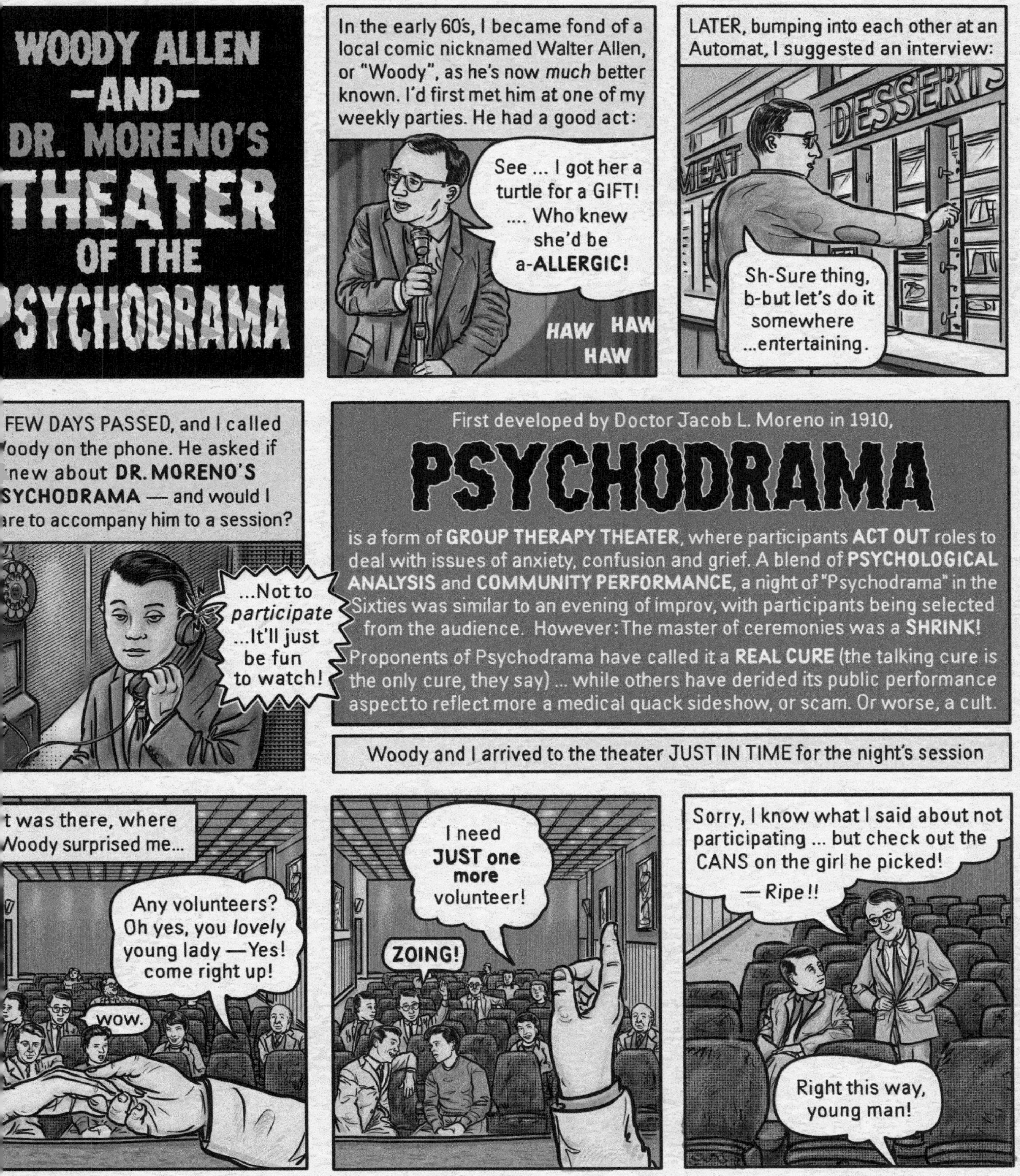
WOODY ALLEN
-AND-
DR. MORENO'S
THEATER
OF THE
PSYCHODRAMA
In the early 60's, I became fond of a local comic nicknamed Walter Allen, or "Woody", as he's now *much* better known. I'd first met him at one of my weekly parties. He had a good act:
See ... I got her a turtle for a GIFT! .... Who knew she'd be a-**ALLERGIC!**
HAW HAW HAW
LATER, bumping into each other at an Automat, I suggested an interview:
MEAT
DESSERTS
Sh-Sure thing, b-but let's do it somewhere ...*entertaining*.
FEW DAYS PASSED, and I called 'oody on the phone. He asked if 'new about **DR. MORENO'S SYCHODRAMA** — and would I are to accompany him to a session?
...Not to *participate* ...It'll just be fun to watch!
First developed by Doctor Jacob L. Moreno in 1910,
PSYCHODRAMA
is a form of **GROUP THERAPY THEATER**, where participants **ACT OUT** roles to deal with issues of anxiety, confusion and grief. A blend of **PSYCHOLOGICAL ANALYSIS** and **COMMUNITY PERFORMANCE**, a night of "Psychodrama" in the Sixties was similar to an evening of improv, with participants being selected from the audience. However: The master of ceremonies was a **SHRINK!** Proponents of Psychodrama have called it a **REAL CURE** (the talking cure is the only cure, they say) ... while others have derided its public performance aspect to reflect more a medical quack sideshow, or scam. Or worse, a cult.
Woody and I arrived to the theater JUST IN TIME for the night's session
t was there, where Woody surprised me...
Any volunteers? Oh yes, you *lovely* young lady —Yes! come right up!
WOW.
I need **JUST one more** volunteer!
ZOING!
Sorry, I know what I said about not participating ... but check out the CANS on the girl he picked! — *Ripe!!*
Right this way, young man!

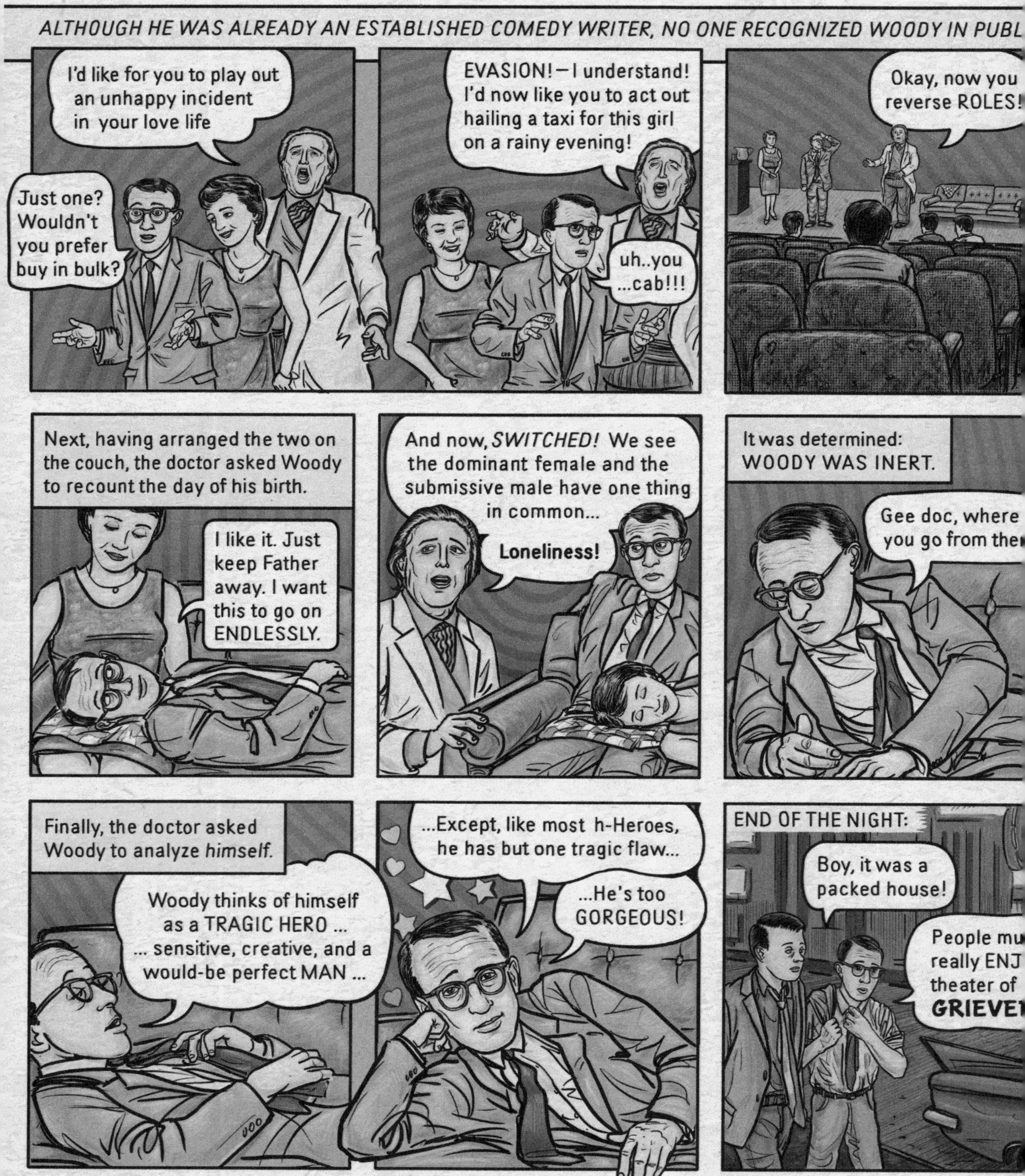
ALTHOUGH HE WAS ALREADY AN ESTABLISHED COMEDY WRITER, NO ONE RECOGNIZED WOODY IN PUBL
I'd like for you to play out an unhappy incident in your love life
Just one? Wouldn't you prefer buy in bulk?
EVASION!—I understand! I'd now like you to act out hailing a taxi for this girl on a rainy evening!
uh..you ...cab!!!
Okay, now you reverse ROLES!
Next, having arranged the two on the couch, the doctor asked Woody to recount the day of his birth.
I like it. Just keep Father away. I want this to go on ENDLESSLY.
And now, SWITCHED! We see the dominant female and the submissive male have one thing in common...
Loneliness!
It was determined: WOODY WAS INERT.
Gee doc, where you go from the
Finally, the doctor asked Woody to analyze himself.
Woody thinks of himself as a TRAGIC HERO ... ... sensitive, creative, and a would-be perfect MAN ...
...Except, like most h-Heroes, he has but one tragic flaw...
...He's too GORGEOUS!
END OF THE NIGHT:
Boy, it was a packed house!
People mu really ENJ theater of GRIEVE

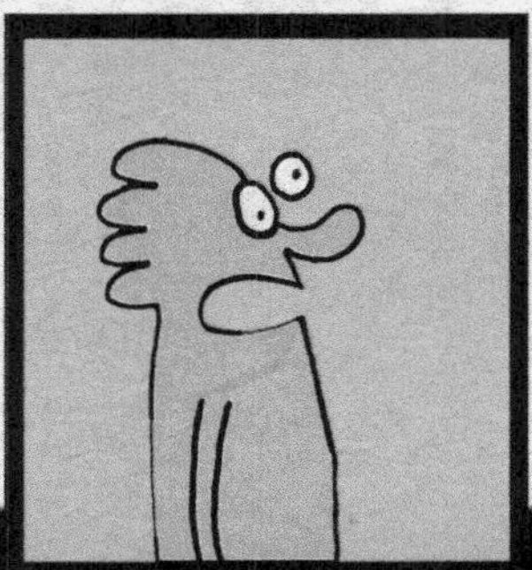

For most of my adult life, I've had breakthrough seizures. I don't know when or where they'll come but quite often they'll happen when I'm out of town, alone, and in front of strangers. They're not dangerous at all, just embarrassing. I've had numerous tests and nobody can figure out why. They were especially annoying when chicken littles trying to help only made things worse before we had the Affordable Care Act (and, as of this writing, will probably lose it). Rather than hide my condition, I've come to embrace it, even draw cartoons about it. I draw cartoons for a living, sometimes I do public readings of them. Here's one such incident that happened last month I'll call...

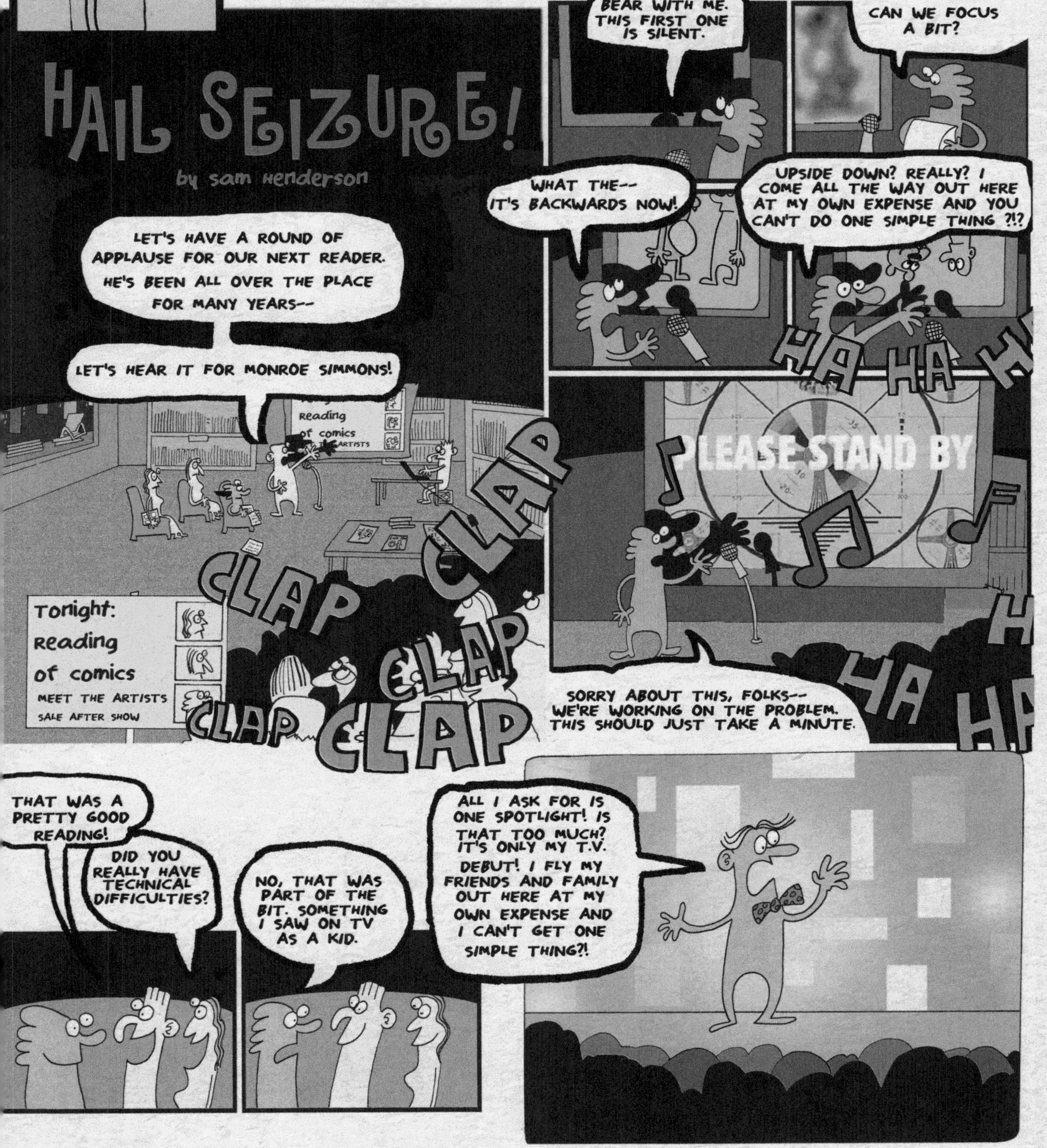
HAIL SEIZURE!
by sam henderson
LET'S HAVE A ROUND OF APPLAUSE FOR OUR NEXT READER. HE'S BEEN ALL OVER THE PLACE FOR MANY YEARS--
LET'S HEAR IT FOR MONROE SIMMONS!
Tonight: Reading of comics MEET THE ARTISTS SALE AFTER SHOW
CLAP CLAP CLAP CLAP CLAP
BEAR WITH ME. THIS FIRST ONE IS SILENT.
CAN WE FOCUS A BIT?
WHAT THE-- IT'S BACKWARDS NOW!
UPSIDE DOWN? REALLY? I COME ALL THE WAY OUT HERE AT MY OWN EXPENSE AND YOU CAN'T DO ONE SIMPLE THING ?!?
HA HA
PLEASE STAND BY
SORRY ABOUT THIS, FOLKS-- WE'RE WORKING ON THE PROBLEM. THIS SHOULD JUST TAKE A MINUTE.
HA HA
THAT WAS A PRETTY GOOD READING!
DID YOU REALLY HAVE TECHNICAL DIFFICULTIES?
NO, THAT WAS PART OF THE BIT. SOMETHING I SAW ON TV AS A KID.
ALL I ASK FOR IS ONE SPOTLIGHT! IS THAT TOO MUCH? IT'S ONLY MY T.V. DEBUT! I FLY MY FRIENDS AND FAMILY OUT HERE AT MY OWN EXPENSE AND I CAN'T GET ONE SIMPLE THING?!

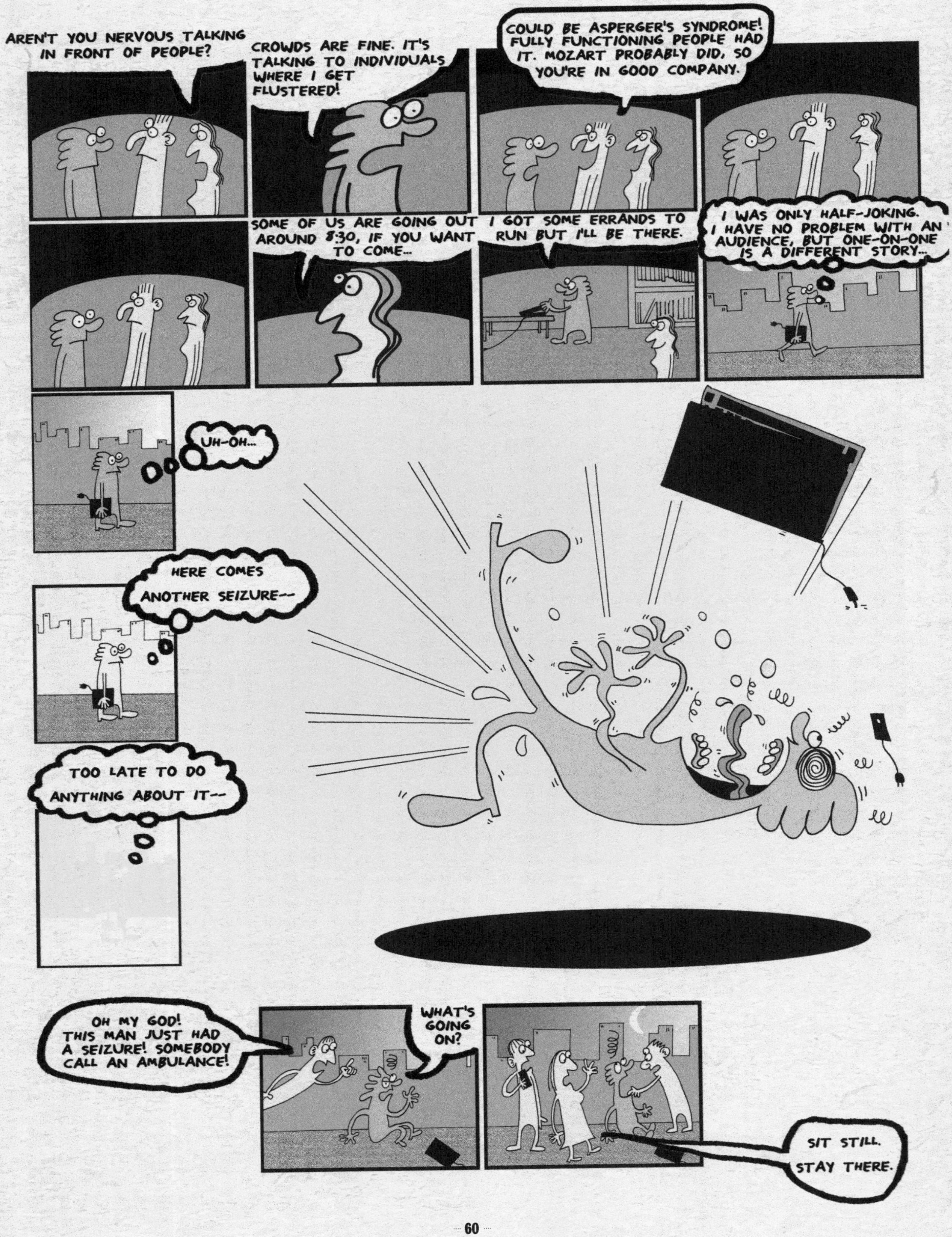
AREN'T YOU NERVOUS TALKING IN FRONT OF PEOPLE?
CROWDS ARE FINE. IT'S TALKING TO INDIVIDUALS WHERE I GET FLUSTERED!
COULD BE ASPERGER'S SYNDROME! FULLY FUNCTIONING PEOPLE HAD IT. MOZART PROBABLY DID, SO YOU'RE IN GOOD COMPANY.
SOME OF US ARE GOING OUT AROUND 8:30, IF YOU WANT TO COME...
I GOT SOME ERRANDS TO RUN BUT I'LL BE THERE.
I WAS ONLY HALF-JOKING. I HAVE NO PROBLEM WITH AN AUDIENCE, BUT ONE-ON-ONE IS A DIFFERENT STORY...
UH-OH...
HERE COMES ANOTHER SEIZURE--
TOO LATE TO DO ANYTHING ABOUT IT--
OH MY GOD! THIS MAN JUST HAD A SEIZURE! SOMEBODY CALL AN AMBULANCE!
WHAT'S GOING ON?
SIT STILL. STAY THERE.

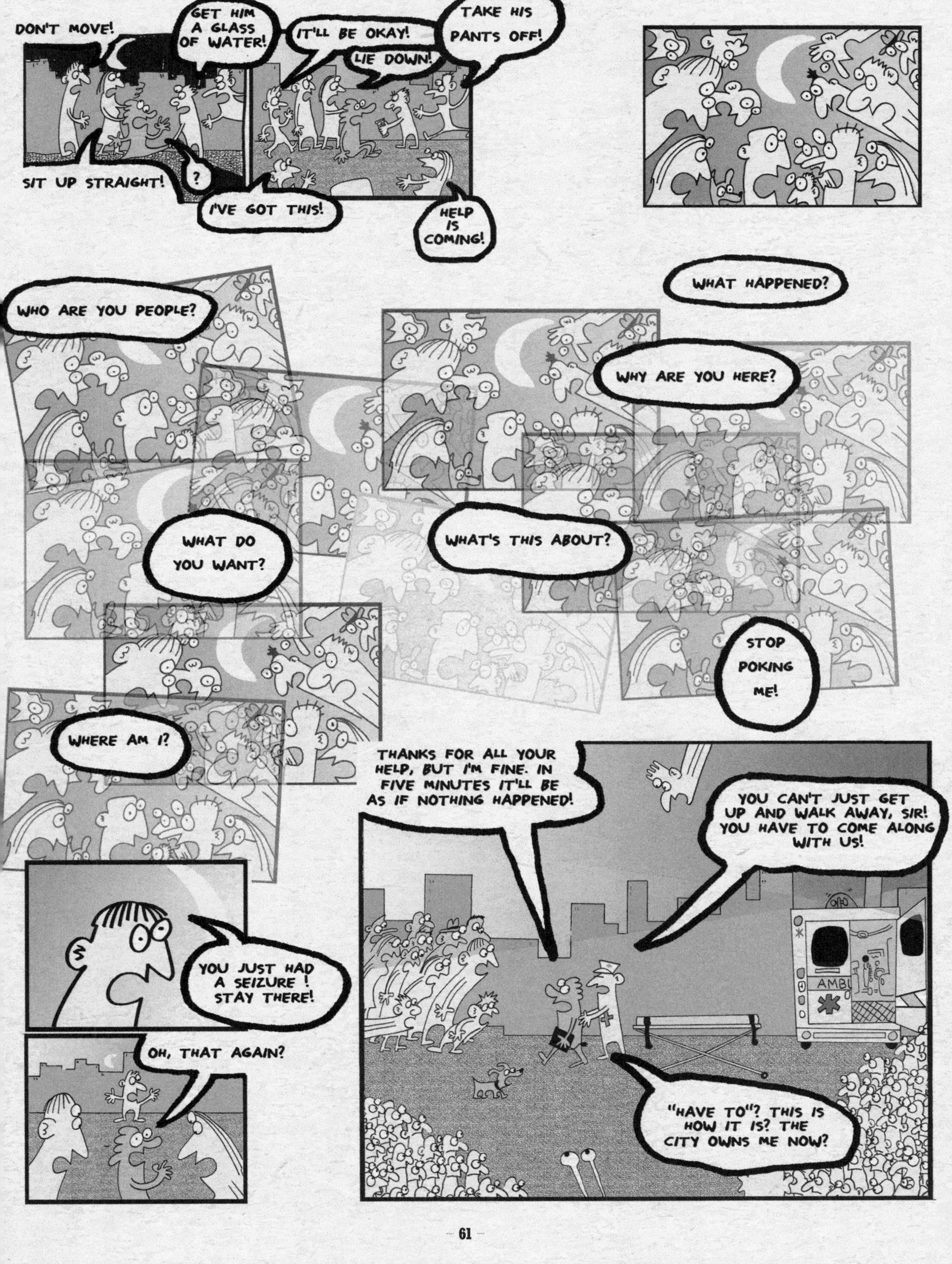
DON'T MOVE!
GET HIM A GLASS OF WATER!
IT'LL BE OKAY!
TAKE HIS PANTS OFF!
LIE DOWN!
SIT UP STRAIGHT!
?
I'VE GOT THIS!
HELP IS COMING!
WHAT HAPPENED?
WHO ARE YOU PEOPLE?
WHY ARE YOU HERE?
WHAT DO YOU WANT?
WHAT'S THIS ABOUT?
STOP POKING ME!
WHERE AM I?
YOU JUST HAD A SEIZURE ! STAY THERE!
OH, THAT AGAIN?
THANKS FOR ALL YOUR HELP, BUT I'M FINE. IN FIVE MINUTES IT'LL BE AS IF NOTHING HAPPENED!
YOU CAN'T JUST GET UP AND WALK AWAY, SIR! YOU HAVE TO COME ALONG WITH US!
"HAVE TO"? THIS IS HOW IT IS? THE CITY OWNS ME NOW?

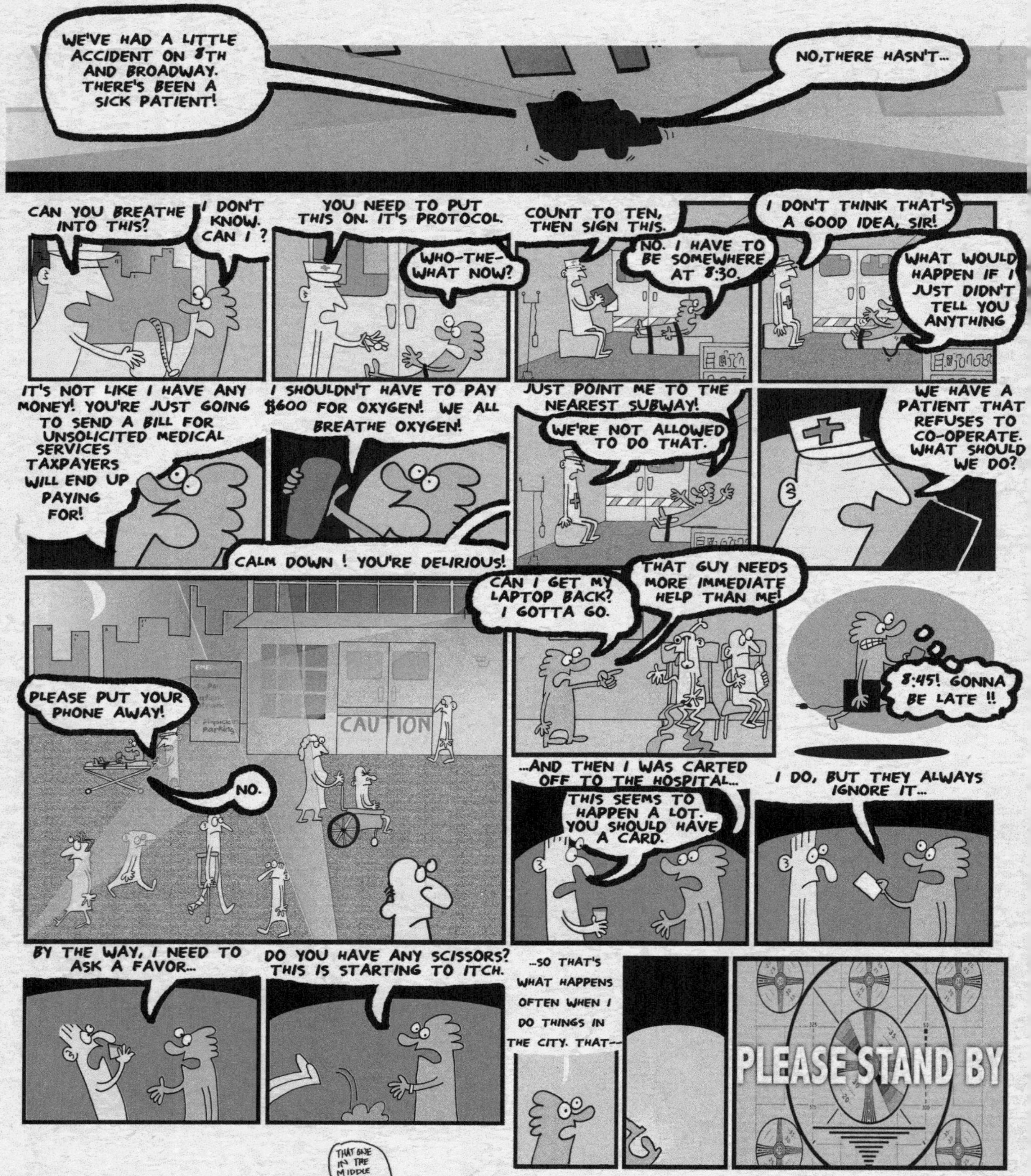
WE'VE HAD A LITTLE ACCIDENT ON 8TH AND BROADWAY. THERE'S BEEN A SICK PATIENT!
NO, THERE HASN'T...
CAN YOU BREATHE INTO THIS?
I DON'T KNOW. CAN I ?
YOU NEED TO PUT THIS ON. IT'S PROTOCOL.
WHO-THE-WHAT NOW?
COUNT TO TEN, THEN SIGN THIS.
NO. I HAVE TO BE SOMEWHERE AT 8:30.
I DON'T THINK THAT'S A GOOD IDEA, SIR!
WHAT WOULD HAPPEN IF I JUST DIDN'T TELL YOU ANYTHING
IT'S NOT LIKE I HAVE ANY MONEY! YOU'RE JUST GOING TO SEND A BILL FOR UNSOLICITED MEDICAL SERVICES TAXPAYERS WILL END UP PAYING FOR!
I SHOULDN'T HAVE TO PAY $600 FOR OXYGEN! WE ALL BREATHE OXYGEN!
CALM DOWN ! YOU'RE DELIRIOUS!
JUST POINT ME TO THE NEAREST SUBWAY!
WE'RE NOT ALLOWED TO DO THAT.
WE HAVE A PATIENT THAT REFUSES TO CO-OPERATE. WHAT SHOULD WE DO?
PLEASE PUT YOUR PHONE AWAY!
NO.
CAUTION
CAN I GET MY LAPTOP BACK? I GOTTA GO.
THAT GUY NEEDS MORE IMMEDIATE HELP THAN ME!
8:45! GONNA BE LATE !!
...AND THEN I WAS CARTED OFF TO THE HOSPITAL...
THIS SEEMS TO HAPPEN A LOT. YOU SHOULD HAVE A CARD.
I DO, BUT THEY ALWAYS IGNORE IT...
BY THE WAY, I NEED TO ASK A FAVOR...
DO YOU HAVE ANY SCISSORS? THIS IS STARTING TO ITCH.
...SO THAT'S WHAT HAPPENS OFTEN WHEN I DO THINGS IN THE CITY. THAT--
PLEASE STAND BY

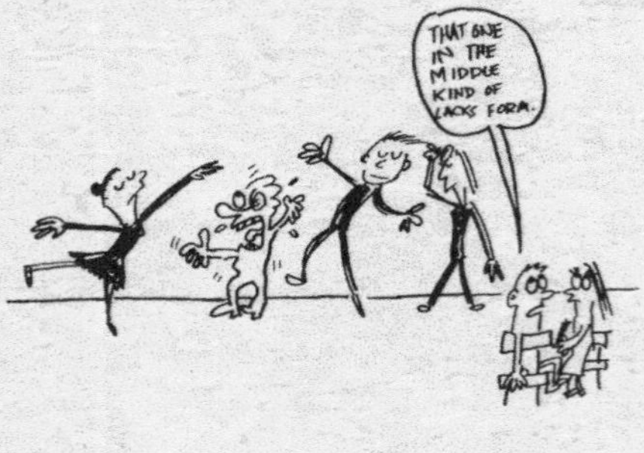
THAT ONE IN THE MIDDLE KIND OF LACKS FORM.

follow mr. henderson on
twitter.com/magicwhistle
or follow this story on
patreon.com/magicwhistle

SLANG & PROFANITY

~A MORAL INQUIRY*

FROM THE RECENTLY UNEARTHED LOST PAPERS OF AN ALABAMA PREACHER'S KID

ESSAY BY HOWARD CRUSE (AGE: 14)

ART BY HOWARD CRUSE (AGE: 70)

* UNEDITED & UNABRIDGED

Howard Cruse
Freshman
Indian Springs School
September 29, 1958

SLANG AND PROFANITY

tap, tap, tap! tap, tap! ♪ Ding!

For as far back as I can remember, my parents have lived with the philosophy that any coloration of the language in the way of profanity or even slang was wrong.

tap! tap! tap!

They went strictly by the Bible verse: "...Let your communication be, Yea, yea; Nay, nay..." (Matthew 5:37)

Until I came to this school, I thought that this was my belief also.

HOW TO THINK FOR YOURSELF

Here at Indian Springs, though, I am learning to think for myself, for perhaps the first time in my life.

And in thinking for myself, I discovered that all my opinions on slang and profanity were simply carbon copies of my parents' beliefs.

THEY WERE NOT MY OWN OPINIONS.

Rumble... So I began to think. Throb...

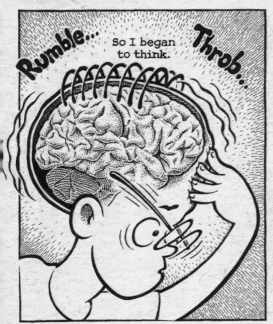

I did not consciously sit down and decide to start thinking.

BINGO!

I simply evolved a philosophy of my own without realizing it until it was complete...

...during the three weeks which I have been at Indian Springs.

Some people refrain from any type of verbal expression simply to assure themselves of their own piousness, and so that they can remain superior over their less refined aquaintances.

Tsk, tsk! Belch!

My parents are not like this. THEY HAVE EVOLVED THEIR OWN PHILOSOPHY, JUST AS I HAVE EVOLVED MINE.

GOOD SON

DOESN'T DIS HIS FOLKS

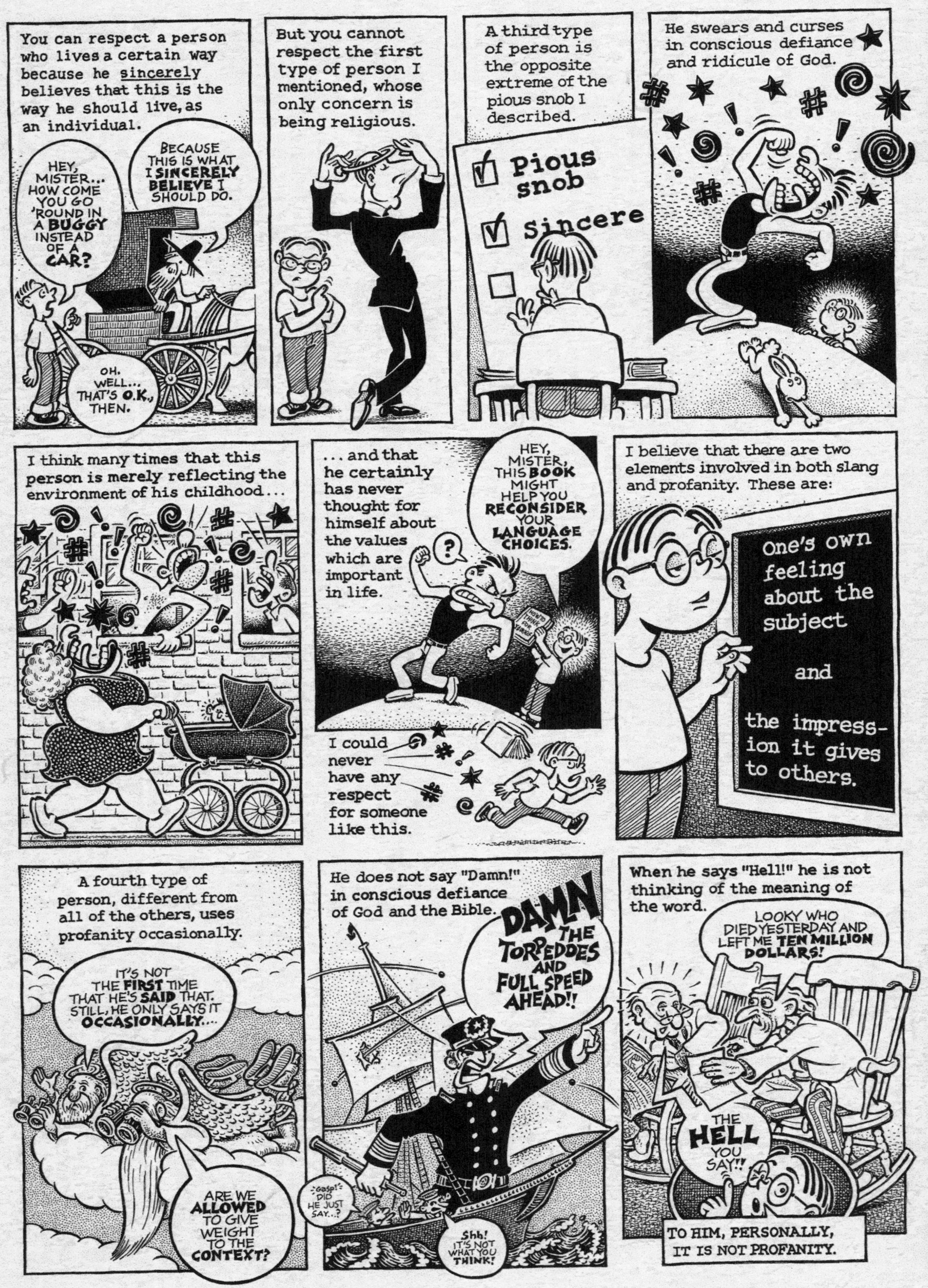
You can respect a person who lives a certain way because he sincerely believes that this is the way he should live, as an individual.
HEY, MISTER... HOW COME YOU GO 'ROUND IN A BUGGY INSTEAD OF A CAR?
BECAUSE THIS IS WHAT I SINCERELY BELIEVE I SHOULD DO.
OH. WELL... THAT'S O.K., THEN.
But you cannot respect the first type of person I mentioned, whose only concern is being religious.
A third type of person is the opposite extreme of the pious snob I described.
Pious snob
Sincere
He swears and curses in conscious defiance and ridicule of God.
I think many times that this person is merely reflecting the environment of his childhood...
...and that he certainly has never thought for himself about the values which are important in life.
HEY, MISTER, THIS BOOK MIGHT HELP YOU RECONSIDER YOUR LANGUAGE CHOICES.
?
I could never have any respect for someone like this.
I believe that there are two elements involved in both slang and profanity. These are:
One's own feeling about the subject
and
the impression it gives to others.
A fourth type of person, different from all of the others, uses profanity occasionally.
IT'S NOT THE FIRST TIME THAT HE'S SAID THAT. STILL, HE ONLY SAYS IT OCCASIONALLY....
ARE WE ALLOWED TO GIVE WEIGHT TO THE CONTEXT?
He does not say "Damn!" in conscious defiance of God and the Bible.
DAMN THE TORPEDOES AND FULL SPEED AHEAD!!
:GASP!: DID HE JUST SAY..?
Shh! IT'S NOT WHAT YOU THINK!
When he says "Hell!" he is not thinking of the meaning of the word.
LOOKY WHO DIED YESTERDAY AND LEFT ME TEN MILLION DOLLARS!
THE HELL YOU SAY!!
TO HIM, PERSONALLY, IT IS NOT PROFANITY.

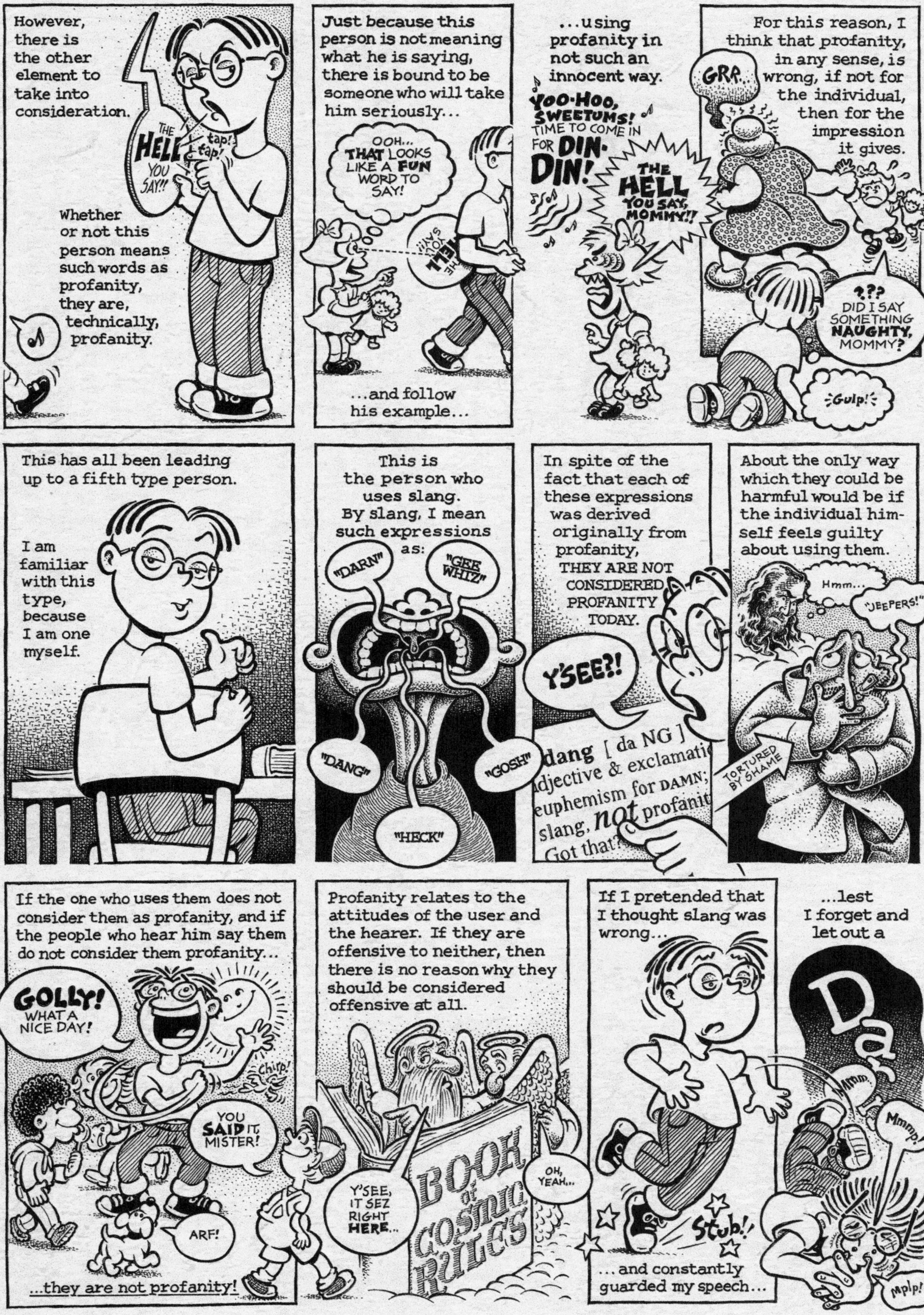

However, there is the other element to take into consideration.
THE HELL YOU SAY!!
tap! tap!
Whether or not this person means such words as profanity, they are, technically, profanity.
Just because this person is not meaning what he is saying, there is bound to be someone who will take him seriously...
OOH... THAT LOOKS LIKE A FUN WORD TO SAY!
THE HELL YOU SAY!!
...and follow his example...
...using profanity in not such an innocent way.
YOO-HOO, SWEETUMS! TIME TO COME IN FOR DIN-DIN!
THE HELL YOU SAY, MOMMY!!
For this reason, I think that profanity, in any sense, is wrong, if not for the individual, then for the impression it gives.
GRR...
?.?? DID I SAY SOMETHING NAUGHTY, MOMMY?
Gulp!
This has all been leading up to a fifth type person.
I am familiar with this type, because I am one myself.
This is the person who uses slang. By slang, I mean such expressions as:
"DARN"
"GEE WHIZ"
"DANG"
"GOSH"
"HECK"
In spite of the fact that each of these expressions was derived originally from profanity, THEY ARE NOT CONSIDERED PROFANITY TODAY.
Y'SEE?!
dang [da NG]
djective & exclamati
euphemism for DAMN;
slang, not profanit
Got that?
About the only way which they could be harmful would be if the individual himself feels guilty about using them.
Hmm...
"JEEPERS!"
TORTURED BY SHAME
If the one who uses them does not consider them as profanity, and if the people who hear him say them do not consider them profanity...
GOLLY! WHAT A NICE DAY!
Chirp!
YOU SAID IT, MISTER!
ARF!
...they are not profanity!
Profanity relates to the attitudes of the user and the hearer. If they are offensive to neither, then there is no reason why they should be considered offensive at all.
Y'SEE, IT SEZ RIGHT HERE...
OH, YEAH...
BOOK of COSMIC RULES
If I pretended that I thought slang was wrong...
Stub!!
...and constantly guarded my speech...
...lest I forget and let out a
Da
Mmm
Mmmp!
Mplp!

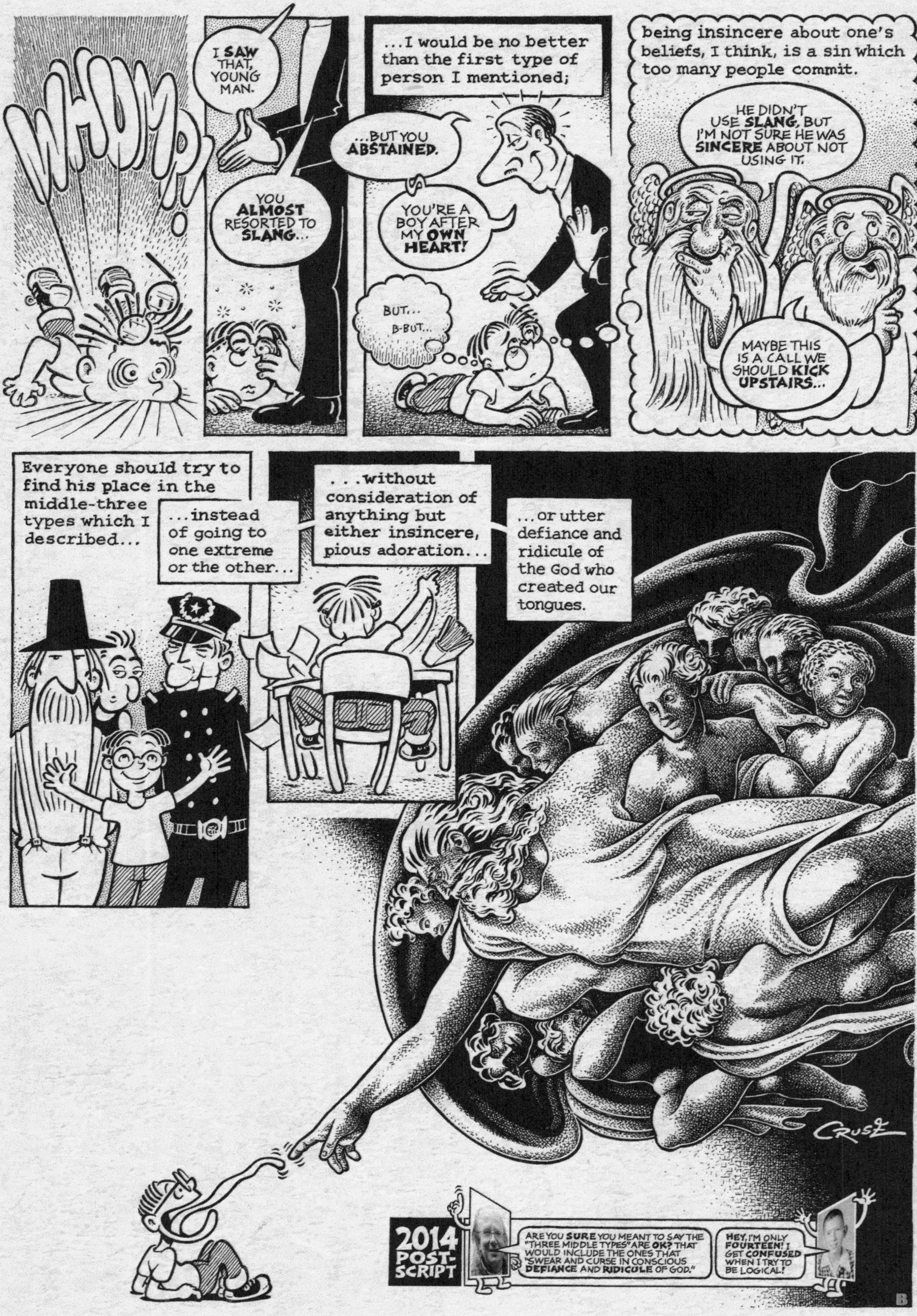
WHUMP!
I SAW THAT, YOUNG MAN.
YOU ALMOST RESORTED TO SLANG...
...I would be no better than the first type of person I mentioned;
...BUT YOU ABSTAINED.
YOU'RE A BOY AFTER MY OWN HEART!
BUT... B-BUT...
being insincere about one's beliefs, I think, is a sin which too many people commit.
HE DIDN'T USE SLANG, BUT I'M NOT SURE HE WAS SINCERE ABOUT NOT USING IT.
MAYBE THIS IS A CALL WE SHOULD KICK UPSTAIRS...
Everyone should try to find his place in the middle-three types which I described...
...instead of going to one extreme or the other...
. . .without consideration of anything but either insincere, pious adoration...
...or utter defiance and ridicule of the God who created our tongues.
CRUSE
2014 POST-SCRIPT
ARE YOU SURE YOU MEANT TO SAY THE "THREE MIDDLE TYPES" ARE OK? THAT WOULD INCLUDE THE ONES THAT "SWEAR AND CURSE IN CONSCIOUS DEFIANCE AND RIDICULE OF GOD."
HEY, I'M ONLY FOURTEEN! I GET CONFUSED WHEN I TRY TO BE LOGICAL!
B

EPISODES in DANGEROUS CLOTHING

RON BARRETT   WAIST:36   INSEAM: 29

BUTTON BLINDS WOMAN ON BUS

CLINICAL RESEARCH POINTS TO CLASHING PLAIDS AS CAUSE OF BIPOLAR BEHAVIOR

HEAVY NECKTIES BLAMED FOR SCOLIOSIS EPIDEMIC IN MEN

NCHANTED HOES LEAD NWARY AN TO RECIPICE

UNATTENDED CHILD EATS SPATS, DIES

NON-RELIGIOUS CIRCUMCISIONS OFTEN CAUSED BY FLIES

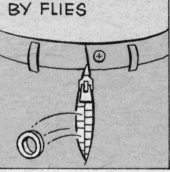

UNDERSIZE HAT PROVEN TO CAUSE TUMESCENCE OF EARS (CLOWN'S SYNDROME)

SCIENTISTS CLAIM EXCESSIVE WEARING OF CUB SCOUT UNIFORMS PROMOTES DWARFISM

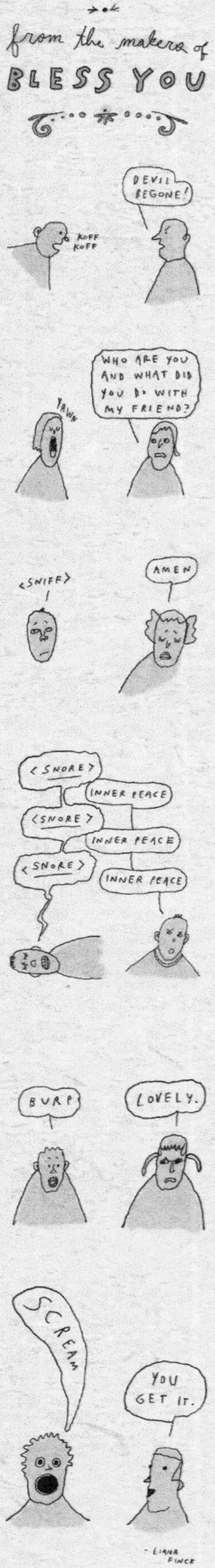
from the makers of
BLESS YOU
KOFF KOFF
DEVIL BEGONE!
YAWN
WHO ARE YOU AND WHAT DID YOU DO WITH MY FRIEND?
<SNIFF>
AMEN
<SNORE>
INNER PEACE
<SNORE>
INNER PEACE
<SNORE>
INNER PEACE
BURP
LOVELY.
SCREAM
YOU GET IT.
- LIANA FINCK

The Doozies

by Tom Gammill

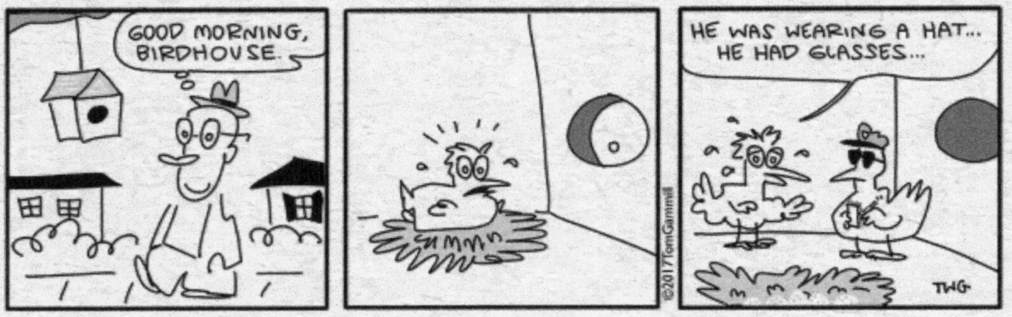
GOOD MORNING, BIRDHOUSE.
©2017 TomGammill
HE WAS WEARING A HAT... HE HAD GLASSES...
TWG

Zen of Nimbus

by Michael Sloan

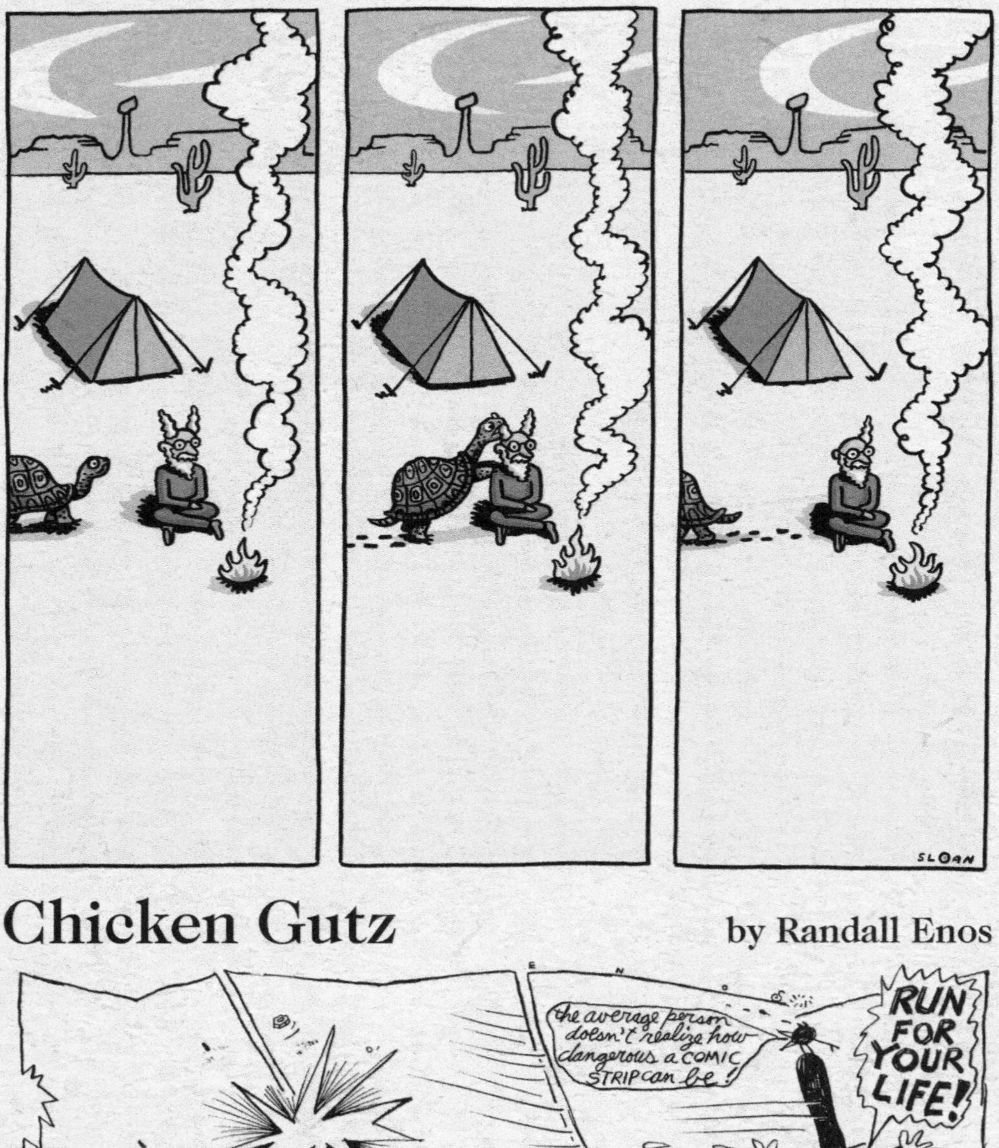
SLOAN

Chicken Gutz

by Randall Enos

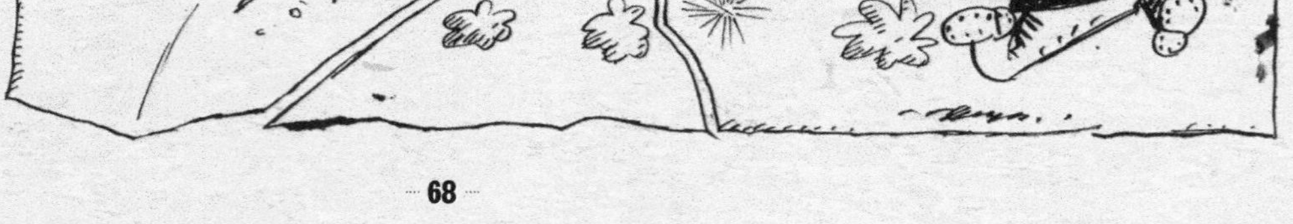
the average person doesn't realize how dangerous a COMIC STRIP can be!
RUN FOR YOUR LIFE!

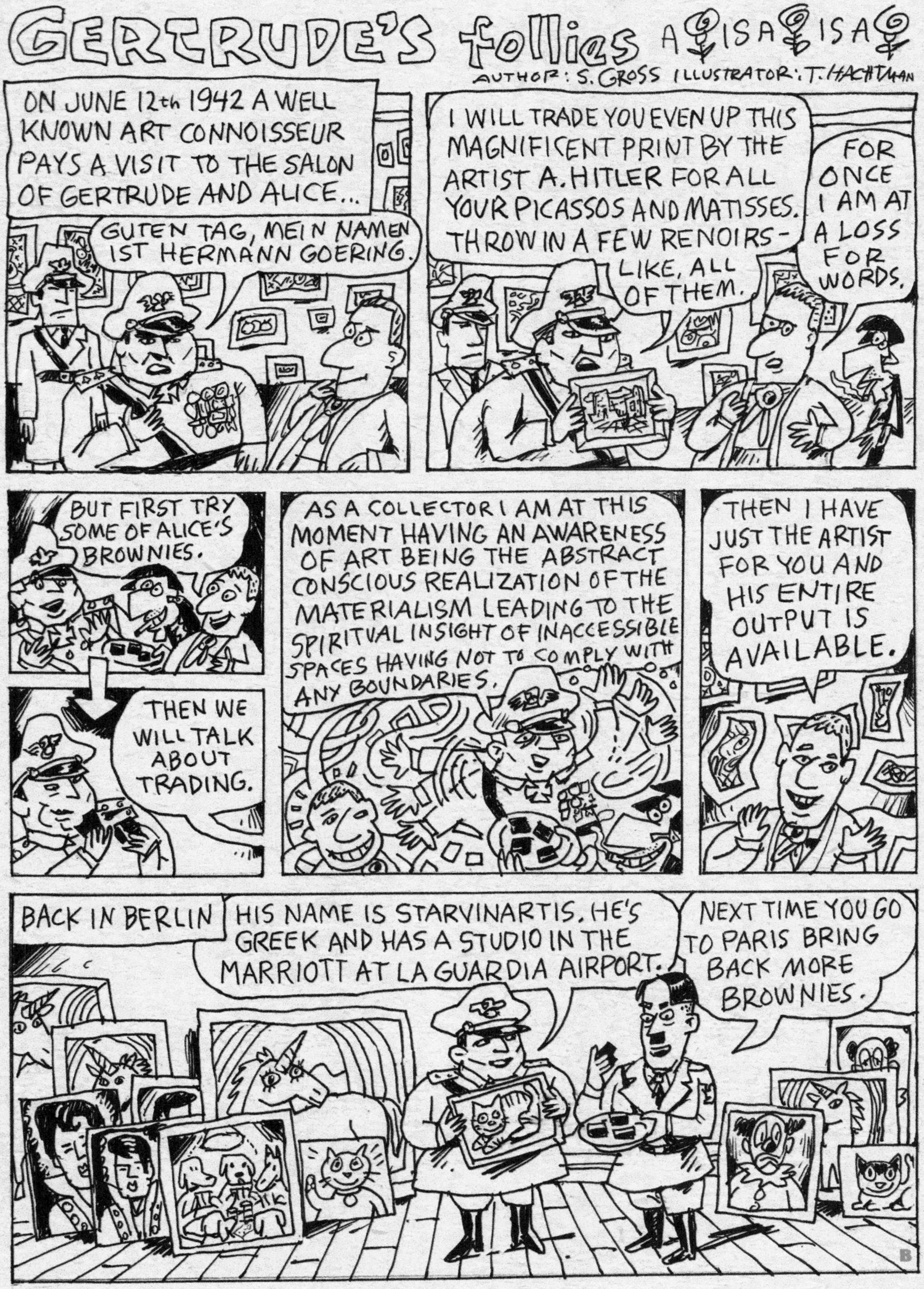
GERTRUDE'S follies A ROSE IS A ROSE IS A ROSE
AUTHOR: S. GROSS ILLUSTRATOR: T. HACHTMAN
ON JUNE 12th 1942 A WELL KNOWN ART CONNOISSEUR PAYS A VISIT TO THE SALON OF GERTRUDE AND ALICE...
GUTEN TAG, MEIN NAMEN IST HERMANN GOERING.
I WILL TRADE YOU EVEN UP THIS MAGNIFICENT PRINT BY THE ARTIST A. HITLER FOR ALL YOUR PICASSOS AND MATISSES. THROW IN A FEW RENOIRS -
LIKE, ALL OF THEM.
FOR ONCE I AM AT A LOSS FOR WORDS.
BUT FIRST TRY SOME OF ALICE'S BROWNIES.
THEN WE WILL TALK ABOUT TRADING.
AS A COLLECTOR I AM AT THIS MOMENT HAVING AN AWARENESS OF ART BEING THE ABSTRACT CONSCIOUS REALIZATION OF THE MATERIALISM LEADING TO THE SPIRITUAL INSIGHT OF INACCESSIBLE SPACES HAVING NOT TO COMPLY WITH ANY BOUNDARIES.
THEN I HAVE JUST THE ARTIST FOR YOU AND HIS ENTIRE OUTPUT IS AVAILABLE.
BACK IN BERLIN
HIS NAME IS STARVINARTIS. HE'S GREEK AND HAS A STUDIO IN THE MARRIOTT AT LA GUARDIA AIRPORT.
NEXT TIME YOU GO TO PARIS BRING BACK MORE BROWNIES.

JOAN'S OTHER KITCHEN

The End may not come with a bang or a whimper, just a "rogue mall" • **By Brian McConnachie**

The Lost Mall of Atlanta

Last Spring, on the shore of the exclusive Breakers Hotel in Palm Beach, Florida, guests were suddenly confronted with the surreal sight of a shopping mall set right at the water's edge. Its familiar shape and imposing authority seemed to banish all concerns of its right to be there, quite the opposite. Instead, witnesses appeared far more delighted than disturbed by this colossal oddity and environmental nightmare suddenly on their fashionable beach.

As more of the curious drew closer, the glass doors whipped open and from the roof several enormous red pennants unfurled, declaring: EVERYTHING 40% TO 60% OFF.

As accustomed to convenience as most of these vacationers were, they may have assumed this was an extravagant promotional stunt which would be to their benefit; and so they threw off any momentary confusion and streamed toward the welcoming edifice.

When the last of them had entered, the doors slid shut and the immense structure slipped silently back into the calm morning ocean from which it came.

Friends and relatives of the missing were frankly suspicious of the eyewitness accounts. Most hired private detectives to find and restore their love ones to them. But within a month, all the detectives were missing as well. The story itself became woefully underreported and soon entered the foggy realm of urban legend.

BRIAN McCONNACHIE is Founder and Head Writer of *The American Bystander*.

Then in early August 2016, at Hilton Head, North Carolina, it happened again. Rising out of the sea like some prehistoric leviathan, the mall slowly drifted toward shore. Beachgoers who believed themselves to be miles from the nearest retail were bluntly confronted with this unexpected challenge to their disposable incomes. Some stood waiting at the water's edge holding up their debit and credit cards while others waded out to meet the marvel halfway, lifting high their fanny packs and shoulder bags. Neither group for a moment suspecting that the only bargain they'd receive that day would involve aquatic entombment.

It's a whole new breed of shopping mall we're dealing with here," said Robert Coalmen, the Department of Homeland Security's recently appointed director of ambulatory structures. "We believe these 'rogue malls' have a hostile agenda — but we're not exactly sure what that is, beyond luring unsuspecting shoppers through their doors and then drowning them for no apparent reason. Every time we try to anticipate their next move, they go ahead and do the exact same move they did the last time. It keeps us off balance," Coalmen said. "This particular mall may be reacting to the dip in consumer confidence, or the increases in online shopping. But why would it lash out?"

"You have to realize, malls are just not that bright," said Marjorie Wellright, Director Coalmen's top profiler. "They're basically right down there with indoor parking lots, storage bins and FEMA trailers. We're not exactly dealing with the Chrysler or the Monadnock here."

The Breakers mall was originally sited in the suburbs of Atlanta, Georgia. Back in the 1980s, malls were being built at such a furious pace, it was inevitable that there would be a serious glut with major fallout. Within three years of its completion, this mall was bankrupt, abandoned, demolished and assigned to landfill.

But it somehow reconstructed itself — and then went rogue. It made its way down the Altamaha River into the Gulf of Mexico. There it may've hooked up with one of the smaller but far more rapacious Eastern European malls that have been swarming to our shores, introducing themselves into our freshwater rivers and estuaries. A mall with ties to the Albanian Mafia was recently spotted in the Mississippi as far north as St. Louis.

Days following the incident at Hilton Head, an 8-year-old girl was found wandering alone on the beach, without identification and in a bewildered state. "Julie X" was wearing a distinctive pink and white flame-retardant pajama ensemble believed to be from the inventory of the Atlanta rogue mall. Though unable to speak, she continually hummed a version of "My Heart Will Go On" from *Titanic*.

Julie X was brought to Washington, where she was personally interrogated by Director Coalmen. Was she put ashore to present the grievances of this mall, or all malls in general but then forgot what she was supposed to say? Possibly. All that is for sure is this: Julie X was a corridor leading nowhere. She has been reunited with her family, who says she acts "different."

If these malls don't get what they want. what happens then? What are they capable of? Have they made any demands? On this point, Director Colemen is firm: "The United States government, does not now, nor will it ever, negotiate with ambulatory retail outlets." But what happens if — *when* — they come after us? Will they follow us home? No president wants it said that on his watch the malls started following the shoppers home like so many disenfranchised panhandlers muttering their contempt for our democratic society while at the same time enjoying the benefits of electricity, running water, Muzak, automatic doors and express checkout lines.

For a time, this phenomenon appeared to be limited to malls — but that is starting to change. In an act more mischievous than malevolent, the building that houses the Commerce Department seems to have swapped places with the Department of Weights and Measures, though no one seems to be bothered by this. Indeed, some who work in the respective buildings have even welcomed the change in their daily routine.

This is dangerous, according to Colemen. People cannot accept this as the "new normal." He has sent the White House no less than 70 tweets warning we

may be facing a catastrophe of apocalyptic measure.

So far, President Trump isn't listening. In an exchange leaked to *The Washington Post*, KellyAnne Conway recently remarked to the president, "Is it just me or does the Oval Office seem closer to Pennsylvania Avenue than it did yesterday? It could be a sign of something. You really might want to read some of these reports that are piling up here."

"I've got very brilliant bright people to keep me totally informed of signs," the president responded. "Their heads are like, huge with extra special sections for their big brains. Look at the size of their heads the next time…"

"Have you taken your meds today?"

"Sure. Of course. Why wouldn't I? Absolutely! Tell me, does this tie make

my pants look baggy? Oh look, there's a bird at the feeder outside the window."

"You are such a bad liar."

"I'm not lying. You're the liar. Who are we having lunch with today? No one ever tells me the lunch plans. Especially those goons from Intelligence. Hey, do you think I'd look good sitting in a huge chair holding a cat on my lap? I'm up for some Russian food. Are you with me? … Tell me, if you could punch any cabinet member in the stomach, who would you want to punch?…Come over here and sit on my lap."

"Mr. President, stop! Read some of this rogue mall stuff. It looks serious."

"It's all fake. There is so much to read. You read it. I want to practice drawing my name. Where did that bird go? Did you see? You know, we never practiced cursive penmanship at Wharton. I've always regretted that. It's held me back. It takes me 55 seconds to draw my name. I want to get it down to 35 but I can't crack 37. Why don't we invite little Marco to lunch and punch him in the stomach. HAHAHA."

"You better read this last memo from Colemen. It's about the Antichrist and the Apocalypse. And you're mentioned."

"Let me see; let me see. Is that a serious thing?…What's this word?"

"War."

"O.K., I knew that…what are all these words?"

"Famine, plague, chaos and madness."

"What's all this writing here?"

"…and the buildings shall turn upon their landlord owners."

"What if I started talking in an English accent? *Jolly-ho old pip!* We should probably order lunch now. Beat the crowd to the kitchen."

"It says: 'Faithless Christians shall be snuck up upon and cudgeled over the head with misshapen logs and then entombed in a bad place. And the last sign proceeding the arrival of the Antichrist is: Buildings shall shrink 25 cubits and depart their foundations then drown their owners in an unnatural procedure. And the accompanying odor will be fetid and inhuman.'"

"Calm down. You're going to make yourself crazy. You'll eat some blinis. You'll drink some soda. You'll feel better. And this will all go away. You'll see."

But will it?…really? **B**

D.WATSON

P.S. MUELLER THINKS LIKE THIS

The cartoonist/broadcaster/writer is always walking around, looking at stuff • By P.S. Mueller

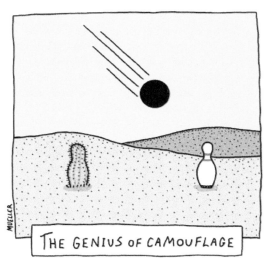

THE GENIUS OF CAMOUFLAGE

Five Secrets of the Men's Room

1) If more than three of us are in there, we skate the urine. A brisk round of "cake hockey" will shake anything loose.

2) The old guy with the towels doesn't work there.

3) Back in the stalls we mutter to ourselves and try to make it sound like we're on the phone. We say unspeakable things in a language no one understands.

4) We fear any physical contact with the floor more than death. Also (this secret is extra) the last stall, occupied or not, is assumed to be "a loaded chamber."

5) No one has ever been born in a men's room.

The Moonlight Guys

As soon as the Moonlight Guys tested the gullibility of Elon Musk, they knew they had it made. Rumors had circulated for years about Musk's willingness to shoot anything into space, no questions asked, as long as he could stand somewhere in front of a chart and display his nearly interesting hair. He glanced briefly at the contract to pay him $40 million to launch a payload about the size of a 2008 Hyundai Accent, and signed it while emitting his famous barely audible low-frequency cackle.

The Moonlight Guys were good to go.

P.S. MUELLER is Staff Liar of *The American Bystander*.

Quantum biophysiologists have long theorized that moonlight, highly concentrated and focused with laser precision, will reverse the aging process of billionaires, even the notoriously reclusive font baron Arvis Manderblad, who literally owns every known word in the developed world. Manderblad is 106 and still sharp enough to realize his only viable plan for any future must involve shaving a good 50 years off his 11-foot beard.

The Moonlight Guys knew this when they tricked Mr. Musk into sending their secret moonlight-sequestering device into lunar orbit. Very slowly, a microfiber net encircled the fabled celestial body and began capturing and beaming a concentrate of silvery immortality to their discreet lab in Schaumburg, Illinois. The Moonlight Guys were able to store the stuff with remarkable frugality in large stainless steel tanks, easily converted after the brewpub collapse of 2018.

Today, thanks to the Moonlight Guys, Arvis Manderblad is happily steering his mountain bike through the Pyrenees, the dark circles beneath Elon Musk's eyes have been transferred to the man in the moon, and North Korea's Kim Jong-un is a fetus.

The Flavorist

Everybody had childhood heroes and aspirations. Back in the Fifties most boys wanted to be astronauts or cowboys, and girls wanted to be lesbians. By the age of 7 and a half, I had been hiding within a childhood disguised as childhood for nearly two years... then I made the decision to live and work openly as a flavorist, and to devote my life to combining artificial substances with chemical additives to create: bottle beef, salmon jelly, prosthetic chicken wings.

Later that year, I found part-time work as a cracker boy at the Snactory, a growing table-food manufacturer in the part of town we all knew then as Nibblers' Row. That job no longer exists — our all-new world has replaced cracker boys with speedy and efficient conveyor belts, powered by distant and oblivious fat men on treadmills.

As a cracker boy, my job was to run test batches between the production and marketing departments. But here's the beautiful part: When things were slow, I would spend time with Dr. Julius Langway, known the world over by marketing people and by table-food manufacturers as "the man who reinvented the cracker."

Dr. Langway was old and half-motorized by then. He suffered from a progressive neurological disorder called "fake-shake," an illness brought on by too many decades of exposure to soy products masquerading as other soy products. Ironically, the process responsible for his malady was both invented, studied and banned by a much younger Dr. Langway and is now used only in

the production of artificial checkers. However, old Langway remained sharp as a tack and set me on the road to success, a road powdered with a mix of asparquilladene, jive-mercury, and polysodium glaxomate.

Dr. Langway's fabled freshness pack eventually gave out and he was, according to his wishes, cremated and mixed into a heap of mine tailings in Nevada — near a place where they dig up nasohydrite for the giant, faceless LLC that makes artisanal quinoa muffins just down the block from you. I went to work for them in 2010, after proving to a group of 500 of my closest colleagues that what they had been eating for the previous three days never came out of a crab.

At about that time, many were predicting that tuna would soon be overfished to extinction, but I was looking ahead and went to work on the problem. Initially, I realized I needed to start from scratch by creating a wholly artificial life form that could swim in the sea and grow to the size of a Belgian horse. I accomplished that early on, but my breeding stock was illegally released by a radical group of so-called Free Artificialists. Do-gooders! And today, I'm sad to say, the world's oceans are teeming with my incomplete, ravenously hungry, utterly flavorless faux albacore monsterfish. (The flavoring agent I had created to make them palatable and complete would have also dulled their appetites.)

Nowadays I sit in the dark, back at the cracker-works. My colossal *doppeltüna* ate the entire cast of *Deadliest Catch*. Still, I did manage to live my life proudly as a flavorist, and even today they let me sneak down to the vats at night to add a little orange to the Cheddaroos.

Great Thoughts of Great Americans

"My first wish is to see this plague of mankind, war, banished from the earth."
—*George Washington*

"No man is good enough to govern another man without the other's consent."
—*Abraham Lincoln*

"Owning a great golf course gives you great power."
—*Donald Trump*

At the Nasty Humorless Men's Club

The first thing we do is warm up the beer and spike it with bitters. The guys who founded this place started that, and we aren't about to change anything just to please a bunch of trend-addled hipster wannabes. Then we file into the meeting room with our hats on. We all wear hats and ties, goddammit, even when we eat or make love to our pinched, unforgiving wives.

Our current president is Falco Wurlitzer, some kind of retired military guy. He pulls around his artificial liver, which also handles all his burps and hiccups, on a special cart made for him by honest-to-God veterans, you ingrateful pieces of human waste. The device connects to a really sore place in his back and makes him really mad most of the time, at least until he's had a half-dozen warm ones. People who have been to his house say he has one of Gen. George Patton's actual tusks, pickled in bay rum and suspended in a glass vessel constructed by Masons.

Most of the time he's not there, and we just sit around playing cards and braying about all those foreigners who want to come over here and force us to learn backgammon. Sometimes we piss and moan about the weather or that crippled dead kid down the block and how we won't pay taxes to have him hauled away. Hasn't he got a family, for crimony jeeps? He might be foreign for that matter! Or maybe it's truck exhaust that's colored him gray. Either way, we're sick and tired of having to step over him.

Every week we invite a special guest to explain himself. Last night we had some idiot covered with face tattoos, and he went on for nearly 15 minutes about using his skin as a living canvas until the Q&A when one of our guys asked him if he wanted to be a puptent and he left. Later we all went down to the basement to look at the old grizzly bear we keep on a chain down there, and if any of those code people with the city hear anything about ol' Groany and tell those godawful carnival people where he is, well, we might do things. **B**

CHUNK-STYLE NUGGETS

...to briefly distract you from the inevitable • ***By Steve Young***

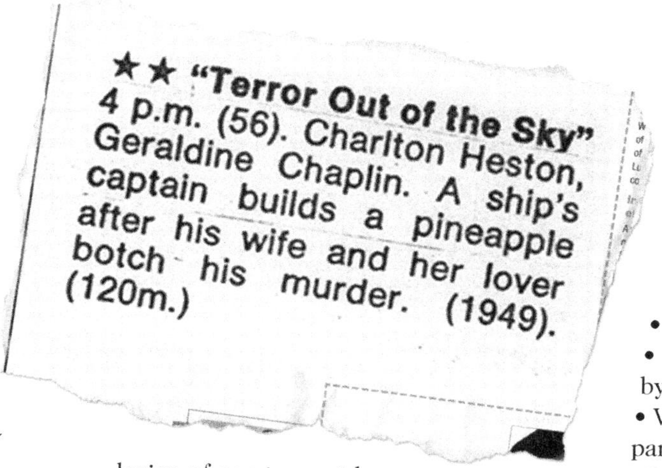
★★ "Terror Out of the Sky" 4 p.m. (56). Charlton Heston, Geraldine Chaplin. A ship's captain builds a pineapple after his wife and her lover botch his murder. (1949). (120m.)

Get to know me!

Here's what's in my wallet right now:

• *Photocopies* of $1, $5, $10 and $20 bills (originals kept elsewhere for safety);
• *Edible Visa card* issued by TastiGroup;
• *New York* dryer's license;
• *World Court at The Hague* cafeteria loyalty card (13th burrito free);
• *Membership card*, Museum of Displayed Items;
• *LuckyBank* scratch-off possible ATM card;
• *Faculty ID*, Apex Mortuary & Pastry Academy;
• *Proof of uninsurance* card, Denial Health;
• *Portrait of* my wallet.

Report of the Youth Marketing Image Research Group

Our research confirmed that teens still consider anthracite to be the "cool" variety of coal. Bituminous coal is mocked as "so whatever" and "totally OMG." This is largely due to the successful efforts by anthracite interests to feature their product in popular coal-related shows for "tweens," in the lyrics of songs sung by top coal-themed boy bands, and in the anthracite-positive *Captain Carbon* superhero films.

Previous attempts to convince teens that bituminous coal is "awesome" have not been successful. The costumed character Bitty, which toured high schools and state fairs last year, was viciously mocked. The Bituminous Life social media app failed to catch on. And the less said about the sponsored rap song "Gonna Get Up in My Bituminous Coal in All That, Yo," the better.

We need to implement a targeted image upgrade campaign ASAP, reaching teens "where they are" and making it "awesome" to join Team Bituminous Coal. Recommendation: Put pictures of bituminous coal on hoodies.

A Reminder From Your *American Bystander* Fire Warden

In the unlikely event that your *American Bystander* magazine becomes involved in a fire situation, activate the nearest Magazine Fire Alert Alarm, then proceed calmly to your designated Nonflammable Assembly Area. Do not take the elevator. Elevators are often full of burning magazines.

Resumé Padders

Use as many as you need!

• Recipient, First-Class Mail
• Exhales carbon dioxide needed by vegetation
• Valued Customer (assorted companies)
• Participant, four laws of thermodynamics
• Reasonably fluent in native language
• Currently dressed

Our IAQ

(Infrequently Asked Questions)

1. What if I forget my sofa's password?
2. Where can I purchase formalwear for my CPR dummy?
3. Can I return a grape for store credit?
4. Is my hamster eligible for a complimentary angioplasty?
5. Does my policy cover damage to a neighbor's thresher?
6. How do I change my spouse's filter cartridge?

Answers: Yes, yes, no, it depends, no, yes

Monologue for Actor Auditions

I am so dysfunctional because of my troubled past! I have difficult relationships with family and friends! I realize I'm speaking loudly and dramatically... the truth is, I'm feeling a lot of dark emotions right now! Which explains the gestures! Wait, I'm feeling better. Sometimes I'm suffused by the sort of peace that's accompanied by a noticeable inner glow. Except then I start to

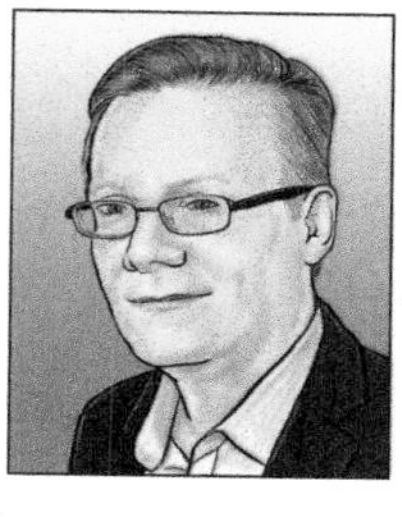

STEVE YOUNG (@pantssteve) is Oracle for *The American Bystander*.

become despondent about my issues. And I get a sort of hunted, fearful look. With sadness. This emotional rollercoaster always resolves with me become appealingly self-possessed as I realize that I am a very, very good actor.

Increase Your Word Power!

Odometer: A device that measures how far an odor has traveled.

Increase Your Word Power!
(corrected version)

Odometer: a device that measures how far former NBA star and Kardashian husband Lamar Odom has traveled.

Increase Your Word Power!
(2nd corrected version)

Odometer: a device that measures how far *Star Trek: Deep Space Nine* character Odo has traveled.

Increase Your Word Power!
(final version)

It is useless to attempt to increase your word power.

What they *don't* tell you

Michael Nesmith's mother was forced to invent Liquid Paper because HE MADE SO MANY FUCKING MISTAKES!

U.S. History Trivia

Ohio and Wyoming are the only states that were admitted to the Union after being wait-listed.

Memory Trick

There's an easy way to remember which are the stalactites and which are the stalagmites. Just go to college, major in geology, and take courses dealing with cave formations in which these features are thoroughly explained.

Fun Fact

Ellis Island's name was shortened from Ellisowicz Islandberger.

Imponderables Corner

Why do AA batteries come in packages of eight, but AA battery *buns* come in packages of 10? B

Navied

SORRY I CAN'T MAKE IT

On June 15, 2017, we had our first reading in NYC. Lots of people came. These people couldn't.

Speech bubble: "Sorry I couldn't be there but this dog with a poorly drawn rifle threatened to cartoon-shoot me if I went."

DONNELLY

I regret many things in life but not attending this reading isn't really one of them.

—*Al Jean*

Very sorry that I'm not able to make it this evening. I am, however, there in spirit, so if you really need me, please consult the nearest Ouija board.

—*Kit Lively*

Dear Everybody,
I deeply regret that I will be unable to attend the *Bystander* reading. I have Vladimir Putin trapped in my basement and it is my patriotic duty to keep him there, and possibly starve him to death. As much as I would love to be among my fellow Bystanders, you can easily see why I must put my country first.

I just wish he would stop glaring at me from beneath the stairs, with those piercing feral eyes.

—*P.S. Mueller*

I'm sorry I tried to take the stage earlier even though I have not yet published any articles in your magazine. I wanted to look big, and for that I apologize, especially to the children of the legitimate readers who were jostled during the so-called scuffle.

I'm sorry I referred to your magazine as *American Beauty Standards* in my introductory letter. I should have made changes to the piece I submitted after learning about my mistake, but I didn't want to put in the effort. On reflection, that choice was at least partly wrong. I'm not sorry about the time it saved me.

I honestly believe I had a shot at going out with Sarah Silverman once but I turned it down because my wife was eight months pregnant with our daughter at the time. Now that my daughter is a snotty teen who never remembers my birthday or returns my earbuds, I'm truly sorry I didn't do that. Now I'm too old.

I wish I had a nice, clear, songbird voice like the good person reading this, but I don't, and that's always been one of my biggest regrets. Half the people who call me on my landline think the automated answering-machine voice they hear is me. They say things to the voice, private things, and then they get mad when the voice doesn't answer. But having a lovely voice isn't everything. It can be masking other problems that are much more severe. The sonorous voice you hear right now could be the voice of a deeply disturbed person. Their words don't necessarily represent me, and for that I'm sorry.

—*Ron Hauge*

I regret I cannot travel from Chicago to be with you there tonight, but the airlines still refuse to recognize my bee colony as a "therapy animal," and the queen gets easily carsick on the Interstate.

—*James Finn Garner*

Hey Mike, pick your favorite one of these:

Ben Orlin wishes he could be here, but he already spent all three of the genie's wishes on waffle toppings.

Ben Orlin is not in the country at the moment. He sends his apologies and, more generally, his condolences.

Ben Orlin wanted to be here, but then his Taoist studies helped him transcend want.

Ben Orlin is unable to attend because he is trying desperately to peel apart the two sides of a plastic grocery bag.

—*Ben Orlin*

[Sorry, Ben. My own Taoist studies have cleansed me of the Poison of Preferences. —Ed.]

Mapquest tells me it would take 37 and a half hours to drive there and I don't do public transportation. So, NO. But y'all have fun, at least the ones who survive the trip there.

—*Billy Collins*

Sadly, I am unable to attend, as I died a few days ago.

—*Larry Doyle*

Mr. Henderson regrets not being able to make it as his toe has been caught in a bowling ball yet again. Fret not because his reading would be unintelligible since he's had the same piece of gum in his mouth for 22 years.

—*Sam Henderson*

I wish I could have been there, but the warlock's curse doesn't allow me within 100 leagues of Avenue A. (Warlocks only measure distance in leagues.)

—Adam Koford

Dear Michael, Readers, and ladies and gentlemen of my target demographic,

It saddens me deeply to miss this live *American Bystander* event, and by "saddens me deeply" I mean "has virtually no emotional impact on me beyond some small dismay to have missed a professional opportunity to meet some accomplished people up to whom I might suck."

If you are deeply saddened or experiencing some small dismay at my absence, please know that I would be there if not for a previously arranged obligation that has me in London just now and a deep commitment to my own convenience.

I'll be in New York in July with a three-week run of my show "Dylan Brody's Driving Hollywood" so perhaps I can make it up to you then.

Tonight, though, enjoy the evening as best you can in my absence, as will I in yours.

As sincerely as is possible in a self-promotional message,

—Dylan Brody

Sorry I can't be with you tonight.

I am in Thailand for two weeks on vacation.

I brought my 10-year-old son with me, so the trip is paying for itself!

—Andy Breckman

[A historical note: This one got a huge laugh when I read it during some technical difficulties. —Ed.]

Dirk Voetberg regrets that he is not able to be here to read his short piece "My piece that was barely rejected by Shouts & Murmurs," which was just barely rejected by *McSweeney's*. Dirk also regrets that *American Bystander* also actually rejected this piece, and that only this regret itself is what was not rejected (barely).

—Dirk Voetberg

I so deeply regret not being able to read or attend *The American Bystander*'s first reading in New York, that I *was* going to start cutting myself, but decided to finally tackle my passion for bulimia.

—Katie Schwartz

[Oh, don't do that. There will be other readings soon, I promise. — Ed.]

Of course, I would like nothing more than to attend this reading — so that's what I'm doing instead: Nothing.

—Daniel Galef

"Regrets" to you — I will be out of town Thursday through the weekend, communing with our UFO overlords at our cabin upstate.

—Scott Marshall

[Please show them the magazine, Scott. I can walk them through Patreon if necessary. —Ed.]

I regret that during the most recent glacial age, ice walls 15 stories tall scoured the middle of the North American land mass and, upon retreating, carved wide canyons in the landscape, which filled with their melt water and precipitation, creating breathtaking sweet-water seas we now call the Great Lakes, the lure of which (especially in summer) has held me mercilessly like a prisoner without reprieve my entire life, or else I would certainly be living in a fourth-floor walkup in Morningside Heights and jump on the 1 train, then the R train, then trudge the scorching asphalt from the NYU station, and join you all at HiFi Bar tonight. I also regret Michael wouldn't pop for airfare.

—James Finn Garner

I recently joined a cult, and to my surprise it turns out that they have some pretty strict rules, some of which prevent me from attending *Bystander*'s first-ever reading.

For example: Travel *is* permitted on Thursdays, but only on those old-timey bikes with the giant front wheel.

I would wish you good luck, but unfortunately all casual expressions of goodwill are also not permitted.

If at some point in the near future I am kidnapped and deprogrammed, I would love to attend your next reading! :)

—Mike Shiell

[That's called "a penny-farthing," Mike. I'll launch the GoFundMe immediately.—Ed.] B

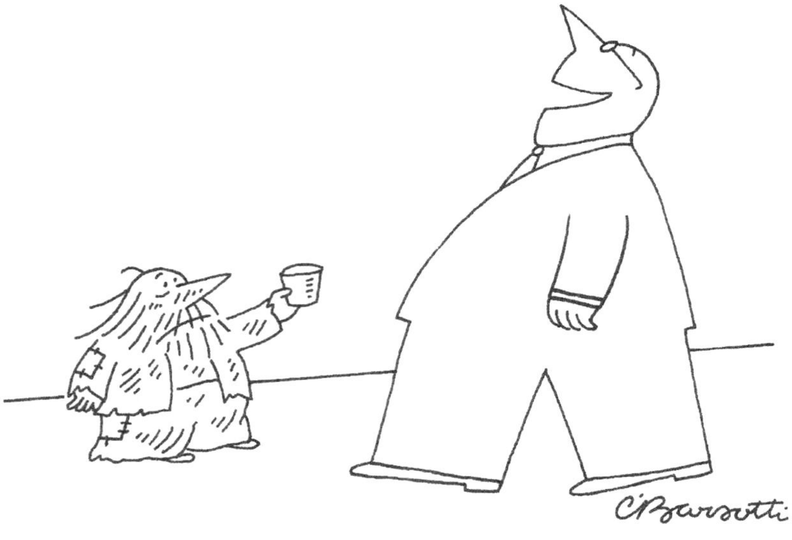
CBarsotti

"Thank you, Lord, for reminding me to count my blessings."

YEAH, I WORKED THERE

My somewhat happy happy years writing for The Ren & Stimpy Show • *by* ***Ron Hauge***

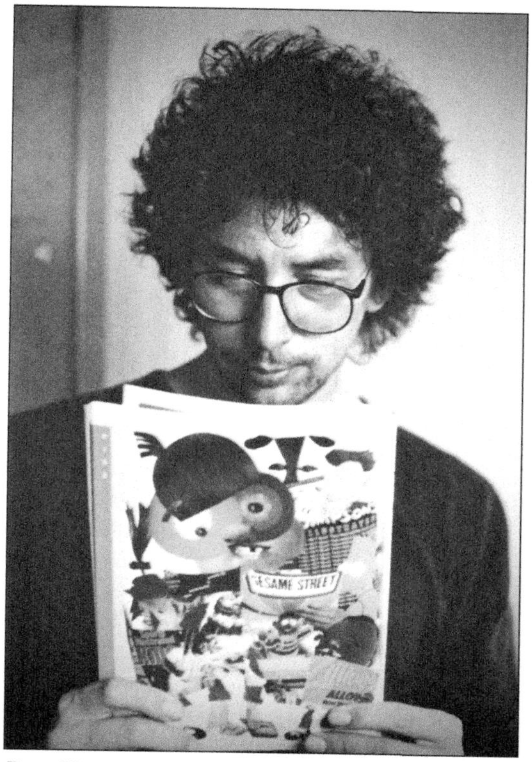

SESAME STREET

Ron Hauge and his marvelous hair, around the time they both worked at **Ren & Stimpy.**

RENÉE EVANS

"Which one is a dog, now?"
—my Dad

I'm pretty sure *The Ren & Stimpy Show* is the only place I ever worked where the showrunner and his executive producers had such a terrible working relationship, they were all in therapy together. I'm not saying that's the only reason the show was good, but I know it helped. Not the therapy part; the need for therapy part. The therapy just drove the showrunner to further madness. And madness drove the show. So, O.K., I was wrong — the therapy "helped." But only by not helping.

Here's how I got the job writing for the show: I was writing for another animated series on Nickelodeon when I went to a Nick party and ran into the showrunner at *R&S*, who was an old acquaintance I admired from the '80s New York cartoon world. Within seconds, I was telling him all about how I was not fitting in at my current show, and how I expected to be fired any minute, possibly at the party, which was the only reason I'd made an effort to come. I told him the show's creator hated me so much, he once asked his young female assistant to leave the room before he would respond to one of my story pitches.

My new savior was delighted. "You gotta come work for us," he said immediately. Then he insisted that his executive producers hire me. He didn't tell them it was because I was trouble.

The showrunner at *Ren & Stimpy* was talented and dedicated and daring, and mighty charming when he wasn't being an ornery Texan — which, in fairness, was only about 8 percent of the time. (His wife's figure on that may vary.) I loved working with him because he would fight to the death for anything he thought was good, and he produced a ton of good. He didn't want to hear any ideas that would water down the show. That led to openly defying and even mocking his mild-mannered producers, who as Nickelodeon execs had to be super-calm and child-friendly and reasonable and nurturing in response or they wouldn't be Nick. Also, they were aware that no one else on the planet could do the job.

I was the first staffer on *R&S* to work solely as a writer, not as a staff artist who wrote. Apparently that puked in the face of the series' creator, John K., who had been ousted not long before I arrived. On my first day, I was introduced as the new writer at a large staff meeting, and the only comment from anyone was from an angry-looking artist who said, "Yeah, whatever happened to John K.'s idea that if you can't draw, you can't write?"

He hadn't been told that I had been a working artist for years, for *The National Lampoon* and other magazines. Or maybe he knew my work and still held the same opinion.

"Don't hate me because I'm a writer," I told him. "Hate me because I'm me." And when the dust finally settled, I'm proud to say he did.

As it turns out, hating-and-complaining was simply a way of life at *The Ren & Stimpy Show*. Everybody (except the super-positive execs!) hated anything or anybody that wasn't one of the original Looney Tunes directors — including flawless new episodes of *The Simpsons*, promising new hires in the art department, another director's outstanding new episode, the cultures of every European nation, beautiful actresses in particular and the remainder of humanity in general. It wasn't personal in that it was always personal, so it was fair.

I later learned that everyone on the ☛

RON HAUGE'S *first job was as a part-time mail order clerk at a rural Montgomery Ward outlet, from which he stole. He later pursued other interests.*

OUTHOUSE
CASTLE
PRODUCTIONS
PRESENTS

Ron wanted to do a followup to Stimpy's cartoon show that would have begun with this homage to another studio, but he left R&S *before this idea could be officially rejected. Ron still likes that there's an outhouse behind the castle, if you can get across the moat.*

creative staff was there because they had been fired — rightly — from another show. We were The Island of Misfit Disgruntled Former Employees.

Because there had never been a writer on the show before me, there wasn't a writers' office when I got there, so I was given a small desk in the office of one of the storyboard artists. The artist, Pete, was the nicest guy in America — but he liked to listen to music while he worked, specifically the stylings of Blossom Dearie. If you're not familiar with her extensive songbook, I suggest you listen to three or four seconds' worth to get the idea. DO NOT LISTEN FOR A FULL FIVE SECONDS.

By the end of the first day, I was doing all my writing on a filigreed metal patio table just outside the offices, with only the constant traffic noise on Sunset Boulevard and the occasional homeless versus hooker debate to distract or inspire me. It was a great spot. Every once in a while a voice actor who arrived early, or who arrived on time and was kept waiting, wandered out onto the patio to pass the time or to have a smoke. That's how you end up talking to a Charlie Callas for 20 minutes about his early days drumming with Buddy Rich, for example. That's how you hear a June Lockhart say something delightfully off-color, which I won't repeat here because we're still friendly and she comes to my block party every year. But it was about Jonathan Harris's "acting."

At some point, our showrunner discovered the building's intercom system, which he then employed like Trump tweets to get the last word with everybody after unsettling meetings with individuals. My friend Larry Doyle was visiting me once when a booming, twangy voice came over the office-wide speaker system with an encouraging, "Anybody who doesn't like working here can QUIT!" This is a good place to remember that he was there because the man he replaced was too hard to work with.

Of course, madness wasn't the only thing driving the show. Pot was also a force. Because our offices were nowhere near the main Nickelodeon offices we were Colonel Kurtz Up the River; almost every day my boss and I started our workday by smoking a joint on his balcony. One of the show's artists told me he used to get his pot delivered to the building by a dealer who would dress up in a full chicken restaurant deliveryman's uniform complete with old-timey paper cap and aluminum hot case. The drugs inside the case were wrapped up and dispensed like food when he arrived at the lunch hour. ("Wowee-zowee, a three hundred and forty-three dollar 'tip?!'

Thanks, mister!!")

No one at Nickelodeon was ever aware of any pot use on the show, and as far as I know, at least while I was there, nobody ever tried to slip a drug reference or endorsement into an episode. We knew kids were watching along with the adults we were really aiming at. Still, the wary executives were always on the lookout for hidden content in our shows. Their assistant once wrangled a moment alone with me and nervously pointed to a word in a new script as he whispered, "Do you know what this means?"

The word was "spode," but it definitely wasn't being used in a way that had anything to do with scenic plate-ware, which I'm both proud and ashamed to say is the only meaning of the word that I knew. The s-word was cut from the script before I could learn what it was supposed to mean in that context, but I always assumed it had something to do with jizz. Again though, not drugs, Concerned Moms and Dads of America.

A lot of ideas suggested at *R&S* got shot down, including our showrunner's notion that everyone in the office should wear a color-coded jumpsuit uniform, with layout artists in one color, storyboard artists in another, etc. He got the idea from watching either a Japanese cartoon or a movie about the future, I forget. I think the only support he got for this was from the sweet hippie girl assistant who wore overalls every day already. Artists and writers get into their professions to avoid uniform-wearing jobs like fast-food cashier, or Private First Class, which are basically the only other two jobs they may be qualified for, at least with more training. But as Frank Zappa once told a stunned audience of anti-military hippies, "You're all wearing a uniform." And I prefer the uniform of the American male television writer, which is essentially the Michael Moore ensemble, minus the classy sport coat, and plus or minus three pant sizes.

Despite our lack of color coordination, there was a lot of collaboration on the show — sort of. When an episode turned out really good, three or four of the artists who worked on it would usually take a writing credit along with me. When an episode failed, they'd leave me hanging as the only writer. Which is fine; more $1.25 foreign-run residual checks for me.

One of the *Ren & Stimpy* episodes I wrote got me my first Emmy nomination, but we lost to a Shakespeare special that many on our staff complained was poorly written.

I did do some drawing on the show. When Stimpy created his own crude cartoon in one episode, my drawings were used as his. I drew it all haphazardly on 40 storyboard panels in a fast sitting, and the final was shot directly from those roughs. The whole idea of this was that Stimpy was the worst artist in the world, but somehow I'm still gratified I was asked to do it.

After about two seasons, I took a short hiatus from *R&S* to be a guest writer on *Saturday Night Live*, near the end of one of their seasons. It's really a tryout for *SNL*'s next season, and I did it with a gifted writing partner, Charlie Rubin. But before *SNL* decided, we were offered a job writing for *Seinfeld*, and we snapped it up. I didn't really have a desk to clear out when I left *Ren & Stimpy*, so before leaving I tidied up the patio a little.

By the mid-'90s, I was writing for *The Simpsons*, where I was not fired after many, many years, and where I had all the non-patio desk I could want. I never worked as an artist there, but I did supervise all the design work for a dozen years. While I was writing there, Matt Groening and David Cohen were struggling to find the right lead actor for their new series, *Futurama*, and I suggested *R&S*'s amazing Billy West — which got me a great *Futurama* show jacket that now hangs next to my great *Ren & Stimpy* and *Simpsons* show jackets in a closet I never use. I think the odd aroma in there is coming from my 23-year-old, lightly worn *Seinfeld* show sneakers, but I'm afraid to check.

I've never worked on a show where any of the actors remembered me after I left. When I worked in New York ages ago, I wrote pretty much every word a TV host said on the air for two years, and when I ran into him two years after that he had no idea who I was. I mean none. Or maybe without me he just had nothing to say. That was Bill Boggs, by the way, just so you know I'm not protecting his name today; in fact, I might be the only one getting it out there. So I was pretty gratified when I ran into Billy West several years after *Ren & Stimpy* and he recognized me from the show. *He* actually approached *me*. We talked for a while about the old *Ren & Stimpy* days and about who was doing what now. Then he said to me, "Hey, I heard one of the writers over there got hired at *The Simpsons*," adding, "I think it was Ron Hauge." **B**

SHOW #
PAGE # 2
SCENE.
BG.
DRAW
DRAW
DRAW
DRAW
SCENE.
BG.
RON HAUGE (ON PHONE)
YEAH SO I TOLD LORNE THAT SIENFELD JUST MADE ME A BETTER OFFER..... SURE.... SURE.... WELL IT'S LIKE I TOLD JERRY,...
FADE OUT/FADE IN – THURSDAY
INTERIOR – RON HAUGE AND PETER AVANZINO'S OFFICE.
FADE OUT/FADE IN – FRIDAY MORNING
INTERIOR – RON HAUGE AND PETER AVANZINO'S OFFICE.
SURPRISE! – RON'S AT HIS DESK!

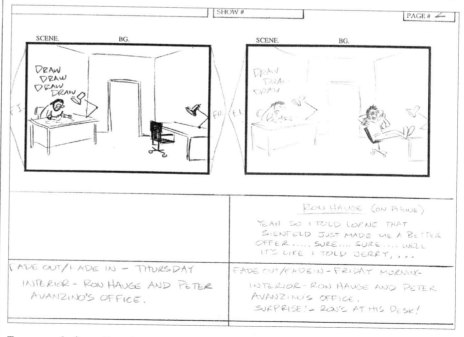

Two panels from Pete Avanzino's storyboard about Ron at Ren & Stimpy, *a gift to Ron when he left the show. Ron didn't tell Pete he was working outdoors because of the distracting, awful music he played. Pete thought Ron just never worked.*

(5K continued from P. 24)

Some might ask, "Are you intentionally trying to get yourself to poop during the race?" To that, I answer, "I guess I care more than you do about charity and the spirit of competition, and I definitely care more than Kevin Sweyer from sales." Others might say, "Gross." Fair enough. But so gross that it's valiant? I think so.

If and when I lose control of my bowels during the race, I'm just going to think of poor animals in need of a happy home. This will give me the strength to keep putting one poop-coated leg in front of the other, even if it means staining the Puppy Prance novelty Hanes Beefy T that I put on and tuck into my shorts after getting it in my swag bag at the starting line. Yes, I'm that serious about this.

All I ask is that if you see me running this Sunday and the inevitable has happened, please think twice before you take a photo or record a video of me. And when you have thought twice and have still taken the photo or video, please post that photo or video online, and please remember to tag me on all relevant social media so all of my co-workers will know the type of person I really am.

Thank you.

—*Nate Dern* B

(Politics continued from P. 39)

Wrap-Up Time

By now, you should have accomplished what you set out to do: charge boldly into a situation of complete gridlock. Now all that is left is for both parties in the discussion to leave, seething with quiet rancor. But, Dear Friends of the Future, it was once customary to include a more graceful parting glance by throwing out a line the people of pre-2016 America used to pretend to believe:

"I may not agree with what you say, but I will defend to the death your right to say it."

This ritual declaration was delivered with humble but heartfelt conviction… And a secret suspicion that, were any of them actually called upon in this capacity, the only risk most would have been willing to take would have been some kind of petty passive-aggressive facial expression. Perhaps a wild-eyed pout, designed to make their former opponent too nervous to ever argue with a stranger again.

After the ritual declaration, you wave goodbye, while possibly adding in a final "Well, YOU started it." Free now to re-enter polite conversation, you rest easy knowing that, no matter how it all played out, obviously you and your side won. B

"I say it's broccoli, and I say, 'Fuck it.'"

NY/NJ COMEDIC ACTOR (40s-50s) available for auditions, readings, runs of any length. Resume and pictures: **DavidCNeal.com.**

IT CAME FROM THE BOTTOM SHELF!
Bottomshelfmovies.com is a film recommendation website focusing on forgotten classics, lesser-known gems, and odd-ball discoveries. It's the video collector's resource for movie reviews, weekly new release video picks, upcoming Blu-ray/DVD announcements, sales alerts, and other cinematic news. **Bottomshelfmovies.com**

JANE AUSTEN MUSIC Live music from the English Regency era for dancing or ambience in the San Francisco area. **jameslangdell@gmail.com**

DOPEY PODCAST
On the dark comedy of drug addiction.
www.dopeypodcast.com

FREAK CHIC STUDIOS
Jewelry, Art & Accoutrements for the Eclectic Heart.
www.freakchicstudios.com
that's Dubyah Dubyah Dubyah dot FreakChicStudios dot See Oh Em. Twitter: @FreakChicStudio / Instagram: Freak Chic Studios / CB Callsign: Freak 2 The Chic. Be a good human and buy my stuff! Ten-four good buddy. Keep the bugs off your glass, and the bears off your... TAIL. Over and out.

THE MISADVENTURES OF LI'L DONNIE
Making Comics Great Again - Since 2017!
donniecrys.blogspot.com or follow "Donald Littles" (w/the asterisk pic) on the facebooks!

MYXPROJEKT
Free long-form Ambient Drone music. Great for relaxation, meditation, sleep. Nod off in style! Money back guarantee.
soundcloud.com/myxprojekt

COMEDIANS DEFYING GRAVITY
Comedians Defying Gravity highlights Chicago comedy: interviews, weekly events calendar and more. CDG is part of ChicagoNow, the Chicago Tribune Media Group's blogging network.**http://www.chicagonow.com/comedians-defying-gravity**

FULL OF WIT Funny poems and more. The Killing Tree by J.D. Smith can be found at most online sellers and at the link.
www.finishinglinepress.com/product/the-killing-tree-by-j-d-smith/

PATSY O'BRIEN
Alt-Celtic Songwriter
Award-winning
NPR - featured.
www.patsyobrienswebsite.com

¿GOT TSUNAMIS?
Or some other annoyingly inconvenient problem at your local beach, port or 5-star resort? Give a shout, we'll sort you out!
http://eCoast.co.nz
jose@ecoast.co.nz
coastal dynamics • tsunamis • erosion • wave pools • surfing reefs • resorts • marinas • marine ecology
Solutions offered worldwide!
No beach out of reach!
The absurdity of advertising coastal engineering services to a bunch of writers and English majors isn't lost on me, but hey, I like the *Bystander*, so why not?

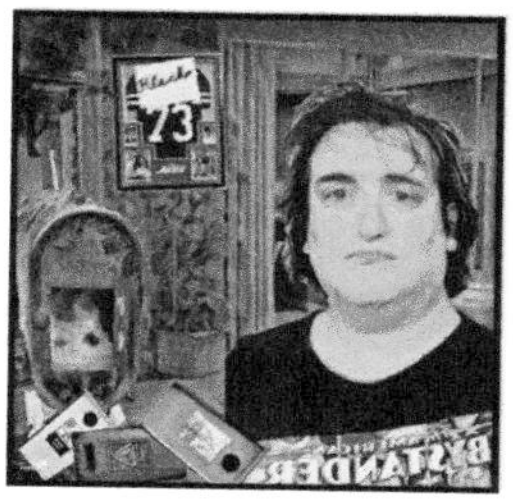

IN MEMORIAM:
Johnson Dunst, Jr., the deaf-mute imbecile who would bring our pre-separated trash and recyclables from the *Bystander* main offices to his religiously-excepted home incinerator just over the border in West Los Angeles, has died. Cause of death is believed to have been his correct knowledge that the life expectancy of a deaf-mute imbecile in AD 1732 was nine combined with his apparent, yet woefully misguided, belief that it is now AD 1732. Mr. Dunst, Jr., leaves no known next of kin, though he was known to smile for days whenever he successfully spelled the word "Klecko" in cursive. We wish him well.

TONY ISABELLA'S NEW BOOK
July 1963: A Pivotal Month in the Comic-Book Life of Tony Isabella Volume One. Obsessive nostalgic fun that inspired the career of the creator of Black Lightning, Misty Knight, Tigra and more. Available in print and digital formats from Amazon. Superman competes in the Interplanetary Olympics. The coming of the Avengers. Baby Huey's criminally negligent parents. Batman's super-powered dog. All this and so much more.

A (VERY GOOD) LITERARY AGENCY
Why, you must have stellar taste to be here. Are you also an extremely talented writer with a book idea? Let's talk. I'm Scott at **sgould@rlrassociates.net.**

www.kingcormack.com

DRUNK MONKEYS
America's finest "two women drinking odd liquors and talking about it" web series may be found at drunkmonkeyshow.com – only one 's', so it's Drunk Monkeys how?

CLASSIFIEDS

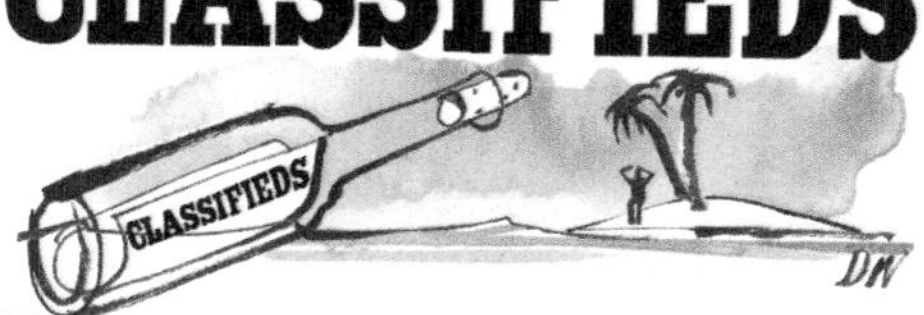

CLASSIFIEDS
DW

Interested in placing an ad? Email **classifieds@americanbystander.org**. The American Bystander reserves the right to reject any ad for any reason. We do not guarantee the quality of the items being sold, or the accuracy of the information provided. Ads are provided directly by sellers and are not verified.

CARTOON COMPANION
Cartooncompanion.com is a new website that discusses and rates the cartoons in *The New Yorker*. Co-hosts Max and Simon trade amusing observations and barbs with each new issue. *TNY* cartoonists have contributed to the site and praised it. Future posts will include interviews of the cartoonists and cartoons that *The New Yorker* rejected.
cartooncompanion.com

DO YOU READ THE OTHER A.B.?
Attempted Bloggery – An art blog about cartoons and other high culture. Published more or less daily since 2011.
attemptedbloggery.blogspot.com

CURRENCY CONVERSION BY MAIL
Convert unwieldy US folding money into small denominations! Send $10 bill get back $5 bill. Send *one* $20 bill receive a completely different bill. Never ask for change again! Do not delay!
Contact **@Specky4Eyes**
Serious inquiries only. No fatties.

YOU LIKE COMICS?
Sure you do! Who doesn't? (well, ignore those dweebs). For the finest in graphic storytelling, look ahead to 2018 for the premiere of BERGER BOOKS, created by the legendary Karen Berger, founding editor of VERTIGO! And the Art Director? The also legendary - except not so much - Richard Bruning! Top notch talent too. Watch for this revolutionary new imprint from indy pioneer Dark Horse.

THE COMIC TORAH
Stand-up comic Aaron Freeman and artist Sharon Rosenzweig reimagine the Torah with provocative humor and irreverent reverence. Each weekly portion gets a two-page spread. Like the original, the Comic Torah is not always suitable for children. "Hyperactive, colorful art brings the story to life." – Publisher's Weekly "If God was a comic artist, this is what She would have drawn." –Harold Ramis "Awesome!" – Alison Bechdel "Sacred & profane at the same time." – Paul Krassner
benyehudapress.com/ct or amzn.to/2npmv4V

STUDY CARTOONING and Illustration at the School of Visual Arts. We offer courses by Tom Motley, Steve Brodner, Carl Potts, and more! Fall courses are enrolling now.
www.sva.edu/continuing-education/illustration-and-cartooning

VISUAL REALIA
Photography, food and everything visual:
www.visualrealia.com.

CONFEDERACY OF DRONES POLITICAL SATIRE
Using humor to shoot down the political hypocrisy of mindless drones.
confederacyofdrones.com

LOTS OF NATIONAL LAMPOON
Lots of Nat Lamps for sale. Various monthly issues and Best Ofs. Mostly in pretty good condition. $4 each or more per issue plus postage. Email me with any particular issue you need at **bardinerman@aol.com.**
Thank you and Godspeed.

COMIC STUDIES at the University of Wisconsin-Madison http://humanities.wisc.edu/research/borghesi-mellon-workshops/past-workshops/comics2

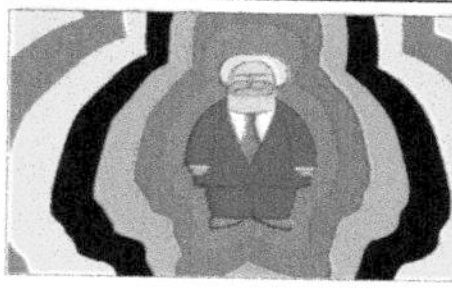

THE MAN WHO KILLED REALITY
The Prefab Messiahs explain all! Observe their hit animated musical video on the Youtubes:
youtube.com/prefabmessiahs

Tres Francais

G	U	E	S	S	#	S	H	I	T	#	K	I	S	S
O	S	A	K	A	#	A	E	R	O	#	A	R	E	A
B	E	T	E	N	O	I	R	E	R	#	M	A	N	Y
#	#	#	E	A	G	L	E	#	#	P	A	N	T	S
O	B	I	T	#	R	O	T	A	T	E	S	#	#	#
M	U	S	#	D	E	R	I	G	U	E	U	R	E	R
E	R	O	D	E	#	S	C	A	R	#	T	U	N	E
R	E	G	I	N	A	#	#	#	F	I	R	S	T	S
T	A	O	S	#	B	A	R	B	#	S	A	T	A	T
A	U	N	A	T	U	R	E	L	E	R	#	L	I	E
#	#	#	G	A	T	E	A	U	S	#	G	E	L	D
A	W	A	R	D	#	#	C	E	A	S	E	#	#	#
S	A	X	E	#	M	O	T	J	U	S	T	E	S	T
I	D	L	E	#	I	K	E	A	#	R	O	M	E	O
N	E	E	D	#	A	D	D	Y	#	I	N	S	E	T

You can't make a website worth a damn.
But we can.
Contact us posthaste.
MerchantAndBlack.com

DELICIOUSLY SATISFYING CONTEMPORARY NOIR
a persuasive Hollywood thriller, taut and gutsy debut novel with clean, brilliant writing. *COLDWATER* by Diana Gould. In all formats, wherever books are sold. (Support your local independent bookstore.) Or, **http://amzn.to/2dJh1Kk**

THE KILLING TREE
Part funny. Part serious. Part cynical. All intelligent. J.D. Smith's fourth collection of poetry, from Finishing Line Press. Advance praise and ordering information available at: **http://bit.ly/2ebGJuw**

WRITING A BOOK? GETTING NOWHERE?
Don't give up – get help (from me!). I'm a ghostwriter/writing coach who partners with you one-on-one to get your book done. Packages range from 45-minute "Copy Therapy" sessions to twelve-week intensive book coaching programs.
For more info, go to **copycoachlisa.com.**

CLOWN NOIR
James Finn Garner (*PC Bedtime Stories*) has a new mystery series for fans of noir, sideshow freaks and Americana. The "Rex Koko, Private Clown" thrillers have won Chicago Writers Association's Book of the Year TWICE! It's *Freaks* meets *The Maltese Falcon*. For info and samples, go to **rexkoko.com**, pally.

TABLETOP TALK - a YouTube channel for gamers by gamers. We create raw tabletop gaming content by filming our games. No scripts, just gaming. **www.youtube.com/user/TabletopTalk**

TOONS BY STEV-O (by Steve McGinn). some cartoons I hope'll make ya laff! drawn fresh in ink & then posted every day - 7 days a week! look for us on Facebook and The Comx Box Syndicate.

THE AMERICAN VALUES CLUB Crossword (formerly the Onion AV Club Crossword): It's rude, it's clued, and you'll get used to it.
Subscribe at avxword.com.

Buy **THE LAFAYETTE CAMPAIGN mybook.to/lafayettecampaign** "Andrew Updegrove brings a rare combination of drama, satire and technical accuracy to his writing. The result is a book you can't put down that tells you things you might wish you didn't know." - Admiral James G. Stavridis, former NATO Supreme Allied Commander Europe

THE VIRTUAL MEMORIES SHOW
What's the best books-art-comics-culture interview podcast you've never listened to? Discover The Virtual Memories Show at
www.chimeraobscura.com/vm/podcast-archive

I LOVE MAKING BEET CHIPS I love it so much that if you come to my apartment I will make some for you. I am not, to my knowledge, a serial killer. **@tinyrevolution**.

GEORGE BOOTH: cartoons, illustrations. Other services: grass fires stomped out and despots deterred. **929-210-0707**

HAVE WHAT IT TAKES TO BE A GOOBER DRIVER?Avoid World's Largest Peanuts envy. Navigate to offbeat tourist sights with the leaders for thirty years–
RoadsideAmerica.com.
Free e-subscription to Sightings. Easy sign-up.
RoadsideAmerica.com/newsletter

<u>SNOW ANGEL</u> IS HERE!
In the tradition of <u>The Tick</u> and <u>Venture Brothers</u> comes this all-new hilarious full-color graphic novel about **SNOW ANGEL,** the newest tween superhero! From American Bystander contributor and Eisner nominee **DAVID CHELSEA**, this massive Dark Horse comic is fun for all ages (except, oddly, 37)! Available at your local bookstore, or email **dchelsea@comcast.com** to learn how you can receive a signed copy! GUARANTEED MERMAID FREE!

AN ILLUSTRATED ZARATHUSTRA
Hilarity ensues as excerpts and epigrams from Nietzsche's timeless classic comes to life in this madcap comic-strip-style dub version. Embrace your Fate and read it online at:
ScottMarshall.org

BOOKS, POSTCARDS, ORIGINAL art by Rick Geary, available exclusively at **www.rickgeary.com**. I also take commissions.

FREE LUNCH!! NO BALONEY!
Attention all hungry cartoonists passing through Chicago:
Contact Jonathan Plotkin
Editorial Cartoonist & Illustrator
Minister of Ways and Means
NCIS Chicago Chapter
Spontoonist@gmail.com
spontoonist.com

COMICS WITH PROBLEMS All problems solved. The Internet's BEST archive of the world's WEIRDEST comic books. **http://www.ep.tc/problems**

HACKER HUMOR You need tech humor, I've got it. Jokes, pitches, consulting, articles, posts. 35+ years experience (in parents' basement).
✉ **rob.warmowski@gmail.com**

YOUR ANDREW JACKSON $20s will soon be worthless! Use one to buy our non-award-winning, non-best-selling comedy anthology, **The Lowbrow Reader**, available from Drag City Books. Or check out the The Lowbrow Reader zine itself, eminently purchasable at **lowbrowreader.com**.

VEGETARIANS EATING HAGGIS PIZZA
Cosmic quarks! It's the <u>Zen of Nimbus</u> comic created by Michael Sloan. Nimbus, the celebrated immobile astronomer, is visited by a variety of repulsive creatures and events. Will they ever disturb his meditations? View the comic and blog, shop for Zen of Nimbus t-shirts and artwork:
www.zenofnimbus.com

EULOGIES WRITTEN ON DEMAND
Need a touching tribute...*stat*? Semi-professional eulogist offers her services. Quick turnaround guaranteed; encomium completed while the body's still warm or it's free. Little knowledge of the deceased in question necessary. Email **megan.koester@gmail.com** for rates.

WELCOME TO DISTRACTIONLAND
Too much time on your hands? Watch <u>RANSACK RABBIT</u> and other engaging animated entertainments.**Xeth Feinberg**, proprietor. As seen on the internet!
www.youtube.com/distractionland

UTILITY RIGHT FIELDER Available Also draws, writes. For more information contact Deerfield (Illinois) Little League. Or visit **kenkrimstein.com.**

UNICORN BOOTY WANTS YOU ...to read some of the most outrageously fun news, pop culture, and opinions on the web! Unicorn Booty serves up original news, film, TV, art, sports, fashion, travel and other weird wonders from around the world. Check us out at **http://unicornbooty.com**.

THE NEW YORK REVIEW OF SCIENCE FICTION
Reading Science Fiction Like It Matters for 28 Years. The first one's free! **http://www.nyrsf.com**

WANTED: MURDERER I'm looking for someone to kill me please, inquiries: **@ZackBornstein** on Twitter & Instagram

STRANGER THAN LIFE
250-page collection of single panel cartoons and strips from <u>National Lampoon</u>, <u>The New Yorker</u>, <u>Playboy</u>, <u>Mother Jones</u> and <u>Arcade Comics</u> by **MK Brown**. Available from Fantagraphics and Amazon. MK happy to inscribe. Contact at **mkbrown88@hotmail.com**

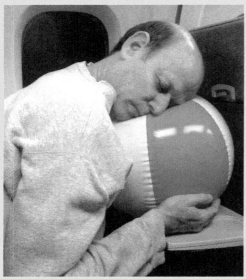

INDEX TO THIS ISSUE

Stuff you might not have noticed • **By Eel Team Six**

(continued) ☞

Eel Team Six *is River Clegg, Evan Waite, Mitra Jouhari, James Folta, Luke Burns & Alison Lieby.*

JONIK

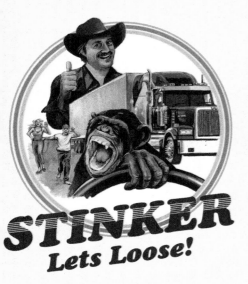

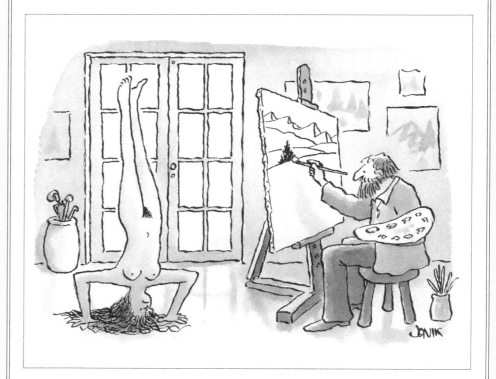

"We must use what we have to invent what we desire."
—ADRIENNE RICH

RESIST! FREE
VOLUME TWO

GRAB BACK!

RESIST! is a new magazine of political comics by mostly female artists. This summer issue features some of the biggest names in comics —
Roz Chast, Kristin Radtke, Lauren Weinstein, Cathy Malkasian, Dan Clowes, Art Spiegelman, and many more — alongside exciting new names, some never-before-published.

The 96-page magazine is edited and produced by **Françoise Mouly**, art editor of The New Yorker, and her daughter, writer **Nadja Spiegelman**.

LIMITED AVAILABILITY

Find it **FREE** at 166 distribution points in over 42 states,
or
ORDER NOW at

www.resistsubmission.com

CROSSWORD #4

BY MATT MATERA & ALAN GOLDBERG

TRES FRANÇAIS

La solution est sur la page 83

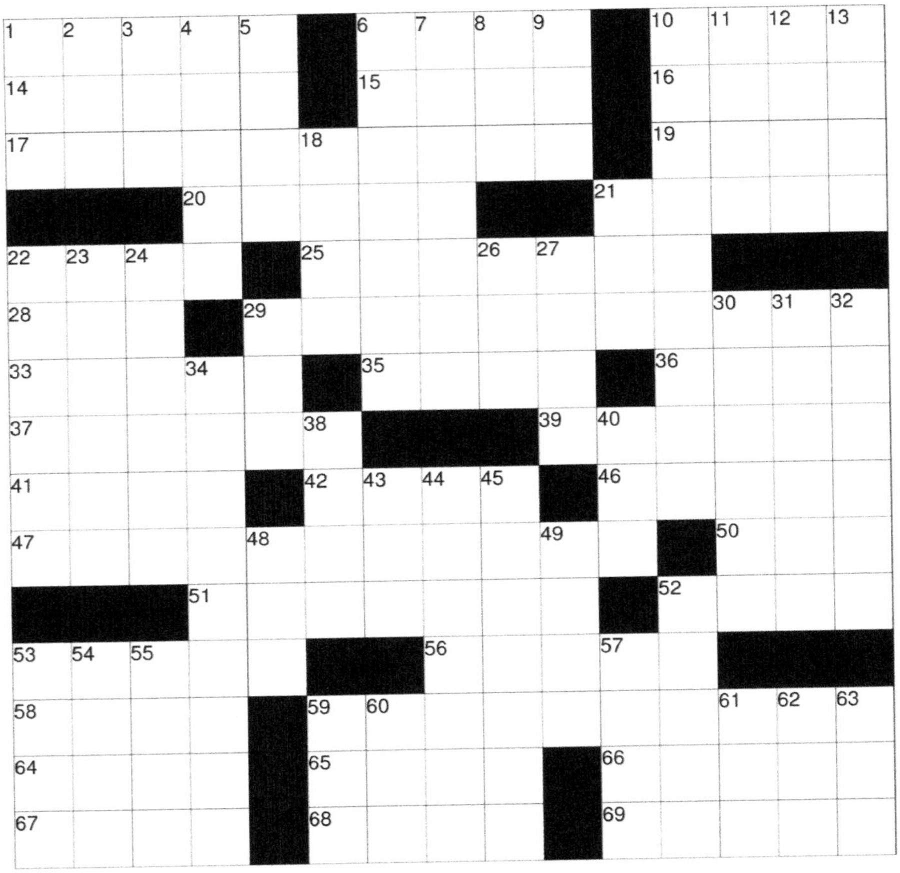

ACROSS

1. It is often educated but hasn't been to school
6. Number 2
10. French
14. It's known as the "nation's kitchen" in Japan
15. Candy bar whose "Irresistibubble" tagline was written by Salman Rushdie (!)
16. ___ 51 (where E.T.s are/n't)
17. Even worse worst enemy?
19. Bucketloads
20. Apollo 11's lunar module
21. 10-Down shows you how to hear them without wearing them
22. Dead reckoning?
25. Slues
28. Greek M's
29. Yet more necessary?
33. Crumble
35. Mufasa's murderer
36. Some muscular people can't carry it
37. "Fidelity" singer Spektor
39. Revolutionary actions
41. New Mexico town with a namesake millennium-old pueblo
42. What tamed the West, by the millions
46. Used, as a table
47. Wearing less than no clothing?
50. Early U.N. statesman or modern presidential statement
51. Rich and often complicated cakes
52. Desex, as a colt
53. 2010 Grammy for "Best Spoken Word Album for Children," *e.g.* (it was won by "Aaaah! Spooky, Scary Stories & Songs")
56. Halt
58. ___-Coburg and Gotha (European royal family)
59. The most absolute perfect thing to say?
64. Eric of Monty Python
65. Where you can sleep with Gjöra, Trysti, or Kjellse
66. "Alfa-" male name?
67. Water for elephants, *e.g.*
68. Residence info, in modern slang
69. Hawai'i, often

DOWN

1. Will Arnett character
2. "It's no ___!"
3. Consume
4. "___ Surfin'" (*Top Secret* song)
5. *Mens* ___ (uncrazy)
6. Argonauts, for example
7. Galileo Galilei, supposedly
8. Pique
9. Rock formation also known as a castle koppie
10. Couples counseling?
11. Hassan Rouhani's country
12. Posted
13. States
18. Not-so-jolly green giant
21. Number 1
22. Reason not to sing?
23. Chiffarobe
24. Shape with equal angles
26. Turkish poohbah
27. ___ toe
29. Group with badges
30. Steal cattle
31. Make a complete ass, oneself, at a party?
32. Imitated God on the seventh day
34. Came to loggerheads
38. Border
40. Beersheba's home (abbr.)
43. *Where the Wild Things* ___
44. Laughed, cried, or both
45. "___ Way" (song from *Magical Mystery Tour*)
48. Skosh
49. Subject of a comedic *Beyond the Fringe* sermon "("An hairy man, but I am a smooth man")
52. Mount
53. "P ___ Ptarmigan" (bad alphabet book entry)
54. N.B.A. star Dwyane
55. Messed-up skating jump?
57. Antidepressant drug type, for short
59. "Paper Planes" singer
60. Approved
61. Paramedic's org.
62. *Now You Holy* ___ *Me* (idea for film about Vatican magicians)
63. Rugrat

CPSIA information can be obtained
at www.ICGtesting.com
Printed in the USA
FSOW03n0131130917
38457FS